EXTRALEGAL GOVERNANCE

Drawing on insights from sociology and new institutional economics, *Extralegal Governance* provides the first comprehensive account of China's illegal markets by applying a socio-economic approach. It considers social legitimacy and state repression in examining the nature of illegal markets. It examines how power dynamics and varying levels of punishment shape exchange relationships between buyers and sellers. It identifies context-specific risks and explains how private individuals and organizations address these risks by developing extralegal governance institutions to facilitate social cooperation across various illegal markets. Adopting a multiple case study design to sample China's illegal markets, this book utilizes four cases – street vending, small property rights housing, corrupt exchanges, and online loan sharks – to examine how market participants foster cooperation and social order in illegal markets.

Peng Wang is Associate Professor in the Department of Sociology, the University of Hong Kong. He is the author of *The Chinese Mafia: Organized Crime, Corruption, and Extra-Legal Protection* (2017). His research interests include organized crime, illegal markets, corruption, economic sociology, bureaucracy, and governance.

Wanlin Lin is Associate Professor at the School of Law, Sun Yat-sen University, Guangzhou, China. Her current research applies institutional economics, law and economics, and game theory to the study of informal property rights, illegal markets, and knowledge governance in China, and interactions between formal and informal institutions.

CAMBRIDGE STUDIES IN ECONOMICS, CHOICE, AND SOCIETY

Founding Editors

Timur Kuran, *Duke University*
Peter J. Boettke, *George Mason University*

This interdisciplinary series promotes original theoretical and empirical research as well as integrative syntheses involving links between individual choice, institutions, and social outcomes. Contributions are welcome from across the social sciences, particularly in the areas where economic analysis is joined with other disciplines such as comparative political economy, new institutional economics, and behavioral economics.

Books in the Series:

PAUL DRAGOS ALIGICA, *Public Entrepreneurship, Citizenship, and Self-Governance*

TERRY L. ANDERSON AND GARY D. LIBECAP, *Environmental Markets: A Property Rights Approach*

ADAM CREPELLE, *Becoming Nations Again: The Journey Towards Tribal Self-Determination*

SHELBY GROSSMAN, *The Politics of Order in Informal Markets: How the State Shapes Private Governance*

MORRIS B. HOFFMAN, *The Punisher's Brain: The Evolution of Judge and Jury*

RANDALL G. HOLCOMBE, *Political Capitalism: How Political Influence Is Made and Maintained*

ROGER KOPPL, *Expert Failure*

PETER T. LEESON, *Anarchy Unbound: Why Self- Governance Works Better Than You Think*

MICHAEL C. MUNGER, *Tomorrow 3.0: Transaction Costs and the Sharing Economy*

JENNIFER BRICK MURTAZASHVILI, AND ILIA MURTAZASHVILI, *Land, the State, and War Property Institutions and Political Order in Afghanistan*

ALEX NOWRASTEH AND BENJAMIN POWELL, *Wretched Refuse?: The Political Economy of Immigration and Institutions*

BENJAMIN POWELL, *Out of Poverty: Sweatshops in the Global Economy (First Edition)*

BENJAMIN POWELL, *Out of Poverty: Sweatshops in the Global Economy (Second Edition)*

JEAN-PHILIPPE PLATTEAU, *Islam Instrumentalized: Religion and Politics in Historical Perspective*

JARED RUBIN, *Rulers, Religion, and Riches: Why the West Got Rich and the Middle East Did Not*

VERNON L. SMITH AND BART J. WILSON, *Humanomics: Moral Sentiments and the Wealth of Nations for the Twenty-First Century*

CASS R. SUNSTEIN, *The Ethics of Influence: Government in the Age of Behavioral Science*

ANDREAS THIEL, WILLIAM A. BLOMQUIST, AND DUSTIN E. GARRICK, *Governing Complexity: Analyzing and Applying Polycentricity*

CAROLYN M. WARNER, RAMAZAN KILINÇ, CHRISTOPHER W. HALE, AND ADAM B. COHEN, *Generating Generosity in Catholicism and Islam: Beliefs, Institutions, and Public Goods Provision*

TAIZU ZHANG, *The Laws and Economics of Confucianism: Kinship and Property in Preindustrial China and England*

TAISU ZHANG, *The Ideological Foundations of Qing Taxation: Belief Systems, Politics, and Institutions*

Extralegal Governance

The Social Order of Illegal Markets in China

PENG WANG
University of Hong Kong

WANLIN LIN
Sun Yat-sen University

CAMBRIDGE
UNIVERSITY PRESS

CAMBRIDGE
UNIVERSITY PRESS

Shaftesbury Road, Cambridge CB2 8EA, United Kingdom

One Liberty Plaza, 20th Floor, New York, NY 10006, USA

477 Williamstown Road, Port Melbourne, VIC 3207, Australia

314–321, 3rd Floor, Plot 3, Splendor Forum, Jasola District Centre, New Delhi – 110025, India

103 Penang Road, #05–06/07, Visioncrest Commercial, Singapore 238467

Cambridge University Press is part of Cambridge University Press & Assessment, a department of the University of Cambridge.

We share the University's mission to contribute to society through the pursuit of education, learning and research at the highest international levels of excellence.

www.cambridge.org
Information on this title: www.cambridge.org/9781009622141

DOI: 10.1017/9781009622158

When citing this work, please include a reference to the DOI 10.1017/9781009622158

First published 2025

A catalogue record for this publication is available from the British Library

Library of Congress Cataloging-in-Publication Data
Names: Wang, Peng (Assistant professor of criminology) author | Lin, Wanlin author
Title: Extralegal governance : the social order of illegal markets in china / Peng Wang, Wanlin Lin.
Description: Cambridge ; New York : Cambridge University Press, 2025. | Series: Cambridge studies in economics, choice, and society | Includes bibliographical references and index.
Identifiers: LCCN 2024061866 | ISBN 9781009622141 hardback | ISBN 9781009622158 ebook
Subjects: LCSH: Black market – China | Black marketeers – Social aspects – China | China – Social conditions
Classification: LCC HF5482.65.C5 W36 2025 | DDC 381.0951–dc23/eng/20250505
LC record available at https://lccn.loc.gov/2024061866

ISBN 978-1-009-62214-1 Hardback
ISBN 978-1-009-62217-2 Paperback

Contents

Figures

Tables

Acknowledgments

This book is the intellectual outcome of a cross-disciplinary research collaboration between two scholars: One is a qualitative criminologist specializing in utilizing sociological concepts and theories in explaining illegal transactions and the underworld economy, while the other is an institutional economist whose PhD dissertation used fieldwork data to examine informal property rights and community governance in China. The first author has spent the past decade investigating illegal transactions and unlawful markets. He has managed to "plant several trees" (i.e., publishing several journal articles, each of which focuses on the essential institutions developed by the participants in a specific market). However, his efforts are far from enough to "nurture a grove/forest" (i.e., publishing a book), which requires a systematic examination of illegal markets and extralegal institutions as well as detailed and comprehensive theoretical discussions and empirical analyses. The idea of writing this book appeared when the second author joined the first author's research team. Continuous discussions and long-term debates on extralegal governance institutions, along with a combination of fieldwork data from several illegal markets, have made this book possible.

The book has greatly benefited from comments and feedback given by a number of outstanding researchers. Ilia Murtazashvili, David Skarbek, Jingyi Wang, and Shitong Qiao read Chapters 1 and 2 and provided constructive comments. Li Ding, Shitong Qiao, and George Lin provided important insights that helped us complete Chapter 5. Cheris Shun-ching Chan, Ling Li, Li Li, and Jack Barbalet helped us build up a theoretical framework for studying corrupt transactions and intermediaries, which are the focuses of Chapter 6. Jianhua Xu and Paul Joosse read Chapter 7 and provided very helpful suggestions. Federico Varese, Xiaoying Qi, Jiangnan Zhu, Ling Li, Li Li, Jing Vivian Zhan, Xiaoli Tian, David Palmer, Sylvia Martin, Hualing

Fu, Ming Wen, Yahong Li, Xiaojun Yan, Hanyu Xiao, Eric Fong, William Hayward, Rebecca Wong, Mark Pennington, Emily Skarbek, Peter J. Hill, Jennifer Murtazashvili, and John Meadowcroft offered helpful suggestions and support at different stages. Special thanks go out to our research collaborators, including Anli Jiang, Jingyi Wang, Mei Su, Mengliang Dai, and Li Li, for sharing their valuable data with us. We also extend our gratitude to our interviewees for participating in our research and sharing their knowledge and experiences with us. Extracts from interviews originally in Chinese have been translated into English by us.

We are grateful for the financial support of the Research Grants Council in Hong Kong (Project Nos. 27615017, 17608821, and 17613224). This support, along with research leave from the University of Hong Kong (HKU), enabled us to conduct fieldwork in China. We are also grateful to the Faculty of Social Sciences at HKU for allowing us to use the Research Clusters PDF Scheme to fund the second author's research position for more than two years at HKU. Several rounds of Seed Fund for Basic Research supplied by HKU enabled us to recruit research assistants for transcribing the interviews and conducting preliminary analyses. Our heartfelt thanks go to Zhang Xiang, president and vice-chancellor of HKU, and his senior management team members for their immense efforts in safeguarding academic freedom and protecting HKU researchers who conduct research on politically sensitive topics. Without President Zhang's support, it would have been impossible for us to complete this book.

At Cambridge University Press, we would like to extend special thanks to Peter Boettke and Timur Kuran, general editors of Cambridge Studies in Economics, Choice, and Society, as well as to our editorial assistant, Sable Gravesandy. Their unwavering support throughout all stages of publishing this book is greatly appreciated. We also want to thank the external reviewers for their anonymous reports and constructive reviews. For our academic writing, we are grateful to Hilary Wright for her long-term help in editing and proofreading all our writings.

Most of all, we would like to thank our family members, who have unconditionally supported us. The first author would like to express his sincere appreciation to his wife, Jingyi, along with his parents and parents-in-law, for their dedicated care of him and his two lovely sons, Hairui and Shichong. The second author would like to thank her parents, Deping Lin and Chujuan Wang, and her close friend Li Ding for their support and encouragement.

PERMISSIONS

Chapter 4 is an updated version of "Governance and informal economies: Informality, uncertainty and street vending in China" (coauthored with Anli Jiang), which was published in the *British Journal of Criminology*, volume 62, issue 6 (November 2022); Chapter 7 is an updated version of "Organized crime in cyberspace: How traditional organized criminal groups exploit the online peer-to-peer lending market in China" (coauthored with Mei Su and Jingyi Wang), which was published in the *British Journal of Criminology*, volume 61, issue 2 (March 2021). The coauthors kindly allowed us to reuse them in this book. The two chapters are reproduced with the permission of Oxford University Press.

1

Introduction

1.1 Extralegal Governance and Lawlessness

How do private individuals mitigate risk and secure social cooperation? Thomas Hobbes, a seventeenth-century English philosopher, believed that life under anarchy was "solitary, poor, nasty, brutish and short" and people should contract with a leader and protector (i.e., the government) who would be able to remove people's basic fears, such as violent death, wounding, and oppression, and protect them from inevitable anarchy (Hobbes 1651). Hobbes's ideas exerted a powerful influence for the next several hundred years (Powell and Stringham 2009). Law and economics scholars, in their early contributions, examined the ways in which anarchy undermines social cooperation and investigated the role of the government, especially "the institution and machinery of the state's law," in providing governance for economic activities and social cooperation (Dixit 2004: 2). For example, in the 1970s, public choice scholars such as Gordon Tullock, James Buchanan, Winston C. Bush, and Warren J. Samuels began their economic analysis of anarchy and published two edited volumes, *Explorations in the Theory of Anarchy* (1972) and *Further Explorations in the Theory of Anarchy* (1974). The early public choice analysis of anarchy shows that in a state of anarchy individuals would face the prisoner's dilemma, cooperation would be limited, and government enforcement would be needed to safeguard long-term contracts and complex transactions.

In the early 1970s, the public choice economists' overall perspective on anarchism "could be described as sympathetic, but ultimately pessimistic" (Powell and Stringham 2009: 508). Anarchy is perceived as an unstable outcome (Nozick 1974) and a solution to the prisoner's dilemma is to create government law enforcement (Buchanan 1974, 1975). The state capacity literature examines two essential components of state capacity – fiscal and legal – and identifies the ability of a state to raise revenue, enforce laws and regulations, and provide "fundamental public goods, including defense, a legal framework, and some degree of productive investment" (Piano 2019: 291; see also Acemoglu et al. 2016; Murphy and O'Reilly 2020). The concept of "State Capacity Libertarianism," which has recently been introduced by Tyler Cowen (2020: online), emphasizes the need for a strong and capable state to "maintain and extend capitalism and markets" and "protect individual rights." However, as Murphy and O'Reilly (2020: 737) argue, state capacity libertarianism contradicts certain strands of political economy literature. As they point out, state enforcement of property rights is either redundant in situations where private institutions and norms can cost-effectively safeguard private property rights (see Stringham 2015; Williamson 2011) or counterproductive when state institutions lack efficiency and their intervention hinders the smooth functioning of private institutions and norms (see Leeson 2014; Leeson and Harris 2018).

A younger generation of researchers "has noticeably less faith in government than their predecessors," and they have investigated how the problems in Hobbesian anarchy can be solved by private or extralegal means of enforcement (Stringham 2005). These researchers find the conventional study of law and economics problematic, because it "takes the existence of a well-functioning institution of state law for granted" (Dixit 2004: 3) and treats the enforcers of the law "as robots who will automatically do what the law asks them to do" (Basu 2018: 35). Despite many modern governments making great efforts to provide effective governance, none is able to guarantee that all social and economic activities are cost-effectively regulated (Skarbek 2011). Extralegal governance institutions therefore "play an important role in protecting property and adjudicating disputes" in circumstances in which state-sponsored governance institutions are ineffective or absent (Skarbek 2014: 6; see also Stringham 2015). Moreover, many governments, especially nondemocratic ones (e.g., Nazi Germany, Soviet Russia, Maoist China, and North Korea), are predatory and incompetent to provide governance (Murtazashvili and Murtazashvili 2020); worse, they severely undermine social cooperation within their societies (Leeson 2014). Law and economics scholars should therefore not only examine the effect of legal rules on economic activities and outcomes but also devote equal attention to "lawlessness and economics" (Dixit 2004) and investigate how private individuals enhance cooperation, enforce property rights, and settle disputes without state law.

In the absence of effective government-provided legal institutions and organizations, individuals who want to obtain benefit from social cooperation are "considerably more creative in finding solutions to their problems than the academics who study them" (Leeson 2014: 3). Private individuals, organizations, and communities devise alternative mechanisms to improve cooperation and eliminate opportunistic behavior. Recent decades have witnessed a growing body of literature, from the disciplines of institutional economics, criminology, political science, sociology, and economic anthropology, examining the formation, prevalence, evolution, and function of extralegal governance institutions and suggesting that various extralegal governance institutions work better than conventional wisdom supposes. For example, Ostrom (1990) unmasks the ways in which local communities govern their common pool resources and overcome collective action problems. Bernstein (1992: 155) investigates "an elaborate, internal set of rules, complete with distinctive institutions and sanctions" developed by the diamond industry to resolve disputes among industry members, with the courts and legal rules playing no role. Leeson (2009) adopts rational choice theory to examine how the world of late seventeenth- and early eighteenth-century pirates was regulated by a "pirate code" and constitutional democracy: Pirate customs served to compensate workers, regulate drinking and smoking, and increase racial tolerance and equality (see also Leeson 2007; Leeson and Skarbek 2010). Stringham (2015) weaves together history and economics to show how private parties devise nonviolent mechanisms to solve the pervasive problem of fraud, facilitate exchange, and protect private property. Skarbek (2014) draws on institutional economics to examine why and how prison gangs form to produce alternative governance institutions facilitating illegal activities in the American penal system. These studies suggest that "private rules and regulations are more common, effective, and promising than most of us believe" (Stringham 2015: 4).

1.2 The Puzzle

Past research has thoroughly examined how and why extralegal governance institutions function more effectively than many believe in both democratic and dysfunctional states (Chamlee-Wright 2010; Grossman 2021; Ostrom 1990; Richman 2017; Shortland and Varese 2016; Skarbek 2014, 2020a). For example, Grossman (2020, 2021) examines the social order of informal markets in Lagos, Nigeria, and finds that market association leaders utilize informal institutions to promote trade, address group disputes, and gain the support of group members in order to avoid and respond to active government interference. Researchers have also studied how informal or extralegal governance institutions operate in authoritarian states.

For example, Murtazashvili (2016) and Murtazashvili and Murtazashvili (2021) have comprehensively investigated the capacity of customary organizations at the village level in the governance of rural Afghanistan, which is widely viewed as a fragile state where people have endured a long history of conflict and political instability.

Moreover, recent decades have witnessed a growing body of literature on informal institutions in authoritarian China, where state capacity is strong. This literature includes the research of Yang (1994), Yan (1996), and Barbalet (2021) on the changing function of *guanxi* in Chinese society, Qiao's (2017) study of strategic interactions among market participants in China's small property right housing market, and the research of Nee and Opper (2012) and Tsai (2002) on the informal financing mechanisms developed by small business owners. However, the ways in which the Chinese state constrains or facilitates the formation and development of illegal markets, as well as how informal or extralegal governance institutions operate within these markets, remain underexplored.

To fill this gap, this book focuses on China's illegal markets and explores different categories of governance institutions that facilitate cooperation within these markets. It explores several theoretically and empirically important questions: How does the state constrain or enable the growth of illegal markets? What are the major market-based uncertainties and political–legal risks faced by illegal market participants? How do governance institutions mitigate risk and secure social cooperation in illegal markets? More specifically, why do participants in a transaction face different types of risk, and why do they view the same risk differently? Why does one form of institutional mechanism work well for governing illegal transactions in one social setting while playing a marginal role in another setting? Why and how do market participants use different forms of governance institution to deal with the same category of risks? Illegal transactions are pervasive, and illegal markets continue to grow both online and offline. How does internet technology affect the social order of illegal markets? To answer these questions, researchers need to collect firsthand empirical evidence and develop innovative frameworks for analyzing illegal markets.

1.3 In Search of an Answer: How the Chinese State Facilitates the Growth of Illegal Markets

China is the perfect example of how in many circumstances authoritarian/centralized states are predatory, rather than protective, as stated by Hobbes in *Leviathan*. Often, the predatory state enables, rather than constrains, the emergence and development of illegal markets in many situations. The role of the authoritarian Chinese state in creating and promoting illegal markets is threefold.

First, China's regionally decentralized authoritarian system, consisting of centralized fiscal and personnel control and decentralized economic governance (Xu 2011), makes local government both developmental and predatory. Under decentralization, the central government has established "a growth-oriented performance evaluation system" (Wang et al. 2019: 3). This motivates local governments facing serious budget shortfalls to rely on the urban-biased land development policy to generate funds to "fulfil the mandates specified in the evaluation system," such as attaining high growth rates and supplying massive infrastructure and public services (Cai et al. 2021: 2333). China can be considered a predatory state due to its lack of political constraints (i.e., "separation of powers at the national level") and its partial protection of property rights; as a result, the Chinese government possesses strong abilities to arbitrarily expropriate property, such as land (Cai et al. 2020: 154). In contemporary China, ownership of urban and rural land is defined as follows: "Urban land is controlled and owned by the state ... whereas rural land is collectively owned" (Sa 2020: 2). The separation of land-use rights and ownership empowers local governments to raise substantial extra revenue from land conveyancing: "The ratio of local governments' financial expenditures to fiscal revenue from land soared from 5.7% in 1999 to 23.4% in 2015" (Zhu et al. 2019: 742). Local governments convey urban land and collectively owned rural land to real estate developers for enormous profits, while residents who possess land-use rights are largely excluded from the decision-making process by local governments and village leaders and are usually undercompensated for what they lose (Cai 2003). Given that land property rights are ambiguously defined and that there is a lack of transparency and grassroots input, villagers need to develop strategies to safeguard their interests. Due to domestic migrants' high demand for affordable housing, informal housing markets and their associated exchange institutions have emerged from the bottom of the hierarchy (Qiao 2017; Wu et al. 2013). The small property right housing market is a typical example and will be examined in this book.

Under such an urban-biased political regime, local governments not only need to promote local economies but also have to control rural–urban migration (Shifa and Xiao 2022). Urban-biased development policies, which systematically discriminate "against agriculture and the rural economy in the allocation of developmental resources" (Bezemer and Headey 2008: 1342), have given rise to a significant urban–rural gap. The enormous disparity in income and living standards between rural and urban residents encourages rural residents to seek job opportunities and better livelihoods in urban areas. To maintain urban fiscal sustainability (Shifa and Xiao 2022), the Chinese government uses its household registration system (*hukou*) to deprive rural-to-urban migrants of equal access to employment, education, health care, and social and political advancement in urban areas. China's uneven development and the discriminatory *hukou* system have led to many migrants from rural areas working as unlicensed street vendors in urban centers (Huang et al. 2018). As the government does not recognize and protect these workers' property rights, such as user rights to public space, street vendors have developed extralegal governance institutions in order to survive.

Second, the authoritarian state has wide powers, but it lacks checks and balances to guard against abuses of power by those who wield it. The lack of political constraint and bottom-up monitoring has led to the rise of a gigantic market for power–money exchanges. Since the 1990s, corruption in China has become rampant and systematic. As Wedeman (2012: 2) points out, "in the case of China, we see rising corruption, high growth rates, and high-speed economic development." The intensification of corruption is linked to the "commodification" of state-owned resources and the transfer of "assets from the command sector to the market" (p. 9). As a result, the primary form of corruption became transactive corruption between public officials and private actors, rather than predatory plunder such as embezzlement of state funds and property. The study of transactive corruption should focus not only on illegal exchanges between officials and citizens, however. Recent studies have started to pay attention to transactive corruption within the public sector. For example, Wang and Yan (2020: 612) observe that corruption in the form of gift-giving and extravagant position-related consumption increases "the efficiency of bureaucrats trying to develop local economies in China, where the political structure is fragmented and the formal incentive system is incomplete." Zhu (2008) and Wang (2016) investigate the buying and selling of public appointments, which is a popular form of transactive corruption in the public sector (see also Hillman 2010; Wang and Wang 2018). These scholars argue that the weaknesses of the formal, rule-based personnel system, such as overconcentration of power in the hands of senior officials and the failure of the state to monitor these officials' misuse of office, allow many public officials to use social ties and bribery to gain promotion. The prevalence of transactive corruption in China offers an ideal opportunity for researchers to make a closer examination of how extralegal governance institutions facilitate corrupt transactions.

Third, the authoritarian state achieves legitimacy by launching campaigns and solving easily identified and easily handled societal problems (Alon et al. 2020; Wang 2020b; Yang and Zhao 2015; Zhu 2011), while illegal markets that are hidden and nonviolent are largely tolerated by the local government. The central government of China is strong in respect of the fiscal resources it controls, but local governments responsible for implementing policies – including anticrime policies – are often weak due to lack of funds (Ong 2018; Wang and Wang 2024). Faced with the rise of illegal markets, such as gambling and prostitution, local law enforcement agencies punish only those who commit violent offenses, preferring to generate extra-budgetary revenue by collecting fines from illegal market participants such as sex workers and gamblers. In other words, because local law enforcement agencies lack the motivation and capability to eradicate or regulate illegal markets, they turn a blind eye to illegal markets that are relatively nonviolent. As communication and information technology developed, illegal entrepreneurs started to use innovative internet-based strategies to market services, such as private loans and gambling, and enforce agreements. As physical violence is not a characteristic of online illegal markets, and online interactions between exchange partners are anonymous, participants in these markets are able to escape police attention and avoid punishment.

These key features of the Chinese authoritarian state – an urban bias, broadly defined powers without checks and balances, and legitimacy maintained by solving easily identified problems – are highly relevant to the growth of illegal markets. The emergence, development, and social order of illegal markets in authoritarian China are different from these in democratic counties. For example, China has witnessed the formation of large-scale markets in informal housing, the buying and selling of government appointments, and unlicensed street vending, whereas these markets are small, or simply do not exist, in democratic countries. The research into China's illegal markets contained in this book therefore enriches the literature on illegal markets and non-state institutions by offering a clear picture of extralegal governance and illegal markets in an authoritarian state. It generates new knowledge concerning the role of the state in enabling or constraining illegal markets, the range of risks, and the complexity of extralegal governance institutions in illegal markets.

1.4 Objectives and Contributions of This Book

This book aims to provide a socio-economic approach for studying the social order of illegal markets as well as risks and institutions within these markets.

It seeks to advance understanding of extralegal governance in authoritarian China, where the economy is experiencing transition (Coase and Wang 2016), private property rights are ambiguously defined (Bai et al. 2006; Zhu 2008), the judicial system is not strong (Gong 2004; Li 2012; Wang 2013b), public-sector corruption is an ongoing concern (Lu 2000; Wang 2016; Wedeman 2012), and illegal markets are thriving (Shen et al. 2010; Wang and Antonopoulos 2016; Wong 2016). Specifically, we examine, both theoretically and empirically, the characteristics of illegal markets, especially their social legitimacy, and the nature of exchange relationships, particularly regarding whether participants are embedded in power-imbalanced relations and face different risks of punishment. We also explore the existence of various types of risks and the ways in which private individuals, companies, and organizations utilize them to mitigate risk and facilitate social cooperation and economic exchange in illegal economies. We adopt a multiple case study design comprising four cases: unlicensed street vending, small property right housing, corrupt exchanges, and online loan sharks. The cases are specifically selected to sample China's illegal markets, which range from offline to online, from public sector to private sector, and from socially acceptable to socially unacceptable (Small 2009).

The first two cases are illegal but socially legitimate, whereas the latter two are neither legal nor socially legitimate. The boom of street vending and the small property right housing market are defining features of China's rapid urbanization and uneven development (Huang et al. 2018; Qiao 2017). Rampant corruption in the public sector and the rise of online illegal markets also characterize contemporary China (Gong 2002; Huang 2018; Wedeman 2012). Due to the fact that different markets include different economic activities, and participants in these markets face different market and political risks and challenges, illegal economy participants need to develop a range of extralegal governance institutions in order to secure cooperation, prevent opportunistic behavior, and counter the threat of government repression. A certain type of extralegal governance institution might work cost-effectively in regulating one category of market transaction, but its role in safeguarding another type of transaction may be marginal. Moreover, participants in street vending and the small property right housing market are willing to coordinate collective resistance to government interference, while corrupt transaction partners and online loan sharks must develop effective institutions to hide their illegal activities and avoid government crackdowns.

The empirical investigation of these four cases enables us to offer insights on a number of essential but understudied issues, including the impact of key features of the authoritarian regime on the development of illegal markets, major market and political–legal risks in illegal markets, and the key forms of extralegal governance institutions developed by market participants in different social settings. The examination of extralegal governance and illegal markets under authoritarianism contributes to the broader study of institutions and illegal markets: It offers a foundation for comparative studies of the governance of illegal markets in democratic and nondemocratic countries. In addition, it offers valuable evidence to government agencies, offering insights into non-state governance institutions and improving agencies' ability to provide the governance needed.

This book contributes to the existing literature in three ways. Firstly, and more generally, it is one of the first English-language books focusing on private rules and regulations in illegal markets and presenting a comprehensive picture of illegal markets and extralegal governance institutions in China. Past research has focused on self-governance or extralegal governance in democratic and dysfunctional states (Chamlee-Wright 2010; Leeson 2014; Murtazashvili 2016; Ostrom 1990; Richman 2017; Shortland and Varese 2016; Skarbek 2014, 2020a), whereas studies of extralegal governance institutions in China are rare, except for Qiao's (2017) research on China's small property right housing, Ho's (2017) research on the function and credibility of institutions in the real estate land, housing, and natural resources sector, and the research of Nee and Opper (2012) as well as Tsai (2002) on the informal financing mechanisms developed by small business owners. We argue that extralegal governance institutions may play a larger role in China than in democratic regimes. This is because the Chinese government is more predatory than democratic governments, and it frequently takes advantage of ambiguously defined property rights to rob its citizens; for example, private land ownership does not exist in China, and local governments, rather than local residents, are always the primary beneficiaries of conveying land-use rights to real estate developers (Hsing 2010; Lin 2009). As a result, informal community-based institutions for protecting private property are common in China.

The prevalence of informal institutions is also due to the importance and resilience of *guanxi* (i.e., social ties) in both the public and the private domains (Barbalet 2018; Bian 2019; Chan and Yao 2018; Li 2011; Qi 2013; Ruan 2019; Wang 2017; Yan 1996; Yang 1994; Zhan 2012). To be specific, social cooperation among Chinese people is to a large extent determined by economic calculation and social mechanisms, with formal institutions playing a comparatively small role. The discussions above suggest that informal institutions in China, specifically extralegal governance institutions, constitute an essential research topic deserving more scholarly attention. This book's examination of the ways in which extralegal governance institutions work in China's illegal markets therefore adds value to the general literature on institutions.

Secondly, and theoretically, this book draws insights from sociology and institutional economics to establish a socio-economic approach to explain risks and extralegal governance institutions in illegal markets. The socio-economic approach considers two dimensions: macro and micro. Macro dimensions, including social legitimacy (distinguishing between legitimate and illegitimate illegal markets) and levels of state repression, are used to examine the nature of illegal markets, the different risks experienced by participants in *different* markets, and the varied forms of institutions employed by market participants. Macro dimensions also take into account the social order of illegal markets when operating online. On the other hand, micro dimensions, including power-dependence relationships and levels of criminal punishment, are helpful for investigating the characteristics of exchange relationships and identifying the different kinds of risk experienced by exchange partners (buyers and sellers) in the *same* market. The construction of this analytical approach is largely based on existing studies that use economics – especially new institutional economics – and sociology to analyze risks, private institutions, and institutional change (Beckert and Dewey 2017; Greif 2006; Leeson 2009, 2014; Liu and Weingast 2017; Skarbek 2014; Stringham 2015). This book therefore not only contributes to the study of illegal markets in China but also facilitates the exploration of illegal markets in general.

Thirdly, and empirically, this book contributes to the understanding of extralegal governance by utilizing rich and valuable empirical data collected by the two authors and their research collaborators. Non-state institutions and illegal markets in authoritarian China have been largely ignored in the existing literature for two main reasons. First, language barriers not only discourage Western scholars from conducting fieldwork and obtaining local understanding of how extralegal governance institutions work in China, but also prevent Chinese scholars from obtaining insights from Western literature and publishing their research findings in international journals. Second, the Chinese government has broadened the scope of academic censorship, meaning researchers have had to restrict their attention to politically correct and otherwise acceptable topics, leaving many essential areas, including self-governance in semilegal and illegal markets, unexplored or understudied.

It is not easy for researchers who study China-related topics to gain access to interviewees and obtain reliable interview data. Researchers who collect empirical data on politically sensitive topics in China, such as corruption, organized crime, and collective resistance, face greater risks than those who study the same topics in democratic countries. Academic research based on survey data collected from over 500 China scholars reveals the repression they experienced: "Roughly 9 per cent of China scholars report that they have been 'invited to tea' by authorities within the past ten years; 26 per cent of scholars who conduct archival research report being denied access; and 5 per cent of researchers report some difficulty obtaining a visa" (Greitens and Truex 2020: 349). Our social connections with interviewees allowed us to collect rich and valuable interview data, which enables us to understand how private individuals in illegal markets avoid external threats from control agencies, such as the police and anti-corruption agencies, and handle internal conflicts caused by dishonest exchange participants.

1.5 Outline of This Book

This chapter emphasizes the lack of good-quality research focusing on how extralegal governance institutions operate in illegal markets in authoritarian China, discusses the rationale for studying the social order of illegal markets in China, and illustrates the contributions this book makes to the literature. Chapter 2 defines "governance" and "extralegal governance institutions," discusses mechanisms of extralegal governance, and provides a definition of illegal markets. It then summarizes the essential contributions made by new institutional economists and economic sociologists, who have developed different approaches to analyzing social and economic order. Over the past few decades, researchers from the two camps have frequently gained insights from each other, but there is still a lack of cross-disciplinary research collaboration. Synthesizing key concepts and theories from both sociology and economics, the chapter develops a socio-economic approach to analyzing illegal markets, as well as the risks and institutions within these markets. The socio-economic approach investigates both the characteristics of illegal markets and the nature of exchange relationships between participants. It reveals that participants in different illegal markets may experience heterogeneous types of risks and uncertainties. Even participants in the same market may face different concerns and uncertainties, or they might perceive the same type of risk differently. This requires market participants to develop innovative approaches in developing extralegal governance institutions to secure transactions and mitigate risks in diverse markets. The socio-economic approach offers valuable insights for the study of China's illegal markets.

Chapter 3 outlines the methodology and explains how the empirical data was collected. It offers detailed discussions about the multiple case study design and the rationale for selecting the four cases, which are street vending, small property right housing, corrupt exchanges, and online loan sharks. The multiple case study design enabled us to make use of interviews, observation, and published materials to obtain an accurate and complete understanding of risks and extralegal governance institutions in different social settings. This chapter covers how informants were selected, the challenges we experienced and how we handled them, and the limitations of our empirical data.

Chapters 4–7 focus on different types of illegal markets. Chapter 4 examines how street vendors protect property rights and address uncertainties without state support. In the absence of state recognition of property rights and state protection, street vendors have to deal with both market-based uncertainties (e.g., resource limitations, competitive bidding, competition for the best vending locations) and uncertainties caused by ambiguous or hostile state regulation. Our findings show that street vendors in our research sites form mutual aid groups based on hometown and ethnicity. Shared norms, values, and routines have been formed among street vendors to facilitate within-group cooperation, which not only helps them solve the problems of resource limitation, competitive bidding, and marketing, and uncertain allocation of public space but also facilitates their collective resistance to government repression. We also observed that street vendors who cannot form or join strong mutual aid groups usually fail to resist government interference and thus face a higher risk of having their properties confiscated by city administrative officials. In our research sites, some street vendors could purchase extralegal protection from the city urban administrative and law enforcement bureau (*Chengguan*) and its officials, who, for department-level and personal benefits, defy higher-level policies and protect street vendors from harassment, eviction, and confiscation imposed by themselves and other city administrative officials.

Chapter 5 investigates the extralegal governance institutions deployed in the small property right housing market. Small property right housing (*xiao chan quan fang*) is housing built on collectively owned land without legal title. Villagers are generally entitled to exchange their own housing plots with others in the village, but exchanging them with outsiders is prohibited and not protected by state law. Small property right housing is illegal, but large-scale residential communities built on collectively owned land have accommodated many immigrants and are often tolerated by local governments, which will intervene or engage in demolition only when they believe the continued existence of this market will give rise to disputes, threaten social order, destroy the local economy, or reduce government revenue (He et al. 2019; Qiao 2015; Zhang and Zhao 2018). Due to the complexity of the small property right housing market (i.e., it is illegal, but socially legitimate and selectively tolerated by local governments), it can be categorized as a special type of illegal market. Participants in small property right housing markets have to develop private institutions to support exchange and avoid government interference.

Our empirical data offers insights into how builders and buyers of small property right housing develop a series of mechanisms to mitigate the risks of contract fraud and government interference. We found that written documents – such as informal certificates of title, contracts of exchange, or lawyers' testimonies – and contract-signing rituals are used to define private property ownership, communicate shared knowledge of the extralegal market outside state law, and help sellers assess buyers' trustworthiness. Sellers also make use of online WeChat groups to facilitate information sharing that sustains the reputation mechanism. More importantly, we found that village committees, functioning as representatives responsible for villagers' self-governance as well as quasi-formal branches of local government, are often capable of enforcing informal property rights. Village committees in many villages perform multiple roles such as builders and sellers of small property right housing and property rights enforcers, whereas village committees in other villages only function as third-party enforcers. In their role as enforcers of property rights and guardians of informal transactions, village committees establish databases as a public good. These databases contain information relating to the registration of ownership and transactions. Village committees also organize collective action (e.g., provision of public goods and collective resistance) and seek political patronage to deter government interference.

Chapter 6 studies the informal institutions used to facilitate corrupt transactions, which are associated with high transaction costs and exchange risks because they are prohibited by state law. Such transactions necessarily lack transparency in order to evade anti-corruption agencies (Lambsdorff 2002). To initiate a corrupt transaction, exchange partners have to employ a private/secret channel to collect enough information to assess one another's reputation for trustworthiness in the social network, which consists primarily of bribe-takers and -givers. In most cases, bribe-givers have to make payment first and trust that the bribe-takers will deliver the promised benefits (Della Porta and Vannucci 2012; Wang 2020a). The asynchronous nature of such exchanges increases uncertainty for exchange partners. The chapter investigates a typical form of corrupt transaction in the public sector: the buying and selling of government appointments. It examines the embeddedness of these transactions in strong-tie relations and the ways in which informal institutions minimize transaction risks under conditions of illegality through the use of "hostages" and *mianzi*. "Hostages" in corrupt transactions include *ganqing* (deep emotional attachment developed through long-term interactions, exchanges, and mutual help) and human capital investment (e.g., time and money) in maintaining exchange relations. *Mianzi* can be simply translated as face, which refers to reputation and social esteem in the social network. The chapter goes on to discuss other essential governance institutions that strongly bind exchange partners and prevent opportunistic behavior but have been ignored by the literature, including disclosing compromising information to anti-corruption agencies and employing corrupt intermediaries.

Chapter 7 examines the governance mechanism of illegal transactions in the illegal online lending market. The popularity of online peer-to-peer lending platforms has brought loan sharks who previously only operated offline into contact with online targets on the internet, where they encounter a new series of challenges. An example of this is the reputation mechanism, which preforms an informational and sanctioning function in offline businesses but plays little part in attracting and screening clients online. Lusthaus (2018a: 193) argues that the anonymity of the internet poses significant difficulties for criminals seeking to "assess trustworthiness and enforce agreements" in the absence of physical interactions. Conventional enforcement strategies, such as violence and unexpected office or home visits, are no longer cost-effective given the lack of geographical proximity of lenders and clients. Loan sharks have thus had to develop new mechanisms to handle defaults. The chapter empirically examines loan sharks' debt-trapping strategies and extralegal governance institutions (e.g., use of social contacts and nude photos as compromising information) to attract clients, regulate exchange behavior, lower the default risk, and enforce repayment.

Chapter 8 presents reflections and conclusions. The multiple case study approach adopted by this research not only "provide[s] a broader array of evidence than do single cases" (Yin 2012: 131) but also enabled investigators to analyze and synthesize similarities, differences, and patterns across four cases to show different categories of risks and institutions and how extralegal governance institutions operate in different illegal markets. It enriches the understanding of institutions and illegal markets by utilizing first-hand data and developing an analytical framework to examine the operation, persistence, and complexity of extralegal governance institutions in China's illegal markets. The analytical framework may attract wider academic interest in illegal markets and enhance researchers' analytical capability. The chapter also discusses the potential of this research to deliver valuable changes to public policy. This research enriches the government's understanding of the complexity and function of extralegal governance institutions and encourages policymakers and legislators to acquire knowledge and skills developed in local communities.

2

Developing a Socio-economic Approach for Analyzing the Social Order of Illegal Markets

2.1 Introduction

In this chapter we present an analytical approach to address the puzzle described previously. Firstly, we provide definitions for "governance" and "extralegal governance institutions." We also discuss the major mechanisms of extralegal governance and what constitutes illegal markets. We then delve into the historical dialogue between institutional economists and economic sociologists concerning economic and social order. This dialogue involves the mutual borrowing of concepts, theories, and insights to better understand society and market. However, the dialogue between the two fields has become less frequent and productive in recent decades. We aim to reinvigorate intellectual exchanges between the two fields by synthesizing key concepts and theories from sociology and institutional economics and by developing an analytical approach for analyzing the social order of illegal markets. This approach examines both macro and micro factors. The macro factors focus on the nature of illegal markets, specifically examining the relationships among the state, society, and illegal markets. Meanwhile, the micro factors explore the exchange relationships between individual market participants.

At the macro level, we consider social legitimacy and state repression in the examination of *the nature of illegal markets*. We utilize sociologist Max Weber's concept of legitimacy and institutional economists Boettke et al.'s theoretical discussions on the morality of illicit markets to differentiate between illegal markets that are socially acceptable and those considered socially unacceptable. The level of state repression, closely related to the social legitimacy of illegal markets and the state's willingness and capability to address them, is also included in the analysis of the nature of illegal markets. As there is a growing trend for illegal businesses to operate online, we will make a point of examining how anonymity and information asymmetry influence the operation of illegal markets.

At the micro level, we adopt the social psychologists' theory of power dynamics to investigate *the nature of exchange relationships* between buyers and sellers. In parallel, institutional economists pay great attention to examining exchange relationships. They have utilized the concept of bargaining power, which concerns the distribution of power among economic actors, and commonly applied sociological concepts such as social relations and social embeddedness in their studies of institutions and the ways in which these institutions influence economic activities. In many exchanges, participants are embedded in unbalanced power relationships, and they need to develop strategies to facilitate exchanges while addressing the risks caused by this imbalance. Moreover, law enforcement agencies often adopt different approaches and levels of punishment when investigating and punishing participants in illegal markets. Their focus tends to be on the investigation and arrest of suppliers, sellers, and distributors of illicit goods and services, rather than buyers. Consequently, we include the varying degrees of punishment faced by exchange partners, because these factors constrain the interactions and exchanges among illegal market participants.

The incorporation of insights from sociology and institutional economics in the study of illegal markets and the nature of exchange relationships helps researchers to identify context-specific risks and uncertainties across diverse markets. This socio-economic analytical approach reveals that participants in different illegal markets may encounter heterogeneous types of risks and uncertainties. Even participants in the same market may face different concerns and uncertainties, or they might perceive the same types of risk differently. This approach also allows us to generate insights regarding variations in the use of governance institutions (e.g., violence, close social relations, and bribery) across the four specific markets that this book covers, which are the central focus of our analysis. It explains why a particular institution may function effectively in one market but not in another. Furthermore, it highlights market participants' innovative approaches in developing new extralegal governance institutions to secure transactions and mitigate risks in diverse markets.

2.2 What Is Extralegal Governance?

Governance is a significant concept for the disciplines of political science, economics, law, and public administration. Public administration scholars define it as "a government's ability to make and enforce rules, and to deliver services, regardless of whether that government is democratic or not" (Fukuyama 2013: 350). In political economy, conventional wisdom holds that government facilitates social exchanges by providing efficient and effective centralized institutions, such as enforcement and rules (Hobbes 1651). In recent decades, however, economists, especially new institutional economists, have noted that government "is but one means of supplying governance" and that governance can often be provided privately (Leeson 2014: 1). They have also argued that creating a state and relying on state-provided governance institutions can be costly because the expense involved in establishing and maintaining the police, courts, and military forces and in enforcing laws and providing public goods is huge (Leeson 2006). These costs are even higher for dysfunctional and predatory states.

Markets can operate effectively without government intervention if extralegal governance institutions develop to "define and enforce property rights, adjudicate disputes, and mitigate the harms of negative externalities" (Skarbek 2011: 702). Such institutions, as Leeson (2006: 41) notes, can be more cost-effective than state institutions, especially "when markets are sufficiently thin or where government is prohibitively costly." We adopt a broad definition of *institutions*, which includes formal and informal rules (particularly norms) as well as organizations that are deployed by private individuals to coordinate individuals' beliefs and enable or constrain their actions (Crawford and Ostrom 1995; Greif 2000, 2006). Institutions can also be understood as an equilibrium resulting from the strategic interaction of private individuals (Calvert 1995; Greif and Kingston 2011; Schotter 1981; Weingast 1997). Therefore, *extralegal governance institutions* refers to non-state mechanisms, often in the form of rules, norms, and organizations, that are used to secure social cooperation, property protection, and enforcement (Leeson 2009, 2014; Leeson and Williamson 2009). Extralegal governance institutions can also be seen as equilibria resulting from actors' strategic interaction.

The terms "extralegal governance" and "private governance" are used interchangeably by law and economics scholars. We have no objection to this, but the term "extralegal governance" is more frequently used than "private governance" in this book because it suggests a sharper contrast with the state-provided legal system. "Private," according to *Oxford Learner's Dictionaries*, means "not for public use," and it is commonly found in terms like "private business" and "private property." The term "private governance" may cause confusion when it is used to refer to non-state institutions that are developed to govern common-pool resources and other resources with public characteristics.

2.3 Mechanisms of Extralegal Governance

When there are no effective state institutions to protect property rights and enforce contracts, private individuals, organizations, and communities that want to reap the rewards of social cooperation have to develop alternative governance mechanisms to overcome the commitment problem, which, according to Frank (2015: 414), is "a situation in which people cannot achieve their goals because of an inability to make credible threats or promises." The problem can be solved by two basic private governance mechanisms: the *bilateral punishment mechanism* and the *multilateral punishment mechanism* (Greif 1989, 2006; Leeson 2014; Milgrom et al. 1990; see Figure 2.1). The former involves "a single person refusing to interact in the future with persons who cheated them in the past" (Leeson 2014: 15). If partners exchange with one another repeatedly and value the earnings potential of future interaction, the threat of terminating the long-term relationship because of uncooperative behavior is sufficient to deter them from seeking short-term gains (Axelrod 1984; Sugden 2004). In most circumstances, the bilateral-punishment strategy is insufficient, however, because the uncooperative partner is free to interact with different partners rather than repeatedly interacting with the same one. The common situation of interactions occurring not only between partners embedded in a long-term relationship but also among the stable membership of a large group deserves more scholarly attention (Dixit 2004). In such circumstances, private individuals are prone to deploy the multilateral punishment mechanism to deter would-be rule-breakers (Greif et al. 1994). Since both the cheated person and their associates perceive uncooperative behavior as an offense, they will coordinate to deliver punishment in a collective manner.

The multilateral punishment mechanism owes its effectiveness to *gossip and reputation* (Giardini and Wittek 2019), which have the power to

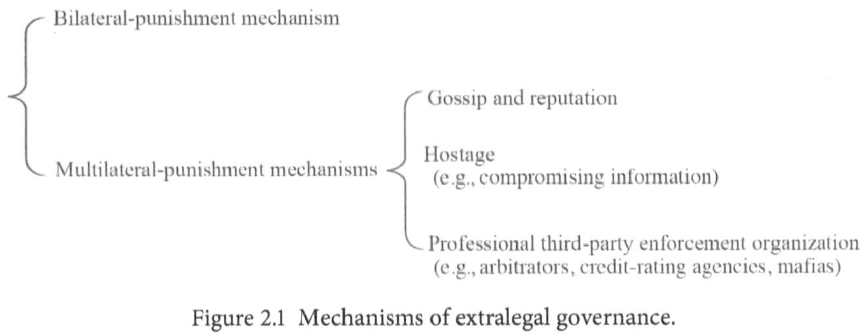

Figure 2.1 Mechanisms of extralegal governance.

effectively enforce social rules and facilitate cooperation in larger groups. Gossip about absent third parties' social information – whether positive (e.g., accomplishments) or negative (e.g., transgression of expected norms of behavior and commitment) – results in the creation, maintenance, and destruction of those parties' reputations (Barbalet 2014; Wu et al. 2016). Gossip facilitates effective reputation-spreading in relatively large groups, serving to deprive individuals with low reputations of future exchange opportunities (Aldrich 2012; Yamagishi and Yamagishi 1994). When the group size increases, however, and group members become more socially and culturally diverse, gossip is no longer an efficient mechanism for transmitting information about uncooperative behavior, making it costly and inefficient to obtain reliable reputation information about potential partners (Ellickson 1991). Such information is also unavailable when a person interacts with a partner outside the group. To overcome the commitment problem, the social mechanisms of reputation and gossip need to be supplemented or replaced by, for example, the use of hostage-taking and professional third-party enforcement agencies.

Hostage-posting can serve as a credible commitment devise used by exchange partners to signal their trustworthiness and enhance cooperation (Raub 2004; Raub and Keren 1993; Weesie and Raub 1996). It helps an individual convince a potential partner that they can be trusted (Williamson 1983). Compromising information, as Gambetta and Przepiorka (2019: 352) note, "can be conceived as a 'hostage,'" and the sharing of compromising information is an important mechanism for criminals, politicians, and other actors who wish to establish credible commitments (Campana and Varese 2013; Gambetta 2009; Schelling 1960; Williamson 1983). Consider a situation in which two agents are desperate to establish cooperation to make money in an illegal market but one or neither of them trusts the other, perhaps fearing the other to be a fraudster, police informant, or undercover police officer. Given that there are no state institutions that can be used to bind the two agents and that there is a lack of trust in the criminal underworld, the agents have to find a solution to make cooperation possible. Scholars have suggested one such solution: the two agents can reveal their misdeeds to each other, with the compromising information then used by them against each other if needed (Gambetta and Przepiorka 2019; Schelling 1960). If they "had no bad things to reveal, [they] would even have the incentive to do something bad" (Gambetta 2009: 59). This sharing of compromising information can effectively bond agents, because if one is cheated by the other, the cheated one can report the cheater's misdeeds to the police, potentially leading to arrest and punishment (Gambetta and Przepiorka 2019).

Moreover, agents can obtain protection and enforcement services, sometimes for a fee, from a third party when "trading opportunities expand beyond the close group," leading to two different systems interfacing with each other (Dixit 2004: 13). For example, the rapid expansion of trade in medieval times in Europe generated a greater demand for governance that was not fully met by the multilateral reputation mechanism, leading to the emergence of professional coordinating organizations, the merchants' guilds, allowing the "rulers of trade centers to commit to the security of alien merchants" (Greif et al. 1994). Similarly, mafia-like organizations and prison gangs act as third-party enforcers of deals and promises in markets where the formal legal system is weak or absent (Chu 2000; Gambetta 1993; Hill 2003; Skarbek 2014, 2020a; Varese 2001; Wang 2017). Credit-rating agencies and arbitrators, as Dixit (2004: 13) demonstrates, function as information collectors and transmitters, accumulating and disseminating enough information to allow certainty about potential partners' intentions and trustworthiness. The sanctioning role of credit-rating agencies and arbitrators should also not be ignored: people often refrain from dishonest deeds because they are afraid that the efficient transmission of information concerning their misconduct by such agencies or arbitrators will lead to loss of reputation and future social exchange opportunities. Furthermore, some community-level organizations or leaders, especially at village level, play a significant role in the enforcement of collective property rights and the deterrence of political threat caused by government interference. Examples include Lagos's market association leaders who help to preserve the informal market (Grossman 2020, 2021) and the Chinese village committees that robustly reduce contract fraud and government inference, which will be examined in Chapter 5.

2.4 What Constitutes Illegal Markets?

How to define illegal markets? The answer to this question may start with researchers' efforts to distinguish between informal and illegal economies. In the 1990s and 2000s, sociologists, especially economic sociologists, attempted to make a conceptual distinction between informal and illegal/criminal economies by examining the means and ends of economic activities. Illegal enterprises get involved in the illicit "process of production and distribution" (means) in order to produce illicit goods (ends), while informal enterprises use illicit means to produce licit final products (Portes and Haller 2005: 405). Social acceptability is also perceived as an essential way of differentiating between informal and criminal economic actions: the former have legitimacy conferred by the broader society, whereas the latter do not (Webb et al. 2009).

However, research boundaries between informal and illegal economies have become blurred in the past few years as researchers have adopted a much broader definition of illegal economies and markets. Illegal markets, as Beckert and Dewey (2017: 2) argue, are "arenas of regular exchange of goods or services for money … in which the product itself or its production, exchange, or consumption violate legal stipulations" (see also Beckert and Wehinger 2013). Beckert and Dewey's definition is inclusive: the violation of legal stipulations does not mean that all elements in the market are illegal, and in many cases, "only certain actions are illegal" (Beckert and Dewey 2017: 2). "Informal" still covers more economic actions than "illegal," however. As Mayntz (2017: 40) points out, "informal economic action escapes state regulation, either because it is not regulated or because, although formally regulated and possibly violating existing rules, it remains invisible to the bureaucracy" (see also Hart 2010). This book adopts Beckert and Dewey's definition to examine illegal markets in which either the goods and services themselves or their production, exchange, possession, and consumption violate state laws and regulations.

2.5 The Dialogue between Institutional Economists and Economic Sociologists

Scholars from both new institutional economics and economic sociology share an interest in studying social interactions, economic activities, and the role of institutions in affecting economic behavior (Velthuis 1999). A review of the existing literature shows that researchers from the fields of economic sociology and institutional economics engage in mutual borrowing of concepts and theories. This intellectual exchange enhances their understanding of social and economic order.

New institutional economics sheds light on the existence of transaction costs and the effect of these costs on economic and social order. This is a departure from neoclassical economics, which assumes "a world of zero transaction cost in which institutions are superfluous to economic analysis" (Nee 2005: 50). Transaction costs, as Meramveliotakis and Milonakis (2010: 1046) note, "constitute the most important explanatory variable for the study of institutions and organizations within new institutional economics." A special contribution made by new institutional economists is that they resort to methodological individualism (which suggests that, besides social institutions and social structure, subjective individual motivation is essential for explaining all social phenomena) and they focus on the cost and uncertainty confronting human interaction. New institutional economists "use standard economic theory to analyze the working of these institutions and to discover the part they play in the operations of the economy" (Coase 1984: 230) and answer "new questions [about] why economic institutions emerged the way they did and not otherwise" (Arrow 1987: 734).

Ronald Coase, the creator of transaction cost theory, examined the emergence of the firm as an alternative mode of economic organization in his seminal article "The Nature of the Firm" (1937). His main argument is that a set of costs is involved in market transactions – including costs relating to discovering price information, locating partners, negotiating and concluding a contract, and conducting inspections – but these costs may be reduced if transactions take place within a firm (Coase 1937, 1960). Building on Coase's insights, Williamson (1975) introduced the term "new institutional economics" in his book *Markets and Hierarchies.* His approach to economic organization "concerns social actions, underlining the affinity of this theory to sociology. The unit of analysis is the transaction understood as a bilateral or dyadic relation" (Richter 2015: 57). Williamson's analysis of economic governance is founded on assumptions of bounded rationality and opportunism. The former assumption shows that decision-makers are not able to take all relevant contingencies into consideration; the latter that economic actors are opportunistic and deceitful (Williamson 1993, 1985). The problem of opportunism and the risk of malfeasance, according to Williamson (2002: 172), can be minimized when governance structures are crafted to be "better attuned to their exchange needs." In other words, private ordering through internal organization (hierarchy) is developed to complement or replace court ordering that is not effective in a transaction environment characterized by incomplete information and opportunism (Richter 2015).

A group of distinguished scholars can make significant theoretical and empirical contributions to institutional analysis and change by developing a series of theoretical concepts and frameworks. For instance, North (1990) defines institutions as "rules of the game," which can be formal or informal, and explores the causal effect of rules on economic performance in a historical context. Aoki (2001) uses the subjective game model, combining the insights of classical and evolutionary game theory, to navigate the institutional linkages and complementarities in corporate economies. Ostrom (1990) pioneers a framework of institutional analysis and development to illustrate how local communities overcome collective action problems and govern their common resources. Their works enrich understanding of how people whose choices and opportunities are constrained by their environments develop solutions to the problems they face.

New economic sociology emerged in the 1980s, and its adherents regard social relations as an essential explanatory element. Mark Granovetter, in his article "Economic Action and Social Structure," stresses the "embeddedness" of economic actions in social processes by pointing out that "[a]ctors do not behave or decide as atoms outside a social context, nor do they adhere slavishly to a script written for them by the particular intersection of social categories that they happen to occupy. Their attempts at purposive action are instead embedded in concrete, ongoing systems of social relations" (1985: 487). Institutional economist Williamson's discussion of the development of institutional arrangements (e.g., hierarchies) to deter malfeasance is criticized by sociologist Granovetter. He argues that Williamson's approach is "undersocialized," as it fails to account for the essential role that concrete personal relations and the inherent obligations within them play in discouraging malfeasance (Granovetter 1985: 489). Williamson's dyadic approach (i.e., his presumption of a dyadic structure to contract) is criticized by sociologists for overestimating the effect of hierarchical power and disregarding the role of social embeddedness in dealing with opportunistic behavior and establishing trust (Granovetter 1995). According to sociologists, the structure of the relationship between economic actors is triadic rather than dyadic, because public exposure of opportunistic behavior in social networks invites third-party intervention and leads to rule-breakers being subjected to social sanctions, such as loss of social prestige and exclusion from future exchange opportunities in the network (Barbalet 2014).

Despite the fact that many sociologists are very critical of economics, some economic sociologists often draw on scholarship from new institutional economics (see Chan 2009), and "the concept of 'transaction cost' soon becomes part of the sociological language" (Nee and Swedberg 2005: 789). Economic sociologists' interest in transaction costs has weakened in recent decades, but their "interest for work by economists on institutions has grown steadily in importance" (Nee and Swedberg 2005: 791). Meanwhile, there has been a "sociological turn in new institutional economics," motivated by the difficulty of utilizing standard economic theory to explain institutions and institutional change (Nee 2005). For example, the embeddedness perspective is incorporated in Williamson's multilevel causal model of the economy, in which social embeddedness is on the highest level, imposing constraints on lower levels of analysis such as institutional environment, governance, and resource allocation and employment (Williamson 2000). Aoki (2001: 53) uses the theoretical treatment of linked games to systematically capture the concept of "social embeddedness," which is helpful for exploring the strategic interaction jointly affected by "the social exchange domain and economic transaction domain."

Other institutional economists, such as North (1990, 1993) and Greif (1994, 2006), also show great interest in the informal elements of institutions that are embedded in social relations, such as culture and belief systems, and they obtain insights from economic sociologists' analyses of how social mechanisms govern economic behavior. More systematically, Ostrom (1990) categorizes "attributes of community," along with "attributes of [the] physical world" and "rules in use," as three institutional components that constrain and regularize the behavior of actors in the action arena. "Attributes of community" refers to the social relationship among communities, often indicated by such variables as population homogeneity, trust, and norms. Ostrom's contribution to economics, according to economic sociologist Viviana A. Zelizer, includes efforts to incorporate the significance of social relations in the explanation of economic governance (Zelizer 2019: 2).

A closer look at new institutional economics and economic sociology suggests that "the contrast between the two fields is less sharp than some scientists might assume" (Richter 2015: 51). It is true that "economic sociology has enormously much to learn from New Institutional Economics' and new institutional economists "may want to be better informed about what has been happening in economic sociology" (Nee and Swedberg 2005: 789). There is no doubt that interaction between the two fields would increase efficiency in knowledge production. The reality of interdisciplinary collaboration is often disappointing, however. There has been little cooperation between economic sociologists and modern institutional economists in recent decades. This lack of cooperation, as Velthuis (1999: 641–642) argues, is due to "the fact that both schools evolve around different institutions (journals, conferences, departments)" and "the intellectual traditions of New Economic Sociology" ("[t]he American tradition represented by Parsons, the French tradition represented by Durkheim, and the German tradition represented by Max Weber") that are hostile toward (old) institutional economics.

New institutional economics and economic sociology differ from each other in their basic assumptions concerning human behavior: the former attributes human interaction to individual rationality (bounded or pure), while the latter examines the various motives of human actions, including rational choice. But a closer examination of key assumptions in the two fields shows that they are often compatible, rather than in conflict, with each other (Richter 2015). For example, bounded rationality in new institutional economics, especially transaction cost economics, is "comparable with Granovetter's concept of embeddedness" (Richter 2015: 67) and Zelizer's concept of relational work. (Relational work focuses on the matching of social ties, transactions, and media for those transactions and on how participants meld personal relationships and economic transactions.) Sociologists' research on embeddedness and relational work highlights the fact that human behavior is motivated not only by monetary rewards but also by nonmonetary rewards, such as trust, reciprocity, and social prestige (Granovetter 1985; Zelizer 2012). This does not contradict the new institutional economists' long-term individual utility maximization hypothesis, which also acknowledges humans' selfish and social motives (Benkler 2006; Williamson 1985).

Richter (2015: 69) notes that new institutional economics and new economic sociology may merge into new socio-economics in the course of time and "what seems indispensable, though, is to enrich economic institutional analysis with sociological … insights." New institutional economists can (or have managed to) improve their analytical skills by learning from sociologists who use "social relations, culture, cognition, norms, structures, power, and social institutions as explanatory variables for the interpretation of economic outcomes" (Beckert 1996: 803). Since the mid 1980s, many sociologists have gained insights from economics and deployed game theory and transaction cost theory to improve their social analysis (Swedberg 2001). Our analyses in this book benefit from the combination of economic sociology and new institutional economics. We use relevant concepts and theories from sociology and new institutional economics to construct a practical analytical approach for studying markets, particularly illegal ones, investigating risk and uncertainty within them, as well as examining institutions used for facilitating transactions and addressing disputes.

2.6 Constructing a Socio-economic Approach at the Macro Level: Examining the Nature of Illegal Markets

By synthesizing essential concepts and theories from sociology and institutional economics, this book establishes a socio-economic approach through which to investigate illegal markets and examine risks and governance institutions within them. The approach analyses the social order of illegal markets from two primary perspectives: the macro level, which illuminates the nature of illegal markets and the relationship between illegal markets, society, and the state; and the micro level, which examines the nature of transactional relationships, focusing on the differential punishments faced by exchange partners and the power dynamics that constrain illegal exchanges. This section discusses the macro-level aspect of our analytical approach. We argue that different characteristics of the illegal market give rise to different categories of risk, which encourage, and even compel, participants to develop different context-specific risk-resolution strategies.

Legitimacy is socially constructed, and it is the outcome of social interactions among a large number of social actors (Johnson et al. 2006; Weber 1956). The concept of legitimacy has been widely used by sociologists to examine public acceptance of an authority, a rule, a leader, an organization, or a practice. This concept can, therefore, be applied to study the social acceptability of illegal markets. Most recently, institutional economists Peter J. Boettke and his colleagues developed the concept of the morality of illicit markets (Boettke et al. 2023). Their research stresses the importance of considering moral legitimacy when analyzing illegal markets.

The moral legitimacy of illegal markets is closely related to state responses to the illegal market. The state may employ very repressive strategies (e.g., wars and massive campaigns) against certain kinds of illegal markets (e.g., hard drugs, human organs, and corrupt dealings) that are socially illegitimate, whereas the state may tolerate or ignore other types of illegal markets, such as the sale of counterfeit clothing, which is considered socially legitimate. Participants therefore experience different types of risk in different markets, or they encounter the same kinds of risk but to different degrees. Furthermore, the development of networked technologies has changed the ways in which individuals do business. The nature of online markets can vary significantly from that of offline markets. Many institutions, such as relationship-based mechanisms that work well in facilitating exchanges and deter opportunistic behavior in the physical world, may play little to no role in regulating online transactions. The anonymous nature of the internet increases the risk of defection and fraud, requiring market participants to develop new strategies.

2.6.1 Social Legitimacy

The state utilizes laws and regulations to delineate "what it considers to be legal or illegal," but members of society may not agree with the state-constructed dichotomy of legal/illegal. This is because some large groups "adhere to norms, values, and beliefs that conflict with the laws and regulations" (Webb et al. 2009: 495; see also Hübschle 2017), and what they consider legitimate may be defined as illegal by state laws and regulations. The term "social legitimacy" should therefore be incorporated into the analytical approach to explain social exchanges and market activities.

Legitimacy is defined by Max Weber (1956) as the subjective belief that a given action of an individual or a given social order is "desirable, proper, or appropriate within some socially constructed system of norms, values, beliefs, and definitions" (Suchman 1995: 574). The concept of legitimacy has been widely applied in the fields of political science and sociology. Political scientists and policy analysts utilize the concept of political legitimacy to examine whether laws and government policies are just or effective, which determines the extent to which a government can coercively enforce its citizens to follow them (Levi 2018; Paletta 2011; Tyler 2006b, 2023). As Levi and Sacks (2009: 311) suggest, "[t]he more a government is effective and fair, the more legitimacy that government is likely to attain, and the more it will possess the potential to elicit compliance without excessive monitoring or punitive action." Researchers in the field of sociology and other fields such as management use the concept of social legitimacy to evaluate whether an individual, group, or organization, as well as their actions and values, conform to societal norms and expectations. This evaluation determines the extent to which they can be accepted and approved by society (Johnson et al. 2006; Suchman 1995). Although social legitimacy and political legitimacy have varying emphases, they are closed connected. For example, if a government policy is unjust and ineffective, the government lacks the political legitimacy to enforce the policy. Simultaneously, such a policy, and at times even the government that designs and implements the policy, lack social legitimacy because society shows low levels of acceptance and recognition for the policy and/or the government.

In the study of illegal markets, the term social legitimacy is used to refer to "the tolerance, acceptance, or moral rejection associated with specific products and services that are offered illegally" (Beckert and Dewey 2017: 12). Researchers who adopt a sociological perspective suggest that the concept of the illegal market needs "internal differentiation" in order "to distinguish between illegal markets that enjoy social legitimacy and illegal markets that are perceived as repugnant" (Dewey 2019: 2). For example, the sale of child pornography, human organs, or heroin is neither legal nor legitimate, whereas trade in counterfeit clothes and software or informal housing is illegal but socially legitimate. Mayntz (2017: 40) describes this phenomenon as the divergence between (formal) legality and (social) legitimacy, arguing that:

> not everything that is formally legal is deemed to be legitimate by "rule takers." Formal rules are issued by a competent authority, but authority may only be claimed by rulers, not granted by the ruled; this can hold for clan chiefs, for CEOs, and for governments … On the other hand, actions formally defined as illegal can be considered legitimate … Where formal legality and social legitimacy diverge, legitimate illegality flourishes.

Recently, institutional economists have begun to consider the moral legitimacy of commerce when analyzing illicit markets. Boettke et al. (2023) utilize the concept of "morality" (moral legitimacy) to examine illicit markets in Soviet and post-Soviet Russia. They argue that illicit markets during the Soviet period were morally legitimate because they "grease the wheels" of commerce. As they demonstrate, throughout the Soviet period illicit markets served as "a means for improvement in living conditions, an opportunity for human betterment, and social cooperation where the scope for commerce had been limited by the predatory nature of the Soviet state" (Boettke et al. 2023: 421). However, illicit markets in post-Soviet Russia lost their moral legitimacy because they transformed into "a means by which to *enable* public predation by 'greasing the palms' of regulators due to political discretion in the privatization process" (Boettke et al. 2023: 411). Boettke et al.'s research offers crucial implications and presents a new avenue of research focused on the relationship between markets and morality.

Illegal but legitimate markets are commonly tolerated by many governments because of their social function. Essential social functions frequently emphasized in the existing literature are that these markets enable entrepreneurs to circumvent and evade predatory states, as well as generate employment opportunities and sources of income for a large part of the marginalized population (Beckert and Dewey 2017: 14; Boettke et al. 2023: 411; see also Dewey et al. 2017; Portes and Haller 2005). Meanwhile, these markets cause limited harm to local communities and the state. For example, counterfeit goods violate state laws but are socially acceptable, especially in developing countries where low-income customers cannot afford to buy brand names. Participants in illegal but legitimate markets do not directly challenge the authority of the state, because violence is usually not used within the market and the objectives of participating in market activities are economic rather than political. In countries where the state is fragmented and state-sponsored benefits are meagre, tolerance of illegal but legitimate markets is a way for the government to care for its citizens (Engwicht 2017: 200).

Illegal and illegitimate markets are not only socially unacceptable, but they also often attract significant attention from law enforcement agencies. To win elections or retain legitimacy, the state, whether democratic or authoritarian, frequently employs hard strategies (e.g., campaigns) to repress these markets. This is because illegal and illegitimate markets not only cause significant harm to local communities but also weaken public trust in, and the power of, state leaders. In other words, the level of social acceptability of illegal markets is closely associated with state attitudes and responses to these markets.

2.6.2 State Repression

Illegal markets are "artificial creations" because they originate from state prohibition (Arlacchi 1998: 203). State intervention in economic life not only "creates a 'formal space' of predictable and enforceable transactions where modern capitalism can flourish" but also provides opportunities for individuals to bypass and escape state controls, giving rise to informal and illegal economies (Portes and Haller 2005: 409). The production, exchange, and consumption of certain goods and services is forbidden or strictly regulated by the state in order to safeguard human dignity and protect the public (Arlacchi 1998). The state provides "a standardized system of coding and rules of exchange" in order to reduce transaction costs, protect private property, and resolve disputes that arise from legal activities; but this coding system, and state services for reducing transaction costs, cannot be accessed by those involved in illegal activities (Palan 2017: 110). Participants in illegal markets must therefore develop their own institutions, such as network-based mechanisms and privatized coercion (mafia groups and "thugs-for-hire") in order to promote cooperation and facilitate economic transactions (Gambetta 1993; Ong 2018).

Moreover, the state plays an essential role in repressing illegal markets. State repression of illegal markets, as Mayntz (2017: 44) points out, "varies in intensity, not only between fully developed modern nation-states and so-called fragile states, but also within states." The differences in state enforcement of prohibitions are due to both capacity and willingness (Engwicht 2017). To be specific, law enforcement agencies, especially in fragile states, not only lack the capacity to implement the law and repress illegal activities but are also unwilling to enforce state prohibitions, because officers are often corrupted by illegal entrepreneurs (Kassab and Rosen 2019). In fully developed modern nation-states, law enforcement agencies that are capable and efficient may still be reluctant to implement the laws against illegal markets that are considered socially legitimate (Engwicht 2017). "Strict enforcement of prohibitions" means that entrepreneurs in illegal markets face "significant risks of incarceration and asset seizure," whereas selective or "lax" enforcement, although it does not pose enormous risks, creates a situation in which "entrepreneurs are not guaranteed complete immunity from enforcement and still risk incarceration and asset seizure" (Beckert and Dewey 2017: 9).

Strong state repression. When the state strictly enforces prohibitions, market participants escape punishment through "hide" (assuring secrecy) and "bribe" (corrupting law enforcers; see Barnes 2017). The sociological and criminological literature on organized crime provides rich evidence of how organized crime groups, as producers and distributors of illegal goods and services, hide their illegal businesses and bribe public officials, especially those in the criminal justice system (Kelly 1999; Lee and Thoumi 1997; Shelley 1997; Wang 2013a). Illegal entrepreneurs usually create legal business ventures as fronts for their illegal activities (Smith 2009; Wedeman 2013; Xia 2008). For example, senior triad members in Hong Kong frequently use intermediaries to create an appearance of investing in entertainment premises, such as massage parlors, nightclubs, and dance halls. These premises are used by senior triad members to cover their prostitution and gambling businesses (Chu 2000). It is difficult for police officers to identify a triad member's role in a business, and the people who are arrested are usually duty managers and sex workers, who do not have any direct connection with the triad members.

Given the high risk of arrest and prosecution, participants in illegal markets assure secrecy by selecting collaborators and exchange partners with whom they are already closely connected. This is, first, because it is not easy for police officers to access secret information concerning the production, exchange, and consumption of illegal goods and services exclusively available to members of criminal networks. Second, strong bonds among criminal collaborators and exchange partners increase compliance and prevent them from betraying each other to the authorities (Von Lampe and Ole Johansen 2004). Close social relations operate as a form of hostage-taking: if a member defects or informs on their fellow associates, they will not only be excluded by other network members but also put their family and relatives at risk (Campana and Varese 2013; van Uhm and Wong 2019). Illegal entrepreneurs who have been betrayed are able to use network information to identify and punish betrayers' most immediate relatives.

Another effective way for illegal entrepreneurs to lower the risk of being punished is to bribe police officers, prosecutors, and judges (Chin and Godson 2006; Godson 2017). Bribery – in the form of money, expensive gifts, or free sexual services – is frequently used by drug dealers and sex ring operators to create mutually beneficial networks with corrupt law enforcement officials (Antonopoulos 2013). Corrupt officials, in turn, provide bribers with services including "protection against extortion conducted by public officials, protection of criminal businesses, protection against police harassment, protection against criminal investigation and protection against legal punishment" (Wang 2013a: 68).

Weak state repression. When the state adopts the mode of selective or lax enforcement of prohibitions, participants in illegal markets still need to develop strategies to mitigate the risk of state intervention. Bribing law enforcers remains an effective strategy to evade state intervention even in a market that is less likely to face severe state repression. Corrupt law enforcers often provide their bribers (illegal entrepreneurs) with private protection such as turning a blind eye to bribers' illegal market activities.

Two other mechanisms developed by participants in illegal but legitimate markets are collective resistance and political patronage. Collective resistance means that individuals are mobilized to unite and fight against law enforcement agencies. By deterring government intervention and resolving the typical problem of free riding, collective resistance is a feasible strategy for marginalized populations (the urban underclass) to pursue their interests. Empirical evidence suggests that organizing collective resistance often requires effective governance institutions, such as smooth information flow, shared rules, a well-organized structure, and strong leadership (Grossman 2020, 2021; Jiang and Wang 2022).

Given that selective or lax enforcement of prohibitions is usually used by the state to regulate markets that are illegal but socially legitimate, illegal entrepreneurs who want to avoid punishment need to justify their illegal activities and increase their public acceptance. In modern nation-states, especially authoritarian regimes, the effectiveness of collective resistance often lies more in its power to challenge the political legitimacy of state repression against illegal market activities than in its physical confrontation with law enforcement agencies, because modern nation-states are able to cost-effectively suppress resistance (Cai 2010; Tufekci 2017). Market participants deploy collective resistance to generate public sympathy toward illegal market participants and public criticism of state repression and even of the ability of the state to govern effectively (Levi et al. 2009; Lin 2022; Tyler 2006a). It is worth noting that, in many scenarios, just the threat of organizing collective resistance by illegal market participants serves as a credible commitment preventing government intervention.

Seeking political patronage is another mechanism by which participants in illegal but legitimate markets mitigate the risk of state intervention. Like collective resistance, political patronage also relies on illegal market participants' collective efforts to enhance the social acceptance of their activities and reduce the likelihood of state intervention. Seeking political patronage differs from collective resistance, however, by relying on the rationalization of illegal but legitimate activities (e.g., through emphasizing their contribution to the local economy) rather than causing tensions with local authorities. By doing so, local government officials show sympathy and significant tolerance toward legitimate illegal markets and the participants within these markets. For instance, a community living in illegal housing can justify their illegal housing project by emphasizing how it provides affordable housing for rural immigrants and promotes economic growth (Zhang and Zhao 2018). Likewise, street vendors can also increase the social acceptability of their businesses by demonstrating the harmlessness of their illegal activities and creating orderly self-regulation to avoid disputes (Grossman 2020, 2021; Hummel 2017, 2021).

2.6.3 Illegal Businesses in the Online Realm

The development of information technologies has had a huge impact on the ways in which market participants conduct their businesses. Sellers and buyers have become increasingly active in exchanging goods and services online. In parallel, participants in illegal markets have also begun to utilize information technologies to create or engage in illegal online marketplaces. Illegal online transactions are associated with even greater risk and uncertainty than offline transactions. The anonymous nature of the internet causes information asymmetry, a major obstacle in online exchanges.

Participants in illegal markets who engage in exchanges in the physical world typically utilize relationship-based mechanisms, such as reputation and gossip, to seek exchange partners and deter opportunistic behavior. However, online exchange partners often cannot rely on information provided by social ties to assess the trustworthiness and reputation of exchange partners. As a result, illegal entrepreneurs face "the risks of doing business with anonymous fraudsters, thieves, and extortionists" (Lusthaus 2018b: 20). Moreover, anonymity on the internet not only prevents potential buyers from assessing "the veracity of any seller's claim" and the quality of goods and services but also leads to moral hazard – "the seller has an incentive to shirk and not complete the transaction after receiving the money from the buyer" (Odabas et al. 2017: 95). Internet technologies allow illegal market participants to operate beyond geographic boundaries, but moving beyond these boundaries makes traditional enforcement methods, such as violence and intimidation, no longer cost-effective.

To address these risks and promote cooperation, participants in illegal online markets who rely on anonymous internet marketplaces (e.g., Silk Road) can use the reputation information generated by the website to identify trustworthy exchange partners. Forum or website administrators enable buyers and sellers to use their platform to rate each other and share information about each other's deeds and misdeeds. This generates reputational information about exchange participants in illegal online marketplaces and promotes cooperative behavior (Décary-Hétu and Dupont 2013; Holt 2013; Odabas et al. 2017). For example, even though sellers and buyers in crypto markets (online marketplaces on the dark web) use encryption software to conceal their locations and identities, sellers of illegal drugs have strong incentives to behave honestly and gain better ratings because "sellers with a better rating history charge higher prices and sell their merchandise faster than sellers with no or a bad rating history" (Przepiorka et al. 2017: 752).

Many participants in illegal online markets who do not rely on institutions provided by internet marketplaces must develop their own strategies to enforce compliance and prevent dishonesty. They often use information hostages, which "is perhaps even more relevant to the realm of cybercrime" (Lusthaus 2018b: 22). Information hostages have become a core mechanism for guaranteeing the stability and security of many illegal online markets. For example, a recent case of cybersex crime in Hong Kong showed that potential members of a sex-video chatroom were required to upload a photograph of their partners in order to join a sex-video chatroom in Telegram Messenger, and members were also required to repeatedly share sex videos and photos of their partners in order to gain the trust of chat group managers and fellow members (Nip 2020). This use of information hostages ensured the trustworthiness of participants and excluded undercover agents and dishonest persons (see also Gambetta and Przepiorka 2019).

2.7 Constructing a Socio-economic Approach at the Micro Level: Examining the Nature of Exchange Relationships

The micro-level aspect of our analytical approach investigates *the nature of exchange relationships*. Drawing on insights from the existing literature on economic sociology and social psychology, our analytical approach focuses on illegal exchanges by entering "into a social space structured around sellers and buyers" (Beckert and Dewey 2017: 2), identifying the different levels of punishment faced by exchange partners (Wang 2020a), and examining power-dependence relations between exchange partners (Emerson 1962; Molm et al. 2000).

According to sociologists, exchange partners may be embedded in imbalanced power-dependence relationships: Exchange partners who are low-power actors are highly dependent on their exchange partners, while exchange partners who are high-power actors possess scarce resources, giving them control over the exchange relationship (Molm 1981). A low-power actor, therefore, needs to develop strategies to mitigate these power imbalances and avoid being exploited. Similarly, institutional economics examines the role of bargaining power (the distribution of power and bargaining opportunities among exchange participants or specific interest communities) in shaping the institutions (e.g., rules and norms) that regulate economic interactions (De Keyzer 2013; Schmitz 2013).

Further, the micro-level aspect of the analytical approach takes the risk of criminal punishment into consideration. This is because law enforcement agencies concentrate on apprehending producers and distributors of illegal goods or services, as well as illegal market participants who resort to violence. As a result, producers and sellers are high-risk actors in the illegal market, whereas buyers are low-risk actors. This imbalance offers a low-risk actor an incentive to extort a high-risk actor by threatening to expose their illegal deal to law enforcement agencies. High-risk actors therefore need to develop extralegal governance mechanisms to lower the risk of being extorted by their exchange partners.

2.7.1 Power-Dependence Relationships

A power-dependence perspective enriches our understanding of exchange relationships among participants in illegal markets. Power-dependence theory, originally formulated by sociologist Richard Emerson (1962) and further developed by Cook et al. (1983), Lawler (1992), and Molm (1994, 1997), looks at "the power aspects of social relations" (i.e., dependence, power, and power-balancing operations), while paying little or no attention to "particular features of the persons or groups engaged in such relations" (Emerson 1962: 32). Actors in a social exchange relationship, whether persons or groups, are mutually dependent, and dependence is the structural basis of power. As Molm (1989: 1394) points out, "An actor's dependence increases with the value of the outcomes that the other provides and decreases with the availability of alternative sources for those same outcomes." However, power is often not equally distributed in the exchange relationship (Cook and Emerson 1978; Cook et al. 1983). In power-imbalanced relationships, actors are not equally dependent on each other, and the less dependent actor possesses a structural power advantage that can be used for obtaining personal favors at the expense of the other exchange partner (Molm 1997).

Existing studies of power-dependence relationships demonstrate that "unequal dependencies produce unequal exchange; the less-dependent actor receives more of the other's potential resources than he or she gives in return" (Molm 1994: 76; see also Cook and Emerson 1978; Cook et al. 1983; Molm 1981). Moreover, a dependency asymmetry may entail systematic exploitation of the lower-power (more dependent) actor by the higher-power actor (Oba and Semercioz 2005; Özen et al. 2016). Although institutional economists have not applied the concept of power dynamics in their analysis of economic actions, they indeed utilize the concept of bargaining power, known as the distribution of power, to study the changes in institutions regulating access to common-pool resources. As De Keyzer (2013: 518) argues, institutional persistence and change are usually determined by the needs of the interest groups that possess the most bargaining power, rather than following "the path towards the highest efficiency or economic rationality" (see also Haller 2007). Both power-dependence theory and the concept of bargaining power stress the significance of power in economic interactions, offering useful insights for the study of exchange relationships in illegal markets.

It is not safe for sellers of illegal goods and services to market their products through public channels. As a result, "the curtailing of marketing instruments on illegal markets makes these markets more demand-driven than legal markets" (Beckert and Wehinger 2013: 12). The more the buyer values illegal goods and services and is less likely to obtain them from alternative sources, the more the buyer is dependent on the seller and the more power the seller gains. In these circumstances, the buyer, a low-power actor, needs to develop extralegal governance institutions in order to obtain exchange opportunities and lower the risk of being exploited by the seller, a high-power actor (see Wang 2020a). In general, low-power actors rely on two power-balancing strategies. The first is to select exchange partners who are known through social relations. Social bonds, characterized by "mutual positive emotions" (Suvilehto et al. 2015: 13811), create moral obligations and require high-power actors to provide favors to low-power actors; and the social embeddedness of illegal transactions reduces high-power actors' motivation to exploit low-power actors and stops high-power actors from charging high prices for low-quality goods and services. The second institution is that low-power actors can reveal their illegal deals to law enforcement agencies if the high-power actors are also high-risk actors who would face severe criminal punishment if caught.

2.7.2 Different Levels of Punishment

Participants in illegal markets may not only be embedded in power-imbalanced exchange relationships, but they also encounter different risks of punishment or varying levels of the same category of punishment. The criminal justice system imposes different types of penalties and different degrees of punishment according to the seriousness of the offense, the characteristics of offenders, and the validity and reliability of evidence gathered by police officers and prosecutors (Sanders et al. 2010). Police officers devote most of their resources to detecting and investigating serious crime – such as burglary, rape, and assault – and pay less attention to less violent or less serious offenses. The vast majority of less serious offenses, especially those committed by young or first-time offenders, and millions of misdemeanors, such as antisocial behavior, shoplifting, or minor assault, are dealt with by outright dismissal or a lesser degree of punishment (Walker 1983). For example, police officers in China prefer not to record crime reports if they believe that the reported case is "too small" and does not deserve criminal investigation (Wang 2020b: 433).

In parallel, though all participants in illegal markets risk arrest and incarceration, they are often treated differently in the criminal justice system and receive different levels of punishment. On the one hand, producers, traffickers, and sellers of goods that are both illegal and illegitimate often cause significant harm to society and if convicted face severe punishment, such as the death penalty or life imprisonment. On the other hand, consumers of illegal goods cause less harm to the community and usually receive lenient or no punishment, perhaps a suspended sentence or conditional discharge. In illegal drug markets, for example, Wang (2020a: 1285) notes that in most countries "drug sellers usually receive a long prison sentence and sometimes even the death penalty, whereas the consumption of illicit drugs usually leads only to short-term detention."

In the illegal market, an exchange partner who risks lenient or no criminal punishment is a low-risk actor who may lack loyalty to the seller, a high-risk actor. Different levels of punishment meted out to different market participants increase the risk of betrayal and can lead to extortion: A low-risk actor may extort a high-risk actor by threatening to reveal their illegal deal to police officers. Engaging in an illegal deal means sharing information about a criminal act, which constitutes a form of hostage-taking (Campana and Varese 2013). A high-risk actor must therefore use extralegal governance institutions to build customer loyalty and handle the risk of extortion. For example, the risk of betrayal and extortion can be mitigated by embedding illegal transactions in social relations. As discussed in Section 2.3, exchange partners use information acquired through social relations to identify reliable and trustworthy exchange partners, and individuals who are connected through social relations care more about the long-term benefits that would be generated by future exchange opportunities than the short-term benefits of opportunistic and selfish actions (Granovetter 1985; Kleemans and Van de Bunt 1999; Van de Bunt et al. 2014).

In addition, traffickers and sellers often have greater ability than buyers to use violence to enforce agreements, and thus sellers of illegal goods can ensure buyers' compliance by threatening violence. For example, the high value of illegal goods and the absence of legal means of obtaining justice generate conflicts, "instabilities, uncertainties, and distrust in the market," making the use of violence an integral part of illegal drug markets (Prieger and Kulick 2015: 1264; see also Casavant and Collin 2001). According to Caulkins et al. (2006), "a seller who is particularly effective in the use of violence may face lower enforcement costs than other dealers" (p. 1), and "the capacity to threaten violence" as an ex ante threat rather than violence per se is often enough to enable a seller to collect debts, prevent users from robbing sellers, and enforce compliance (p. 5). Third, hostage-holding is another ex ante mechanism that elicits compliance and stops low-risk partners from betraying their high-risk partners. The hostage could take the form of a physical asset, cash, or compromising information.

High-risk actors can also conceal their identity by employing intermediaries or moving their businesses onto the internet, which is built on anonymity. Senior triad members, as mentioned in Section 2.6.2, use the disguise of investing in entertainment businesses. In the online illegal market, sellers and buyers of drugs "could publicly discuss, plan, and participate in illegal activities" because e-commerce markets provide them with "verifiable pseudonyms and securely obfuscated real-world identities" (Ladegaard 2020: 532). The use of intermediaries and the anonymity of the internet make illegal transactions nonidentifiable, preventing high-risk actors from being caught by police officers or extorted by low-risk actors.

2.8 Exploring China's Illegal Markets: Insights from the Socio-economic Analytical Approach

As discussed in Section 2.1, both Weber's concept of legitimacy and Boettke et al.'s theoretical interpretation of the morality of illicit markets offer crucial insights for studying the nature of illegal markets, which constitutes the macro-level aspect of the socio-economic approach. We therefore argue that illegal markets can be divided into two major categories: legitimate illegal markets and illegitimate illegal markets. This categorization not only inspires us to investigate both socially legitimate and socially illegitimate illegal markets in China, but also provides a solid foundation to further examine why participants in different markets face varying levels of risk caused by state repression.

In the macro-level aspect of the socio-economic approach, the examination of the role of state repression is crucial, because the level of state repression is highly relevant to the social legitimacy of illegal markets. State prohibition and repression significantly influence the social order within these markets. To survive, participants in illegitimate illegal markets must deal with two different categories of risk. They first need to address the significant risk brought by law enforcement agencies. In past decades, the Chinese government has shown zero tolerance toward serious and organized crime, as well as illegal markets that cause significant harm to local communities (Wang and Wang 2024). The central government frequently utilizes campaign-style law enforcement, mobilizing all available resources (e.g., judicial, fiscal, and propaganda) to crack down on any criminal elements the government believes challenge the authority and legitimacy of the party state. Facing extensive law enforcement measures and a strong state, participants in illegitimate illegal markets have to conceal their illegal businesses or bribe law enforcers, such as police officers, while avoiding confrontations with the state and refraining from using violence that could attract police attention. Second, participants in illegitimate illegal markets need to address market-based uncertainties (e.g., seeking trustworthy partners, addressing conflicts, and preventing opportunism), relying on nonviolent institutions such as close social relations and information hostages.

Participants in legitimate illegal markets usually face lenient punishment – fines or confiscation rather than criminal punishment. To address uncertainties and risks caused by law enforcement, they have more choices than those in illegitimate illegal markets. Their choices include bribing law enforcers, using collective resistance to challenge the political legitimacy of state repression, and seeking political patronage (e.g., rationalization of their activities) to prevent state intervention. To handle market-based uncertainties, they commonly cooperate and exchange with others beyond their close relations, and they also employ innovative strategies to facilitate cooperation and transactions. These strategies include forming informal associations, developing norms and rules, and establishing cost-effective channels of information transmission.

The micro-level aspect of the socio-economic approach inspires us to concentrate on the exchange relationships between individual participants (e.g., buyers and sellers). Because of power imbalances and varying levels of criminal punishment, different participants encounter varying risks and uncertainties arising from exchanges. In power-imbalanced social relations, participants can be divided into high-power and low-power actors. It is therefore crucial to make such a distinction and to examine the strategies developed by low-power actors to gain opportunities for engaging in exchanges with high-power actors and to protect themselves from exploitation by high-power actors. Moreover, we need to differentiate between high-risk and low-risk actors when exchange participants face notably different levels of criminal punishment, and also investigate the methods high-risk actors use to lower the risk of extortion by low-risk actors who may threaten to report criminal activities to law enforcement agencies such as the police and anti-corruption agencies.

Additionally, the advancement of internet technologies has facilitated the rapid growth of illegal businesses in cyberspace. Internet anonymity and information asymmetry have not only significantly impacted the nature of illegal markets and exchange relationships but also caused considerable transaction risks for exchange participants. Conventional institutions, such as the threat of violence and social relations, often play almost no role in fostering cooperation in the online setting. Therefore, we need to take illegal online markets into account and investigate the major risks caused by internet anonymity and information asymmetry, as well as innovative strategies used to enforce compliance and deter dishonesty.

2.9 Conclusion

Drawing on insights from sociology and new institutional economics, this chapter has developed an analytical approach that explains the social order of illegal markets. It is suggested that illegal markets can be analyzed through both macro-level and micro-level dimensions. Macro dimensions include social legitimacy and levels of state repression, both of which are closely related and offer valuable insights into the different categories of illegal markets and their associated risks. Participants in legitimate illegal markets usually face no or light criminal sanctions, whereas those in illegitimate illegal markets are faced with severe criminal punishment once convicted. As a result, participants who face severe punishment must develop strategies to lower the risk of detection and avoid police attention. Additionally, when traditional illegal markets go online, participants in those markets face substantially increased risks because of the anonymity of the internet.

Micro dimensions focus on the nature of exchange relationships between sellers and buyers, enabling researchers understand the existence of differences in the risks experienced by these participants. These exchange partners can be high-risk or low-risk actors, because sellers and buyers may face different levels of criminal punishment. They can also be high-power or low-power actors, because their exchanges may be embedded in unbalanced power relations, and thus exchange participants have to deal with the risks caused by such an imbalance. Combining macro and micro dimensions enhances researchers' ability to identify context-specific risks in illegal markets and understand how different types of extralegal governance institutions can be used to mitigate risks. This combination also enriches the existing literature by explaining how the same types of institutions function in different situations.

Although we drew on a broad literature review when developing our analytical approach, the approach is still far from complete because it does not include all aspects of illegal markets and unlawful transactions. Individual researchers suffer from limited knowledge and cognitive bias, both of which have a negative effect on creativity and innovation. Further development of this analytical approach therefore demands further interdisciplinary collaboration. Moreover, institutional complexity is prevalent in illegal economies, and market participants are more innovative in developing governance institutions than might be supposed. This means that the institutions mentioned in this chapter are not complete, and researchers need to continue to observe what happens in illegal markets, why certain types of institution are developed, and how these institutions work in practice. In addition, even though this book uses four cases to examine the social order of illegal markets and the risks and extralegal governance institutions within them, it is not comprehensive due to the limited number of markets selected and the potential for neglecting certain institutions that play no role in the chosen markets while performing essential functions in others.

3

Unmasking China's Illegal Markets

Research Design and Fieldwork

3.1 Introduction

This chapter offers detailed discussions about multiple case study design and the rationale for the selection of the four cases in this study (unlicensed street vending, small property right housing, buying and selling of public appointments, and online loan sharks). We conducted field research, consisting of a total of 318 in-depth semistructured interviews, focusing on these four cases. This chapter explains how informants were selected, how the interviews were structured, and how we handled the challenges and ethical issues we encountered. The chapter also briefly discusses the limitations of our research design and empirical data.

3.2 Multiple Case Study Design

Qualitative research methods such as interviews and participant observation are commonly adopted by researchers to study private rules and informal institutions. For example, Grossman (2021) spent many months conducting interviews with traders, market leaders, and government officials in Lagos to examine the role of private trade associations in promoting trade and resolving disputes, both between traders and the local government and among traders themselves, in an informal sector. Murtazashvili (2016) utilizes empirical data collected through a large number of interviews, group interviews, and careful field observations to study customary institutions at the village level in Afghanistan. Qualitative research methods are particularly helpful for examining extralegal governance institutions because they provide rich empirical data that enhances our understanding of how informal rules and institutions operate in informal and illegal markets. Researchers may not be able to uncover these issues through other research methods.

This book adopts a qualitative research method and a multiple case study design. A case study is "an empirical inquiry about a contemporary phenomenon (a 'case') set within its real-world context – especially when the boundaries between phenomenon and context are not clearly evident" (Yin 2009: 18; see also Gerring 2006). The case study method is very helpful for addressing both *descriptive* questions ("What is happening or has happened?") and *explanatory* questions ("How or why did something happen?") (Yin 2012: 5) and can be applied to a single case or multiple cases. Yin (2012: 7) notes that although "the multiple-case design is usually more difficult to implement than a single-case design … the ensuing data can provide greater confidence in your findings." Researchers in the interdisciplinary field of institutional analysis have noted the importance of using qualitative research methods, such as multiple case studies, to study institutions (Poteete et al. 2010; Skarbek 2020b). These methods allow researchers to use different types of evidence, such as archival materials, interviews, and observation, to study thick concepts and obtain "a more accurate and complete understanding of institutions" (Skarbek 2020b: 411).

Because an analytical approach combining micro and macro elements was generated in Chapter 2, this book needs to adopt a multiple case study design in order to better understand the characteristic of illegal markets, the nature of exchange relationships, and how private individuals mitigate risks and secure cooperation in different illegal markets. It is important to strike a balance between the number of cases and the level of detail: Focusing on one or two cases would produce a highly detailed, precise description of specific types of risk and extralegal governance institutions, but this could not cover all the dimensions mentioned in the analytical approach or illustrate the range of risks and the complexity of the institutions involved. Selecting a large number of cases is very helpful for illustrating different forms of risk and informal institution, but a large number also poses significant challenges, such as collecting sufficient data and analyzing each case in depth. We have therefore selected four cases, each of which illustrates particular aspects of illegal markets, as shown in Table 3.1.

Unlicensed street vending and the small property right housing market are illegal but socially legitimate; state enforcement agencies usually tolerate these activities and adopt soft policing strategies. Street vending creates an enormous number of job opportunities for marginalized populations in China, so it enjoys a high degree of social legitimacy. Chinese *chengguan* (a city's urban management or administrative officers) adopt four soft strategies to enforce the law and regulate unlicensed street vending: "turning a deaf ear when cursed [by street vendors and passersby], providing help [to

Table 3.1 *The use of analytical dimensions to identify core features of cases selected*

Dimensions / Cases	Macro dimensions			Micro dimensions	
	Social legitimacy	Level of state repression	Offline/ Online	Imbalanced power relationships	Differential punishment imposed on exchange participants
Unlicensed street vending	High	Low, occasionally medium	Offline	Not obvious	Not significant
The small property right housing market	High	Low, occasionally medium	Offline	Not obvious	Not significant
Corrupt transactions in buying and selling public appointments	Low	High	Offline	Obvious	Significant
The illegal online lending market	Low	Low before 2018; high after 2018	Online	Obvious	Significant

street vendors], playing the vulnerability card, and making friends during prolonged interactions [with street vendors]" (Jiang 2020: 5). *Chengguan* strictly enforce laws and regulations only when the city is inspected by upper-level government agencies, competes for the National Sanitary City award or the National Civilized City award, or during the National People's Congress and the People's Congress of the City. Without state support, street vendors need to develop extralegal governance mechanisms to address a number of market-based uncertainties, such as competitive bidding among vendors, socio-spatial disputes over public space, and uncertainty caused by inconsistency in law enforcement.

Small property right housing refers to housing built on collectively owned village land. It is a widespread practice in many peri-urban areas of Chinese cities, and the housing is mainly sold to people who are not from the village, such as migrant laborers. The practice is illegal but socially acceptable; because it is "generally cheaper and more affordable than urban commercial housing, urban middle- and low-income groups and migrants prefer informal settlements over commercial housing" (Zhou and Yau 2021: 915). Due to the illegal nature of the market, participants in the small property right housing market have to develop strategies to overcome both market-based risks, such as opportunistic behavior on the part of the exchange partners, and political–legal uncertainties, such as government interference or crackdowns. Local governments may interfere with the local small property right housing market when they believe that their intervention is unlikely to cause collective resistance. Expropriating collectively owned land while selling land-use rights on the market results in massive quantities of land conveyancing fees as extra-budgetary revenues.

Studies of unlicensed street vending and the small property right housing market improve understanding of macro dimensions by revealing how formally illegal but socially legitimate markets work, but, as Table 3.1 shows, they do not improve understanding of micro dimensions, such as the differential punishment imposed on exchange participants and the imbalances in power relationships. This prompts us to consider the informal job market in the public sector (i.e., the buying and selling of public appointments) and the illegal online lending market. Neither of these markets is legal or considered legitimate, and participants within them must navigate risks caused by differential punishment and imbalanced power relationships.

The corrupt buying and selling of public appointments and the illegal online lending market are neither legal nor socially acceptable. Examining these markets improves our comprehension of illegal markets from a macro perspective. Participants in these markets must put aside their moral scruples and will suffer severe punishment if arrested and prosecuted. After President Xi initiated his nationwide anti-corruption campaign in 2012, the Chinese government significantly increased its scrutiny of personnel matters, and those who buy and sell public appointments now face both Party disciplinary punishment and severe criminal punishment. Since the Chinese government began its "Sweep Away Black and Eradicate Evil" campaign in 2018, targeting organized and gang crime, online loan sharks have also faced an extremely high risk of criminal punishment. The selection of corrupt transactions and the online illegal lending market as case studies contributes to the understanding of how private individuals react to state repression in illegitimate illegal markets.

The selection of these two cases also enhances the study of illegal markets from a micro perspective, because participants in these two illegal markets are embedded in imbalanced power relationships. To be specific, senior government positions in the government are scarce resources, and lower-ranking officials who seek to buy public appointments are highly dependent on the sellers, who are higher-ranking officials (Wang 2020a).

In online loan-sharking, the sharks must develop strategies to control the exchange relationship with borrowers, most of whom are untrustworthy, and compel them to make repayments; otherwise, the sharks are likely to lose the money they loaned. The imbalanced power relationship promotes compliance, but it often leads to the exploitation of the less powerful actor (who takes out a loan or buys a public appointment) by the more powerful actor (who offers the loan or sells the public appointment).

Buyers and sellers in these markets experience different levels of punishment: Sellers of public appointments and loan sharks risk severe criminal punishment, whereas their buyers and borrowers encounter little or no punishment. This imbalance often leads to the actor at less risk coercing the actor at greater risk by threatening to reveal their illegal deal to law enforcement agencies. In addition, the case of the illegal online lending market makes a special addition to this book, because it is the only case used by this book to show how illegal market participants address risk and promote cooperation online. Empirical data concerning this case reveals new forms of risks caused by internet anonymity and innovative strategies developed by market participants to make up for the lack of cost-effectiveness of traditional offline strategies, such as relationship-based mechanisms and violence to promote compliance in an online environment.

3.3 Fieldwork and Data Collection

For the study of illegal markets, as well as risks and extralegal governance institutions within these markets, a multiple case design was deemed more powerful than a single case design, because participants in different markets deploy different strategies or use the same strategy differently to reduce risks and enhance cooperation. But a multiple case study has its disadvantages. For example, conducting multiple case studies can be very costly and demand substantial time. Yin (2012: 131) also notes that "doing multiple-case studies takes more effort and may require a team of researchers rather than a solo investigator." This book includes four case studies in order to offer a granular depiction of risks and non-state institutions in different social settings, and it is therefore a product of collaboration between two scholars of different disciplines who collected empirical data for all four cases. This section focuses on our experiences during fieldwork and data collection. This book also benefits from empirical data collected by our research collaborators, who generously allowed us to use their interview data. This section consists of four parts, each of which focuses on data collection for a particular case. Each part discusses how interview respondents were selected, how the interviews were structured, and how we dealt with ethical concerns and other challenges during our fieldwork.

3.3.1 Street Vending

Street vending is prevalent in most Chinese cities. However, most street vendors are unlicensed, and their activities are considered a violation of city bylaws. Given that China is a huge continental country, where levels of economic development and sociocultural contexts vary widely in different provinces and cities, urban management officers often develop context-tailored methods of regulating street vending. Similarly, street vendors' strategies to promote cooperation and handle state intervention vary from city to city. The ideal way of collecting empirical evidence is to select a number of cities, including first-tier cities (e.g., Beijing, Guangzhou, Shanghai, or Shenzhen), second-tier cities such as capital cities of provinces, third-tier cities, and small cities or counties. But doing fieldwork in multiple cities is unfeasible and less productive for individual researchers. Instead, we selected Guangzhou, a first-tier city, and Guilin, a third-tier city. We chose these specific cities because we had already established social connections with urban management officers and street vendors.

The regulation of street vendors in these two cities varies with respect to the frequency and level of fines imposed on unlicensed vendors. Nevertheless, the major strategies used to manage street vending are almost identical: soft policing strategies with occasionally strict enforcement of laws and regulations (see Figure 3.1). The strict enforcement creates a clean urban image during inspections by upper-level government agencies and major political events. This book focuses on comparing risks and extralegal governance institutions in different illegal markets, rather than examining subtle differences in the daily regulation of street vending or the ways in which street vendors promote cooperation and interact with city management officers in different cities. Therefore, we believe that two research sites are sufficient for understanding how street vendors handle market-based uncertainties and respond to state intervention.

Qualitative methods were used to collect data, including semistructured interviews and participant observation. Our research team approached two groups of people. The first group comprised 88 city administrative or management officers at different levels, and the second group comprised 56 street vendors. We also conducted repeat interviews with some participants, which allowed us to gather additional data. In total, we conducted 179 interviews between 2014 and 2021. The snowball sampling method of

Figure 3.1 Urban management officers confiscating an unlicensed street vendor's stall and merchandise (author's photo).

recruiting participants was used: We approached research participants with whom we had already established connections and asked them to identify other potential subjects. We designed interview questions based on participants' occupations and personal experience. Questions asked of frontline city management officers concerned their daily interactions with street vendors, challenges they faced when regulating unlicensed street vendors, securing vendors' compliance, and dealing with noncompliant vendors. Questions for senior officials focused mainly on the regulatory framework applicable to street vendors, a historical overview of government responses to street vending, and how they cooperated with other departments, such as the police, in the process of regulating street vending. Questions asked in interviews with street vendors included the problems and challenges they faced in order to survive, how they negotiated access to public space, the ways in which they cooperated or competed with other vendors, and their strategies for avoiding fines and protecting their goods and equipment from confiscation by city officers.

One member of our research team engaged in participant observation both as a street vendor and as a city management intern. This not only enabled us to identify and create connections with potential interviewees, but also offered excellent opportunities for the researcher to observe the daily practice of regulating street vending and street vendors' daily interactions with customers, other vendors, and city administrative officers from a neutral perspective. This was very helpful when assessing the reliability and validity of the interview data collected from vendors and officers. During the process of participant observation, all street vendors who did business near her pitch and all colleagues with whom she interacted were informed about her identity as a researcher. But ethical issues could arise in certain circumstances; for example, the observer might not have been able to inform street vendors and city management officers who became embroiled in conflict or violent confrontation that they were being observed by a researcher. The solution to these ethical issues was that the observer took field notes recording interactions between street vendors and city management officers that did not include any personally identifiable information. This method can be justified because (1) there were always large numbers of passersby present, so the observer's presence was insignificant and did not increase the risk to people being observed; (2) it ensured the observer's safety; and (3) it facilitated objective observation, recording exact details of what happened in these daily interactions between street vendors and frontline officials without opinion or interruption.

3.3.2 Small Property Right Housing

With China's rapid urbanization and economic growth, small property right housing markets have proliferated in the peri-urban areas of cities (see Figure 3.2). To maximize profits and meet increasing demand

Figure 3.2 Small property right housing in Zheng Ge Zhuang, one of the largest informal housing communities in Beijing (author's photos).

for affordable housing, villagers, village committees, and external private developers (real-estate investors) build small property right housing on collectively owned land. These dwellings are then sold to buyers such as labor migrants, the retired, and villagers. In order to understand the operation and persistence of the extralegal housing market, we conducted fieldwork with a range of market participants, such as house builders, buyers, and village committee members, in three cities, including two first-tier cities, Shenzhen and Beijing, and one third-tier city, Sanya, which is a tourist city in China's Hainan province.

We began by using the snowball sampling method to generate a pool of participants. Through recommendations made by friends who had personal connections with buyers and owners of small property right housing, we were able to conduct formal interviews with them. Reassured by existing interpersonal relationships, these interviewees were often willing to share their experience, knowledge, and opinions about the market. We then contacted other appropriate interviewees by ourselves. We visited the sites of small property right housing projects, where we invited any sellers and potential buyers who happened to be there to be interviewed. We also joined public WeChat (China's most popular social media platform) groups organized by small property right housing agents, who invited anyone interested in selling or buying small property right housing to join the group. All chat group members therefore became potential interviewees. Due to the lack of social connections and interpersonal trust, sellers and buyers we met in person on the sites of small property right projects, as well as chat group members, were often hesitant to accept our invitations. To gain their trust, we kept showing up, chatting with them in person or online whenever there was an opportunity, and participating in their gatherings (e.g., sports). As a result, some of them grew to trust us and agreed to be interviewed. In total, we conducted forty-one interviews in 2018 and 2019, including villagers (n = 15), members of village committees (n = 3), private developers (n = 3), agents (n = 5), buyers (n = 12), and government officials (n = 3).

To investigate the social order of the small property right market, our interviews with villagers, buyers, sellers, and village committee members focused on the following aspects: categories of small property right housing and their physical and spatial features, interactions between buyers and sellers and specific risks they encountered, the approaches and mechanisms market participants use to mitigate risks, the reasons for the success or failure of their risk mitigation strategies, and the multiple roles played by village committees. Interviews with agents focused on strategies they suggested to their customers, both buyers and sellers, for securing transactions; the operation of the price mechanism in the market; and the reasons why they believed that participants in the small property right housing market can or cannot deter government interference. Government officials were invited to share their experience of and opinions about law enforcement actions against informal housing in their city, such as evictions of informal settlement dwellers. We paid particular attention to factors that affected local government decision-making on whether to intervene in the extralegal housing market. The data collected from all participants reveals how local people secure market transactions without state support, how they reduce both legal and political risks in the small property right housing market, and why village committees as third-party enforcers are effective in mitigating these risks and protect the market.

Selection bias often occurs during the identification of interview participants. Because the number of our formal interviewees is relatively small, the participant pool and the data thus derived may not be representative. We therefore adopted two strategies to overcome this problem. First, in addition to formal interviews, we participated in two types of informal group discussion. We conducted informal conversations with housing buyers and villagers in places near the small property right housing projects. These conversations sometimes attracted neighbors and passersby. We also joined several online chat groups composed of small property right housing buyers, sellers, and agents and followed their daily conversations. Although we did not directly use the evidence gained from these informal discussions, it was nevertheless useful in several ways: (1) It helped us evaluate the reliability of the data collected from formal interviews; (2) it enabled us to capture market participants' concerns about the informal property rights associated with the small property right housing market; (3) it helped us generate a comprehensive list of interview questions that could then be asked during formal interviews; and (4) it enriched our knowledge of the small property right market. The second strategy was to incorporate published materials (e.g., news reports, academic publications, and government documents) and records of judgments from China Judgments Online, an official database developed by the Supreme People's Court of China.

We also visited a number of local communities where small property right housing projects are located. Our field trips not only revealed the scale, land-use patterns, and public infrastructure of small property right housing communities, but also deepened our understanding of the relationships and daily interactions among market participants, the role of village committees in the market, and the extent of villagers' involvement in the market, which further indicated the capacity for collective action of participants in the extralegal housing market. Taken together, these evidentiary sources enabled us to inquire into what mechanisms people employ to enforce informal property rights and mitigate market uncertainties and legal risks. The empirical evidence also enabled us to assess the efficiency and effectiveness of these non-state mechanisms and examine how these mechanisms work.

3.3.3 Corrupt Transactions

China's economic reforms not only gave rise to rapid growth and a better social welfare system but also made government jobs particularly attractive, because being a senior public official brings high social status and enormous opportunities for personal aggrandizement. In other words, government appointments and public power have become commodities corrupt officials trade for personal gain, giving rise to a giant illegal market where power trades for money and power trades for more power.

President Xi's anti-corruption campaign, which began in 2012 and continues to the present day, is the most far-reaching and the harshest in China's modern history. This campaign has found millions of officials guilty of corruption. These officials are in the Party, government, and military and range from top-ranking officials to street-level bureaucrats. The Party's Discipline Inspection Commission identified the buying and selling of public appointments as a major form of public sector corruption (Wu 2016: 185; see also Bakken and Wang 2021). In his seminal work, *China's Crony Capitalism*, Pei (2016: 78) quotes President Xi as saying that "corruption in personnel matters is a prominent problem; the practice of appointing officials in violation of the rules is widespread."

This widespread buying and selling of government appointments arose for several reasons. First, China's dramatic marketization policy gave rise to the commodification of state-controlled resources, because these resources could now be bought and sold at market prices (Wank 2001, 2002). Government appointments, as Wang (2020a: 1289) argues, "have also been perceived as commodities that are sold for profit" (see also Hillman 2010, 2014; Zhu 2008). Given that a high-ranking public official is entrusted with power that can be misused for personal gain, many Chinese people are keen to buy public positions (Fewsmith 2013). Second, the cadre management system has long suffered from weaknesses such as "concentration of power over personnel issues and the difficulties of monitoring top administrators"; these personnel problems were serious even before Xi's anti-corruption drive (Zhu 2008: 558; see also Pei 2016: 81).

We became interested in studying the buying and selling of government appointments in late 2011, when we conducted fieldwork in the city of Chongqing, the largest municipality in southwest China with a population of 32 million. Before the downfall of the city's former Party chief Bo Xilai in 2012, his "Chongqing model" attracted global attention. This model included the "singing red songs" campaign, which praised the Chinese Communist Party, and the "smashing black" campaign, which cracked down on organized crime groups and their "protective umbrella" (corrupt officials who offer protection to local criminal organizations; see Broadhurst and Wang 2014; Lafarguette 2011; Wang 2013a). Our research focused on the political–criminal nexus (collusion between public officials, especially those from the criminal justice system, and local gangsters) and corrupt networks established in the public security bureaus. We conducted interviews with police officers (n = 2), prosecutors (n = 2), journalists (n = 2), academics (n = 3), and community members (n = 3) to understand how corrupt networks were formed and used for illicit profits and how lower-ranking police officers created strong ties and emotional bonds with upper-level officers in order to gain promotion.

President Xi's "hunting tigers [corrupt officials in the high ranks of power] and swatting flies [rank-and-file officials]" campaign revealed the powerful corrupt networks in which public officials profited hugely by colluding with businesspeople and selling promotion opportunities to lower-ranking officials. In early 2015, we started a second round of data collection on the buying and selling of government positions in other Chinese cities. During the initial stage of data collection, most interviewees mentioned the significance of *zhong jian ren* (literally, intermediaries) in corrupt activity when they talked about how public officials achieve promotion and engage in corrupt transactions. This piqued our interest, so we decided to incorporate questions about intermediaries into our interviews. Many of our colleagues believed the study of corruption and intermediaries would be impossible because of its high political sensitivity, but we managed to conduct fifty semistructured interviews with academics (n = 9) and state officials (n = 41), including military officers, police officers, and public servants from different government departments and agencies. Additional interviews were conducted with businesspeople, whose experience of socializing with government officials enhanced our understanding of the embeddedness of corruption in social networks.

The key to successful evidence collection was to make use of our established social connections with public officials, who became both interviewees and intermediaries, facilitating our access to other public officials. We expanded the number of interviewees and enriched our empirical evidence by developing relationships of trust with several public officers, who also acted as intermediaries for the research. For example, JJ was a public official and a researcher. We made contact with JJ through a third person. Knowing that JJ needed help with collecting data, writing up articles, and publishing them in reputable journals, we volunteered to assist, helping him draw up interview guidelines, analyze interview data, and polish his writing. Our long-term assistance obliged JJ to return the favor; he helped us gain access to a number of his colleagues, most of whom were mid- and high-ranking government officials.

Intermediaries such as JJ played a central role in the process of data collection. First, intermediaries enabled us to gain access to interviewees. Intermediaries usually accompanied us when visiting their friends, all of whom were public officials. For the sake of maintaining face, interviewees seldom declined our invitations, even though most of them believed that the topic was too sensitive to talk about. Second, the involvement of intermediaries in the interview process guaranteed the reliability and validity of the interview data we collected, because the nature of the relationship between the intermediaries and the interviewees made interviewees stick to the truth.

All interviewees were informed about our identity as researchers, the aim of our study, our procedures for coding and using interview data, and their right to withdraw. They were also informed about how we removed their personally identifiable information and made personal information anonymous. Our interviews focused on corruption cases in the public domain concerning the buying and selling of public appointments. Participants were encouraged to share their perceptions, knowledge, and analysis of several issues surrounding corrupt transactions: the reasons for the widespread use of bribery in seeking promotion; the extent to which tie strength and bribes facilitated corrupt transactions; the cultural meaning of money in corrupt exchanges; the role of intermediaries in making corrupt deals; the risks encountered by exchange participants; and the impact of the anti-corruption campaign on the ways in which people engaged in corrupt transactions. To avoid facing ethical dilemmas and breaking confidentiality, a core principle of research ethics, participants were only allowed to discuss corruption cases that had already been made public in the state media, and they were not allowed to mention specific names relating to illegal conduct if doing so would have involved reference to unpublished data. If that happened, we immediately reminded the participant to stop revealing sensitive information, and, if the interview was being recorded, the information was wiped from the recorder immediately after the interview.

The Chinese government has significantly strengthened its control over public officials, so being interviewed by overseas researchers, even from Hong Kong, on sensitive topics could endanger officials' career development. It has become increasingly difficult to recruit new interviewees; even intermediaries have become unwilling to assist. We were also interviewed by national security officials, who warned us off our research topic, suggesting that we focus on topics that contribute to society and safeguard the government's image. We therefore made almost no progress in collecting empirical data after 2016. Given that corruption is a very complex social phenomenon, the sixty-two interviews that we conducted with state officials (n = 45), academics (n = 12), community members (n = 3), and journalists (n = 2) are far from sufficient to offer a detailed or comprehensive account of corrupt transactions. Nevertheless, it is one of the first attempts made by researchers to study corruption from both macro and micro perspectives.

3.3.4 The Illegal Online Lending Market

As Huang (2022: 1) argues, between 2007 and 2020 China's peer-to-peer lending market "experienced a drastic boom and bust, and ended up with zero surviving platforms." Peer-to-peer lending platforms were perceived by the Chinese government as a highly risky sector that involved a substantial number of fraudulent schemes and questionable lending practices. Our research focuses on a specific part of China's peer-to-peer lending market: online loan-sharking targeted at university students (see Figure 3.3, showing an online post by a loan shark stating "Since December 2017 we have started to market our business [online lending] on university campuses and have expanded our operations to over seventy universities. We now invite new business partners to join us."). There are three reasons for selecting this case. First, the illegal online lending market offered us the opportunity to investigate how traditional offline loan sharks move their businesses online, which produced information about major risks and risk reduction strategies in the illegal online market. Second, and more specifically, online loan scams targeting university and college students have attracted enormous public attention, and journalists and scholars have published a large number of articles that were essential sources, helping us to understand the ways in which online loan sharks create scams and exert control over student borrowers. Third, collecting empirical data was feasible, because we

Figure 3.3 An illegal peer-to-peer lending company's post announcing its expansion to over seventy universities and inviting new business partners to join it (author's photo).

have personal relationships with several university teachers who manage student affairs and police officers who have experience of handling cases involving online loan sharks.

In order to expand our pool of participants and gain the trust of victims and their teachers, classmates, and relatives, we offered free legal aid to victims of online loan sharks. Student victims told us of their reasons for borrowing money from illegal lenders, showed us the original loan agreements they had signed with loan sharks, outlined their online interactions with loan sharks, and described their suffering and the methods they used to attempt to escape the debt trap. Student victims' teachers, classmates, and relatives described their experience of being text-bombed by loan sharks as well as their attitudes toward victims of online loan sharks. Interview data gained from university teachers helped us understand the rise of online lending targeted at students and the ways in which universities deal with the problem, especially how and to what extent universities protect their students. A member of our research team helped several student victims to negotiate with online loan sharks directly.

We chose not to interview loan sharks, for two reasons. First, it was unsafe for us to meet loan sharks, many of whom were gangsters; and second, empirical data collected from victims and police officers, as well as direct negotiation with loan sharks through phone calls, provided enough data for us to understand loan sharks' deception techniques and aggressive enforcement actions. In several cases, we reported student victimization to their universities and to local police. Obviously, researchers should be noninterventionist in research sites, and reporting criminal activities to police officers infringed this noninterventionist stance, but we felt the reporting was justified for two reasons. First, the loan sharks threatened their student victims with retaliation if they sought help from the police. Second, our assistance in reporting cases to the police helped us to understand how local police officers dealt with cases of online loan-sharking targeted at university students. During our fieldwork, we observed that police officers largely tolerated online loan-sharking and frequently declined to record offenses committed by loan sharks. By contrast, they instantly adopted a very aggressive approach to online loan-sharking after the central government started its "Sweep Away Black and Eradicate Evil" anti-crime campaign in 2018.

From 2017 to 2018, we conducted thirty-six interviews with police officers (n = 6), lawyers (n = 8), victims (n = 8), clinical psychologists (n = 3), and others (n = 11) familiar with the illegal online lending market. The interview data enabled us to understand the challenges loan sharks face when they offer illegal lending online and the ways in which they attract student borrowers and design their internet-based scams. The data also contained details about the process of victimization, which further illustrated the innovative strategies developed by illegal online lenders to secure transactions and enforce loan repayment. The empirical data collected in China suggests that the development of internet technologies not only brings offline loan sharks into contact with suitable targets on the internet but also enables crime groups to obtain compromising information via photography, video, or audio recording, which can then be used as blackmail to enforce agreements.

To complement the empirical data, we also conducted searches in CNKI (China National Knowledge Infrastructure, China's most comprehensive academic resource) before and during our fieldwork. The use of keywords such as *xiaoyuan dai* (student loans), *luo dai* (naked loans), *P2P wangluo daikuan* (peer-to-peer online lending) helped us identify 1,143 journal articles and 369 news articles. An overview of these journal articles and news reports not only improved our understanding of China's illegal online lending market but also helped us develop interview questions.

3.4 Conclusion

This chapter has presented our research design and fieldwork. We employ a multiple case study design, incorporating four cases for consideration: unlicensed street vending, small property right housing, buying and selling of public appointments, and online loan sharks. The primary reason for selecting these four cases is to show the analytical power of our socio-economic approach, encompassing both macro and micro dimensions, in analyzing the social order of illegal markets. This chapter has also provided details about our fieldwork, including our interviewees, the methods used to gain access to participants, major challenges encountered and how we addressed them, and ethical considerations.

Our selection of cases and empirical data suffer from two major limitations. First, this book is not able to include many further intriguing illegal markets because collecting sufficient empirical evidence concerning these markets is not feasible for us alone. A comprehensive examination of illegal markets in China may require researchers to incorporate more cases into their studies, such as gambling, prostitution, and the trade in endangered animal parts, but it is too ambitious to include so many illegal markets in this book. Our objective is to generate scholarly interest in illegal markets and bring our analytical approach for the study of illegal markets to a wider audience. For more cases to be covered, a collective project might be the solution: An edited volume could take in a wider range of cases, with experts specializing in different illegal markets being invited to contribute chapters.

Second, although the empirical evidence collected is extremely helpful in illustrating the workings of illegal markets and the ways in which illegal transactions are secured, the sample size for qualitative interviews is still small, and selection bias may occur in our qualitative research. To address these drawbacks, we used published materials to complement our empirical data. News articles, journal articles, government documents, and court judgments are valuable resources to show what happens with street vending, the small property right housing market, corruption, and the online illegal lending market in China; what kinds of risks and uncertainties participants have to face; and how the government and the judicial system respond to these markets. Published materials were also used to examine the validity and reliability of the empirical data we collected from interviewees.

4

Unlicensed Street Vending

4.1 Introduction

How can individuals in legitimate illegal markets protect property rights and address uncertainties? This chapter addresses this question by focusing on unlicensed street vending in China. Street vending forms an essential part of urban economies in developing countries like China, and most street vendors operate outside state regulation. They encounter market-based uncertainties and uncertainties caused by unpredictable enforcement. Empirical data collected in two Chinese cities, Guangzhou and Guilin, suggests that street vendors form private governance organizations to overcome resource limitations, allocate pitches, and resist government interference. Street vendors who cannot rely on effective private governance organizations may purchase protection from a third party (e.g., agents of the state) to secure informal rights over a particular spot and avoid confiscation of their wares and equipment. The case study of unlicensed street vending enhances our understanding of illegal markets, particularly those that are morally legitimate yet legally unauthorized.

4.2 Uncertainty and Street Vending

Even though some illegal markets are socially acceptable in society, participants in these markets still need to develop and maintain governance institutions, not only to protect property rights and facilitate market transactions but also to respond to active government interference. An example of this is street vending in developing countries. Street vendors have to

This chapter is an updated version of A. Jiang and P. Wang, (2022), "Governance and informal economies: Informality, uncertainty and street vending in China," *British Journal of Criminology*, 62(6), 1431–1453. Permission has been granted by Oxford University Press.

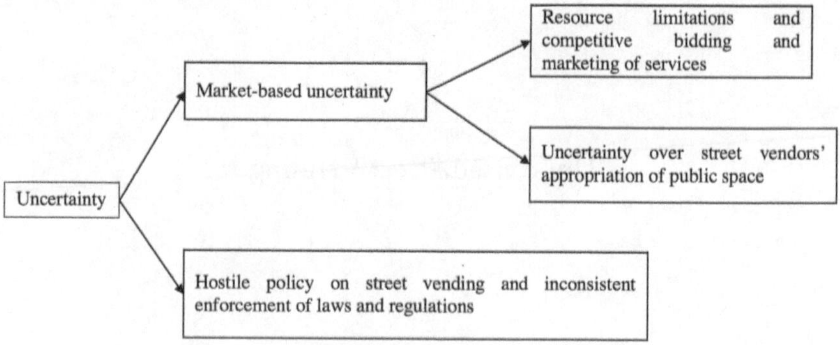

Figure 4.1 Uncertainties encountered by street vendors.

safeguard two types of property rights: informal user rights to a particular spot (e.g., a certain area of pavement) and ownership of their wares and equipment (e.g., mobile carts and weights and measures).

Street vendors face two major types of uncertainty: market-based conflicts and political–legal uncertainties (see Figure 4.1). They "lack access to regulated banking systems" (Martínez et al. 2018: 23) and thus have limited resources to invest in a street vending business. Street vendors "might haggle over intrusions that result from competitive bidding and marketing of services to potential clients" (Bonnet and Venkatesh 2016: 646). Outside the formal state regulatory system, street vendors compete among themselves for advantageous physical locations, characterized by high traffic flow and low risk of detection, in order to make more money.

Political–legal uncertainties caused by unpredictable enforcement of laws and regulations threaten the very survival of street vendors. In developing countries such as China, where enhancing the appearance of the city to attract investment is perceived by local government as more important than the livelihoods of the urban underclass, the right of street vendors to trade in public spaces is largely suppressed, and vendors also risk having their wares and equipment confiscated by city administrators (Huang et al. 2014; Xue and Huang 2015).

Despite significant market-based conflict and government hostility toward street vending, a large number of street vendors still manage to survive. Our assumption is that street vendors form social rules and private governance organizations to deal with resource limitations, coordinate activities, and solve internal disputes. They may employ collective negotiation and resistance to handle uncertainties caused by unpredictable law enforcement (see Bhowmik 2010; Cross 1998; Crossa 2009) or make regular payments to grassroots officials for protection (see Lata et al. 2019).

An investigation into street vendors' responses to uncertainties can learn much from the literature on the mafia, which suggests that mafiosos can be effective protectors, safeguarding unlicensed street hawkers' businesses and ensuring that their preferred vending locations are not encroached upon by competitors. For example, in *The Triads as Business*, Chu (2000: 54–55) shows that triad members in Hong Kong protect their hawkers' interests by "limiting new entrants," not allowing hawkers to "sell the same kind of goods as others in the area," and deterring "people who attempt to report the illegal hawking activities to the authorities." Federico Varese, in *The Russian Mafia* (2001), offers an ethnography of the interaction between kiosk owners and criminal racketeers. Drawing on rich empirical data, Varese offers a detailed explanation of how criminals supply kiosk owners with "some protection against competitors and assistance in obtaining credit, although at very tough conditions." Existing research into the involvement of criminal racketeers in protecting street vendors' interests inspired us to investigate whether local gangs play a similar role in protecting the interests of unlicensed street vendors in China.

4.3 Street Vending in China

Street vendors are typically self-employed informal-sector practitioners who operate small-scale businesses in public spaces such as squares, streets, and stations (Bhowmik 2005). Some street vendors are stationary; others are mobile. Along with rapid economic growth and the increasing gap between the rich and the poor and between coastal and inland areas, China has witnessed a boom in the informal urban economy, especially street vending. This section discusses the causes of the rise of street vending in China and the key features of state regulation of street vending.

4.3.1 The Rise of Street Vending

Since China launched its economic reform and opening up in the late 1970s, the country has witnessed rapid economic development and an explosion of rural-to-urban migrants (Parodi et al. 2012). Most migrants enter low-end formal sectors such as manufacturing, construction, and service industries. However, China has also witnessed a growing number of migrants working in the informal sector as street vendors (Huang et al. 2014; Xue and Huang 2015). There are several reasons for this. First, coastal cities gradually became saturated with cheap immigrant labor, and unskilled and inexperienced migrants could not find work. Second, migrants who work in the formal sector face poor working conditions, long hours, low wages, and insecure jobs. The low entry requirements and flexible working hours of street vending are attractive to many rural-to-urban migrants (Huang et al. 2018; Xue and Huang 2015).

The number of street vendors in China is estimated at 25.53 million (He 2008). In Guangzhou, one of our fieldwork sites, the estimated number of street vendors was 500,000 at the end of 2013 (Ma 2013). In 2020, the estimated number of vendors in another fieldwork site, Guilin, was between 50,000 and 80,000.[1] Street vendors have attracted media and academic attention because they suffer from aggressive state regulation, often under the pretext of protecting a city's modern image. City administrative officials call street vendors "walking devils," accusing them of polluting the environment, disrupting traffic, and creating considerable noise. Vendors are held to be unhealthy and untaxed and are often blamed for traffic congestion (Flock and Breitung 2016; He 2008). Unauthorized street vending in China is illegal, and street vendors are subject to intensive regulation by *chengguan* (the urban administrative and law enforcement bureau). Street vendors are chased, expelled, threatened, and occasionally beaten by city administrative officials, and their merchandise is often confiscated (Human Rights Watch 2012). The state regulation of street vending, which can be characterized as *historical regulatory ambivalence* and *legislative regulatory ambivalence,* causes vendors enormous uncertainty.

4.3.2 Historical Regulatory Ambivalence

Regulatory policy toward street vending varies in different historical and political contexts. In the 1980s, street vending played a significant role in alleviating poverty and was a sign of a prosperous local economy; it was therefore largely tolerated and even encouraged by local governments. Street vending in Guangzhou flourished as never before; vendors became a unique feature of the city at that time, and the city was held up as a good example for other cities to follow (Xue and Huang, 2015). In order to make space for street vending, the government even removed fences beside roads. However, the political climate gradually changed in the 1990s. China's economic development accelerated and authorities started to buy into a new image of the modern city. Governments at all levels became obsessed with creating modern cities that attracted investment, and city administrators launched a series of campaigns to remove street vendors in order to succeed in the National Civilized City and National Sanitary City

[1] Interview C4N178 (city administrative official), 2021.

competitions (Huang et al. 2014). Since the early 2000s, local governments have been encouraged to apply relatively gentle regulation of street vendors to enhance social harmony, but in practice city administrators have employed increasingly aggressive strategies against street vendors (Huang et al. 2014). A historical review shows that state regulation of street vending in China is "not a neutral classification but rather one made and remade by the state to satisfy its political purposes" (Xue and Huang 2015: 157).

4.3.3 Legislative Regulatory Ambivalence

Local governments possess the power to formulate their own regulatory policies on street vending; cities adopt regulatory policies and deliver levels of penalty based on local conditions, such as the level of economic development and number of rural-to-urban migrants. For example, a street vendor who occupies one square meter of public space for a vending business without permission will be fined RMB 200 in Guangzhou, whereas in Shenzhen (another city near Guangzhou) the fine is RMB 500–1000.

Even within one city officials sometimes adopt contradictory regulatory measures in different urban spaces. In Guangzhou, for example, street vending is prohibited in areas such as the central business district, administrative centers, city parks, and traffic stations, while street vending in some urban villages[2] (i.e., villages in the city), old neighborhoods, overpasses, and outlying districts may be tolerated. Street vending in certain regions is tolerated by city authorities during most of the year but can suddenly be prohibited for specific periods, such as during the National People's Congress and the People's Congress of the City. Street vendors must therefore have local knowledge about the changing practice of law enforcement in different areas at different times.

Due to the lack of national legislation on regulating street vendors, the law enforcement work of city administrative officials is based on a mixture of regulatory policies, rules, and laws made at different levels of government. For example, the Regulations on Urban Road Management are used as a legal basis for regulating street vendors who illegally occupy public roads. The Law of the People's Republic of China on the Prevention and Control of Atmospheric Pollution forms the legal basis for punishing street vendors who cause air pollution. The Regulations on the Administration of City Appearance and Environmental Sanitation can be used when

[2] Urban villages, also known as villages inside urbanized areas, "provide an important source of rental housing for low-income populations" (Wu 2016: 852).

punishing street vendors who make public space dirty. The Measures for the Investigation and Punishment of Unpermitted and Unlicensed Business Operations are used to penalize unlicensed street-level entrepreneurs. The lack of unified national legislation and the fragmentation of local provisions mean that frontline officials can interpret all these regulations as they see fit. Unsurprisingly, this leads to serious contradiction and uncertainty.

4.4 Establishing Private Governance Organizations

Our empirical data shows that street vendors develop innovative strategies to deal with uncertainty (Figure 4.2; see also Chu 2000; Varese 2001). Suffering from social exclusion and lacking access to state-based institutions, street vendors have no choice but to seek support from each other and develop their own survival strategies. We found that street vendors in our research sites formed mutual aid groups based on ethnicity, kinship, dialect, and hometown. Ethnic, cultural, and religious homogeneities play an essential role in facilitating group cooperation (see Skarbek 2011). Moreover, we observed that street vendors who are not bonded by ethnic and hometown ties are also able to form cohesive groups, facilitating effective cooperation and coordination within the group. They are able to do so because they live near one another, work next to one another, help one another during daily business, or share the same experience of being harassed by law enforcement agencies.

According to Webb et al. (2013: 604), "common norms, values, beliefs, and routines" are formed over time to enable street vendors to coordinate actions and accomplish tasks. Common interests (e.g., survival and profit-making) and the threat posed by law enforcement agencies encourage

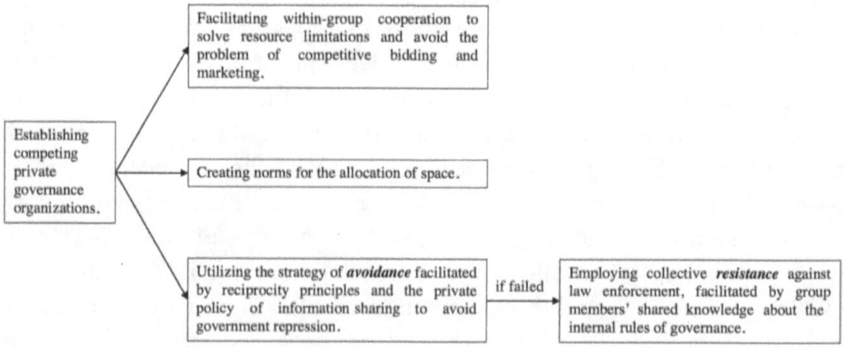

Figure 4.2 The establishment of private governance organizations by street vendors to redress uncertainties.

street vendors to follow the principle of reciprocity and to adopt private pro-trade policies (e.g., information sharing and prevention of competitive marketing among group members). Figure 4.2 depicts the implementation of private governance organization by street vendors to address risks and uncertainties, which will be discussed in detail in Sections 4.4.1–4.4.3.

4.4.1 Overcoming Resource Limitations and Avoiding Competitive Bidding and Marketing

Street vendors often face severe resource constraints because most of them are low-class and cannot easily access the formal banking system. To handle these constraints and increase sales, street vendors in our research sites share information about good-quality supplies, share warehouse storage costs, and join the informal system of consignment. They also develop effective mechanisms to handle the problem of competitive bidding and marketing.

Sharing information about good-quality and well-priced supplies. When one of our research team members began participant observation as a street vendor, she was invited by another street vendor to join a QQ group and a WeChat group,[3] both of which were created by street vendors in Guangzhou to share information about good-quality and well-priced supplies and risk avoidance strategies. Figure 4.3 shows that a male street

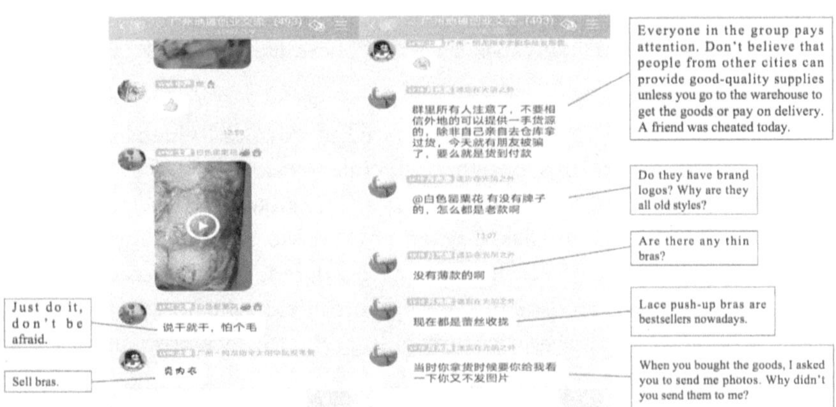

Figure 4.3 Sharing information about well-priced supplies and risk avoidance strategies in a QQ group.

3 QQ and WeChat are the two most frequently used communication apps in mainland China.

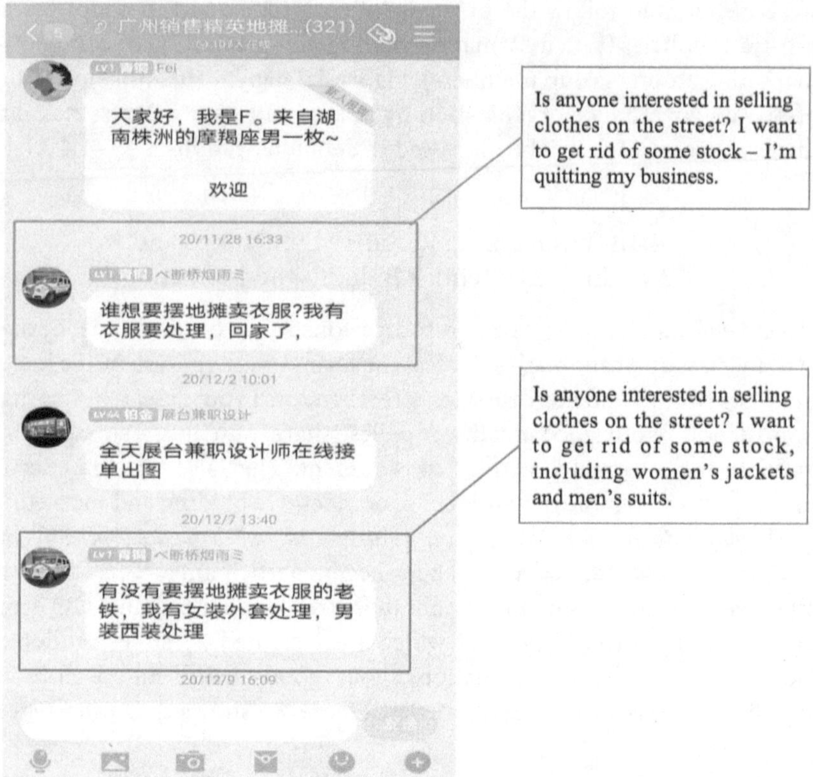

Figure 4.4 Sharing information about well-priced supplies in a QQ group.

vendor who decided to sell lingerie shared photos and videos in the QQ group of goods he recently bought. A female vendor warned group members not to trust so-called firsthand wholesalers outside the city; she showed interest in the lingerie and asked whether these were branded goods. After noticing that the style of the lingerie was outdated, she criticized the male street vendor for not sending her these photos before he bought the goods. She also suggested that a special type of lingerie, the lace push-up bra, was popular at that time.

In another case, a street vendor announced in a QQ group established by local street vendors that he planned to leave the city and therefore wished to sell inventory at an unusually low price (see Figure 4.4). Street vendors frequently share this type of information (supplying goods at a lower price in order to deal with excess stock), which helps them find well-priced supplies.

Sharing warehouse storage costs. A majority of street vendors live in urban villages, where they also store their goods. Interviewee Yi, a male vendor in his thirties, sells porcelain tableware, which requires a lot of storage space. However, a large enough room would cost RMB 600 per month, which is too expensive. To lower the cost, Yi joined with three other street vendors to rent a room together.[4] Sharing storage costs is not uncommon. Another street vendor, Dong, rents a one-bedroom flat near a subway station and installed a large shelf. He rents part of the shelf to two other street vendors, who each pay him RMB 2 per day. According to Dong, the renters are part-time street vendors who have day jobs. They use Dong's shelf because it saves them travel time. As Dong recounted, "After they get off work, they can take the subway to my flat, take their goods out, then they can start to vend. You know, they cannot take their goods to their workplaces during the daytime. Two yuan [per day] is a reasonable price."[5]

Joining the informal consignment system. To increase sales, street vendors have developed an informal system of consignment: They give their goods to other street vendors (consignees/distributors) whom they trust, and the informal consignment agreement is made based on the negotiations between consignee and consignor. Here, the consignor is also a distributor responsible for selling goods owned by other street vendors. For every item sold, the distributor usually gets 10 percent of the price as commission (or profits are shared based on a percentage agreed by both parties). During her participant observation, our research team member, Anli, was asked by Meili, a female vendor who sold earrings, whether she was interested in earning money from selling earrings. According to Meili, Anli could buy some earrings from her with a 40 percent discount, or she could help Meili to sell earrings when they did their vending business together and Anli would get a commission of RMB 3 per item. In order to sell earrings at a good price, Meili also collaborated with formally registered jewelry store owners, who usually charged a much higher commission fee. Meili therefore preferred to rely more on the informal system of consignment established by street vendors.

Avoiding competitive bidding and marketing. Street vendors develop the practical norm of avoiding selling the same products, which prevents competitive bidding and marketing of commodities and services. At our research sites, vendors who sell similar goods cannot set up next to each other. For example, when our research team member Anli conducted participant observation as a street vendor, she joined forces

[4] Interview C4N13 (street vendor), 2014.
[5] Interview C4N115 (street vendor), 2015.

Figure 4.5 Street vendors avoid selling similar goods (author's photos).

with a vendor who sold dried fruit and nuts. She realized they were the only vendors selling dried fruit and nuts on that street and wondered why. Her vendor partner, Wei, told her that avoiding competition is an unwritten rule for street vendors. He also revealed how this informal rule is practiced:

> You see, other vendors sell barbecue, roast chicken, and other goods, but no one sells dried fruit and nuts. That is why I pick this spot ... this norm is also applied to others. If I have already been here selling dried fruit and nuts, other vendors will not sell the same goods nearby; if they do want to sell dried fruit and nuts, they should pick another place. This is our unwritten rule.[6]

Further observation echoed what Wei said: Many vendors sold clothes on that street, but when Anli checked what they sold, she found they each sold different types of clothes, such as suits, T-shirts, coats, pyjamas, or underwear. Figure 4.5 shows that street vendors on the overpass sell different categories of goods, such as potted plants, kids' toys, underwear, or belts; street vendors at a different location sell pants, underwear, skirts, toys, wallets, or belts.

Empirical data also shows that street vendors who contravene the norm are socially excluded by other vendors. Female street vendor Xia, who sold women's high-heeled shoes, explained that when she started on that street, she sold sandals, but then decided to sell women's high heels instead,

[6] Interview C4N12 (street vendor), 2014.

because a girl who had long been there also sold sandals. When Xia was asked about her reason for choosing to sell other goods, she explained:

> It was not good for my business, because she [the girl] came first, she had already had her own customers and she had already established good relationships with other street vendors there. But I was a newcomer, I felt that I was not welcomed by others. Even *chengguan* [city administrative officials] treated me worse. Street vending has a first come, first served rule. She came first, so she had priority to decide what kinds of goods she was willing to sell ... At the beginning, when I sold the same goods as her, I found myself not only her competitor but also a norm-breaker [and therefore socially excluded by other vendors]. It was not good for business. That is why I had to make a change.[7]

To sum up, by sharing information about well-priced supplies, splitting storage costs with others, and forming an informal consignment system, street vendors largely manage to overcome the problem of resource limitation. They also get over the problem of competitive bidding and marketing by collectively enforcing the norm of avoiding selling the same products in the same area.

4.4.2 Creating Norms for the Allocation of Space

To establish a high degree of certainty over their appropriation of public space, street vendors develop practical norms of space allocation (e.g., the rule of first possession). Unlike Thailand and India, where street vendors are entitled to establish vendor associations to protect their property rights, coordinate their actions, and solve disputes relating to allocating space, street vendors in China are forbidden by the government to form their own associations. The absence of formal governance structures encourages Chinese street vendors to develop informal norms for distributing space and solving disputes. At our research sites, street vendors create an informal norm for allocating and occupying spots in vending areas: the first come, first served rule. Once a street vendor occupies a spot they usually mark that spot on the road (see Figure 4.6). The informal user right to that spot becomes exclusive: Other vendors are not allowed to occupy that spot unless they gain permission from its "owner."

In the summer of 2014, when our research team member Anli started participant observation as a street vendor, it was hard for her to find a place to set out her stall. The 300-meter-long street had been occupied by more than 200 street vendors during the night. Vendors set up right next to each other, leaving no space for newcomers. She wrote in her fieldnote:

7 Interview C4N19 (street vendor), 2014.

Figure 4.6 Sprayed words in Chinese meaning "occupied" (author's photos).

> City administrative officials are usually off duty at 6 p.m. ... Street vendors will show up very early, usually before 5 p.m. They do nothing but just wait on their own spots because *chengguan* are still there ... but the problem is that I cannot find a space to set up my business. It seems clear that all the spots are occupied by other street vendors, and they watch me very carefully when I approach their spots, because they see I have a bag of goods to sell ... I have been here for two weeks, and many times I tried asking them to move a little bit and give me a little space, but it never worked. Some of them just ignored me; others asked me to find another place in an unfriendly tone. Some even made fun of me, saying, "You look young and pretty, you should find an office job and street vending is less suitable for you; if you cannot find a job, then find a boyfriend."[8]

Anli eventually found a spot to conduct her business after weeks of negotiation and socialization with some of the vendors. This indicates that at our research sites street vendors respect the first come, first served rule. The strict implementation of this informal rule not only secures their user rights to public spots but effectively expels competitors.

[8] Anli's fieldnote on July 30, 2014.

4.4.3 Avoiding and Resisting Government Repression

Government interference has always been a primary concern of street vendors. State regulation in developing countries like China is commonly described as "uncertain and mostly hostile" (Xue and Huang 2015: 156; see also Donovan 2008; Popke and Ballard 2004). To handle government repression, street vendors rely on information sharing among group members to make the strategy of *avoidance* effective. Avoidance, also known as the cat-and-mouse game, refers to vendors sharing information to enhance their ability to spot the approach of law enforcement and evade penalties (e.g., fines or confiscation of stock and equipment such as freight tricycles and weights and measures).

Dong, who has been a street vendor in Guangzhou for fifteen years, shared his understanding of how the cat-and-mouse game plays out:

> City administrative officials are enemy number one for street vendors; they frequently fine street vendors and confiscate their goods and equipment. Many of us have had this experience. There is a tacit agreement between those officials and street vendors: When officials show up on the street, vendors need to "cooperate" with them, which means that street vendors must pick up their stalls and run away. Usually, those officials will take a picture [of the "clean" street] as evidence of successful law enforcement. Street vendors will not return until officials go away.[9]

During large events and campaign periods,[10] city administrative officials adopt a much harsher enforcement approach toward street vendors (Huang et al. 2014). In response, street vendors have developed two main strategies to stay safe. First, they frequently check information posted in online chat groups, where members share sightings of law enforcement activity and inform their friends about any imminent threat of law enforcement. Figure 4.7 shows that street vendors exchanged information about law enforcement actions in the Dongpu area (where *chengguan* "rob" vendors of their goods), which helped nearby vendors escape the confiscation or destruction of their property. Second, a group of street vendors sometimes place a member at the entrance of the city's administrative and law enforcement bureau to monitor administrators' schedules and actions, continuously updating information online for group members. These

[9] Interview C4N115 (street vendor), 2015.

[10] In our research sites, city administrators usually remove street vendors during designated dates of inspection for the city's candidacy for the title of National Sanitary City, during periodic inspections by upper-level government, and during significant events such as the Asian Games in the city of Guangdong and the Annual Cultural Tourism Festival in the city of Guilin.

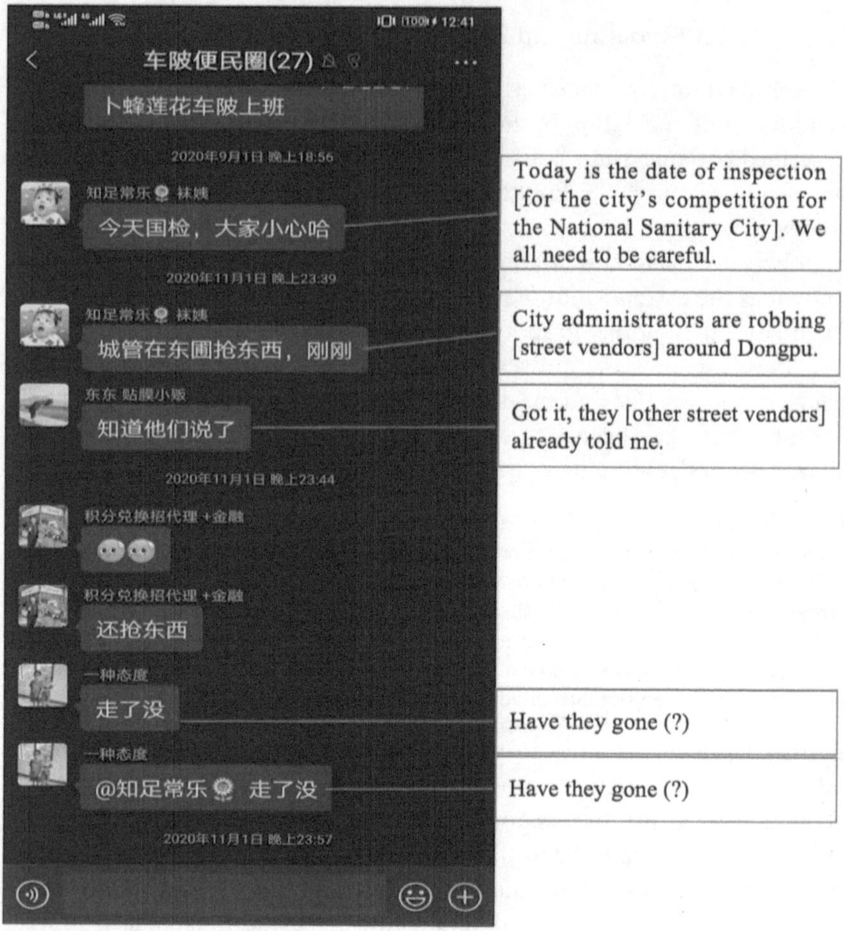

Figure 4.7 A vendor's posts in an online chat group warning his friends of city administrators' strict enforcement.

strategies help street vendors protect their property and reduce the risk of punishment during large events and campaign periods.

Street vendors' avoidance strategies do not always work well, especially when local authorities suddenly change attitude to street vendors from tolerance to aggression and hostility. As a result, street vendors have to resist eviction and confiscation by city administrative officials. *Resistance* refers to the use of threats and street violence against law enforcement as well as the use of crowds to generate situational stress to affect the discretionary decision-making of street-level bureaucrats. We observed several cases of collective resistance facilitated by the formation of shared knowledge among street vendors about a group's internal rules of governance: For example, if one member of the group has a physical or verbal conflict with street-level bureaucrats, all members will back that member up. In an interview, a city administrative officer told us:

> In my jurisdiction, that is the TY street, there are many street vendor gangs or groups based on hometown ties ... It is difficult for us to remove them. Once we ask one of them to leave, she or he will call his or her fellow members to come and threaten us ... In this case, we can do nothing but call the police for help ... Especially when we attempt to confiscate their stock, vendors backed up by other vendors can be very uncooperative. Some of them even use violence against us, making our enforcement actions extremely difficult.[11]

Another city administrative official remarked:

> These street vendor gangs are not formed in one or two days but over a long period. They have stable structures and use violence to resist law enforcement actions, especially when we attempt to confiscate their goods and equipment. One of my colleagues who worked in the CB street was stabbed seven times during a law enforcement operation. In areas like CB, where there are many street vendors, conflicts occur every two or three days ... We have to confiscate their goods very efficiently and leave the "battlefield" immediately [before vendors' friends arrive].[12]

Street vendors' collective resistance against law enforcement is facilitated by shared knowledge. Knowledge of the group's rules is generated by long-term interaction and cooperation among street vendors. Shared knowledge is explained by Skarbek and Wang (2015: 291) as a situation where "not only do all members know the rules, but they know that everyone knows the rules, that everyone knows that everyone knows the rules, and so on." Shared knowledge helps street vendors overcome coordination problems and successfully resist law enforcement. Zhao, a male vendor who sells plastic household products, told us:

> Our [street vendor] group has seven members. We all come from the same county in Henan province, and we all sell plastic household products that are made in Henan. We are closely bonded. If one of us is in trouble [with city administrative officials], others will immediately come and help ... if they need help, I will definitely help, because I know that if I need help, they will help me too.[13]

At our research sites, street vendors without hometown ties were still able to build camaraderie through long-term interaction and experience of mutual aid. For example, it was very common for them to take care of each

[11] Interview C4N28 (city administrative official), 2014.
[12] Interview C4N32 (city administrative official), 2014.
[13] Interview C4N115 (street vendor), 2015.

other's customers when someone was leaving; some became roommates and "business partners" in order to reduce living costs. Assisting each other to fight law enforcement actions therefore becomes a norm. Our interviewee Xinrong recalled collectively resisting law enforcement: "One day, two city administrators asked us to leave. I hesitated. A bold male vendor openly refused their order, saying, 'None of us will leave.' After that, I chose to stay there. None of us left that day."[14] Xinrong was asked what would have happened if that male vendor had been violently punished by city administrative officials. She replied, "We have been doing business together on that street for several years. Of course we would back him up, because we are on the same side ... Helping him is helping myself."[15] Long-term participant observation showed us that when street vendors outnumber city administrative officials, vendors prefer not to cooperate with officials. Their collective resistance helps them stay in business and protects their stock-in-trade.

Street vendors also crowdsource moral and tactical support from the public. City administrative officials were notorious for abusing vulnerable groups including street vendors (Xu and Jiang 2019). Media coverage of conflicts between city administrative officials and street vendors has severely damaged the reputation of city administrative officials. As official Xia revealed in an interview, officials tried to avoid attracting public attention during law enforcement actions, so media coverage made things worse.[16] Although Xia perceived media reports as incomplete and biased, he did acknowledge that these reports have tarnished the reputation of his department.

Here is an example of how street vendors use crowds to create situational stress to resist law enforcement. Sun and his wife sell barbecue food on CB street. One day, a group of city administrative officials told them to leave. They turned off the barbecue and dealt with the hot oil in the pot, but officials cursed them for being too slow. Sun pointed out that hot oil needed care to avoid burns. The official retorted, "You have already broken the law, you deserve it if you burn yourself." This angered Sun, who said, "I earn money through honest work. Which law have I broken? Do you think you are better than me? [You are] just a dog with a uniform." The official and Sun started to push and shove each other. Sun's wife started to yell "City administrative officials are beating people again!" and began crying very loudly. Passersby gathered to watch and discuss the conflict. The situation spiraled out of control and the officials left.

[14] Interview C4N7 (street vendor), 2014.
[15] Interview C4N7 (street vendor), 2014.
[16] Interview C4N30 (city administrative official), 2014.

4.5 Purchasing Third-Party Protection from Agents of the State

Empirical data suggests that at both research sites street vendors who form strong groups (in which members are closely connected and activities are well coordinated) can use collective action to avoid and resist government intervention, whereas street vendors who are more loosely linked show less capacity to resist government repression. These street vendors have to rely on alternative protective mechanisms, one of which is purchasing protection from agents of the state or corrupt street-level bureaucrats (see Figure 4.8).[17]

A number of street vendors at both research sites (Guangzhou and Guilin) establish a high degree of certainty over their appropriation of public space by making regular informal payments to agents of the state, who offer protection by defying higher-level policies and creating a "grey space" (see also Huang et al. 2014; Lata et al. 2019; Yiftachel 2009). The empirical data collected from Guilin illustrates this. In order to earn extra-budgetary revenue that is commonly used for staff bonuses, city administrative officials in Guilin have designated a "grey space," a street near a large local market, as a vending area for over 100 street vendors. Officials protect those vendors who pay them rent against harassment, confiscation, and eviction by other city administrators; meanwhile, they drive other unlicensed vendors off the

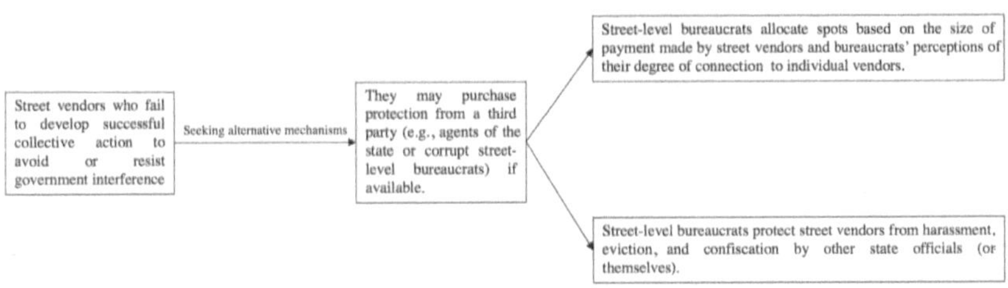

Figure 4.8 The purchase of third-party protection by street vendors.

[17] At our research sites, street vendors who possess different forms of social capital or social networks develop different ways of handling risks and uncertainties. For example, street vendors who are local residents may prefer to purchase "official licenses" from agents of the state, because their connections with city administrative officials help them occupy favorable locations in the regulated areas. However, the number of spots in the regulated areas is much smaller than the number of street vendors. Most street vendors are rural–urban migrants who do not have connections with city administrative officials. As a result, the primary solution for most rural–urban migrants is to develop cohesive groups to facilitate cooperation and resist government repression, and purchasing protection from agents of the state and corrupt street-level bureaucrats then becomes an alternative, and not a primary, solution.

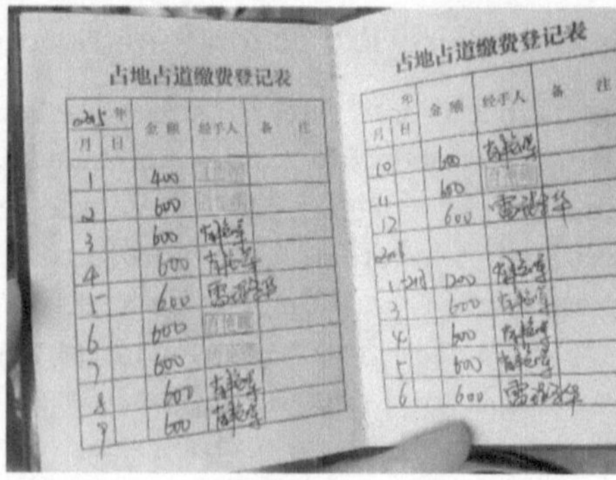

Figure 4.9 The authorized "license" showing the monthly rental payment.

street. An authorized "license" containing rental payment information is granted to each "registered" street vendor (see Figure 4.9). The monthly rental fee, ranging from RMB 400 to RMB 1,000, is determined by two main factors: First, the better the spot, the higher the charge; second, street vendors who have established close ties with officials occupy the best spots.

Street vendors who have already established close ties with city administrative officials are usually able to gain "licenses," whereas vendors lacking these ties frequently find their applications turned down. To create personal connections with those in power, some vendors turn to intermediaries, such as relatives, friends, and fellow villagers who have personal relationships with individual officials. To create and maintain close ties with individual officials, vendors commonly send them gifts and bribes. As a result, a hierarchical structure of street vendors has formed: Those who have strong ties with officials occupy the best spots; those with weak ties occupy less attractive spots; and those who have no ties are not allowed to do business on the street.

Song's booth is located at an intersection opposite a major market. It is one of the best spots in the area because there are a lot of passersby. When Song was asked how he got such a good place, he said, "It is very simple. My brother-in-law works in the city urban administrative and law enforcement bureau."[18]

A typical way for street vendors with no or weak social ties with city administrative officials to gain permission to do business on a regulated street is to go through the formal application process. But getting permission depends on luck. One street vendor, Qiu, noted that it was not easy to get

[18] Interview C4N134 (street vendor), 2017.

permission because few booths were available.[19] In order to get a booth, Qiu begged an administrative official several times. He eventually gained a spot after giving a senior official expensive cigarettes. Even though he had to pay a monthly rent of RMB 600, he was still satisfied with the deal because he did not have to worry about confiscation and eviction. Qiu's experience was common at our research sites. As another street vendor complained, "I don't want to exaggerate, but the truth is that almost no one can gain permission [from city administrative officials] without a personal relationship with those officials or bribing them."[20]

Social relationships with individual officials also determine who can occupy a spot over the long term. For example, a female street vendor, Ku, lost her booth when she gave birth to her child.[21] This frustrated her because she had paid the rent and a city administrative official had promised to let her continue her business after she came back. After noticing that her booth was occupied by another street vendor, she went to the local administrative officials' office, baby in her arms, and asked why her place was occupied by another vendor. But nobody was willing to explain. Ku later noticed that the vendor who replaced her was a close relative of a city administrative official. She later became an employee of another vendor, who told her to purchase vegetables from other vendors, most of whom had failed to obtain permission from city administrative officials. Ku was paid a monthly salary of RMB 1,000, which was significantly lower than her previous income. Ku's experience is not an exception. At our research sites, a number of street vendors at the bottom of the social structure either become employees working for, or suppliers of goods at low prices for, vendors who manage to gain permission to do business.

Setting up "grey spaces" brings advantages for both parties. On the one hand, street vendors who get "official licenses" receive genuine protection from city administrative officials. Official protection is effective because city officials turn from being robbers, extortionists, and repressors to being protectors and facilitators. On the other hand, city administrative officials receive large informal payments; this is prohibited, but tolerated by upper-level government, and officials thus regulate street vendors in a cost-effective way. When the local government is inspected by upper-level government or competes for the National Sanitary City award, city administrative officials can effectively create a clean image by ordering street

[19] Interview C4N135 (street vendor), 2017.
[20] Interview C4N143 (street vendor), 2017.
[21] Interview C4N146 (street vendor), 2017.

vendors off the street. Street vendors who are "protected" by city administrative officials have enormous incentive to cooperate, because if they do not obey orders they will lose their spots.

At our research sites, local gangs play no role in regulating street vending and do not offer protection services to street vendors. This is because authoritarian China has developed widespread social control measures, such as campaign-style policing and routine policing, that target street-level gangs (Varese and Wong 2018; Wang 2020b). As Atkinson-Sheppard and Hayward (2019: 629–630) point out, "'the street' in China is one of the most closely monitored and controlled areas of public spaces in the country." Local law enforcement agencies adopt a zero-tolerance approach toward street-level violence and extortion, and a successful crackdown on street gangs is an essential way to show the government's ability to maintain social stability. The local government's enthusiastic implementation of policies against street violence leaves no space that can be filled by profit-driven, street-level gangs.

4.6 Conclusion

This chapter has analyzed how street vendors in two Chinese cities protect property rights and deal with uncertainty. The criminalization of street vending reduces vendors' access to governmental and legal institutions and thereby encourages them to develop private governance institutions to handle market-based disputes and unpredictable law enforcement. Street vendors at our research sites form private governance organizations to facilitate cooperation (see Figure 4.10). First, the principle of reciprocity and the benefits of mutual aid encourage members of organizations to share warehouse storage costs, avoid selling the same products, institute an informal system of consignment, and develop a collective way of deterring competitive bidding and of marketing goods and services. Second, street vendors respect and follow the norm of first possession to avoid conflict among vendors and protect their informal user rights to public spots. Third, the government's hostile approach of evicting street vendors compels vendors to share information to avoid government repression. In addition, shared knowledge among street vendors helps them overcome the coordination problems of collective resistance, making street-level bureaucrats unable to enforce their eviction and confiscation policies.

This research also suggests that street vendors who are unable to form and maintain a strong, cohesive, effective private governance organization tend to purchase protection from agents of the state and corrupt street-level

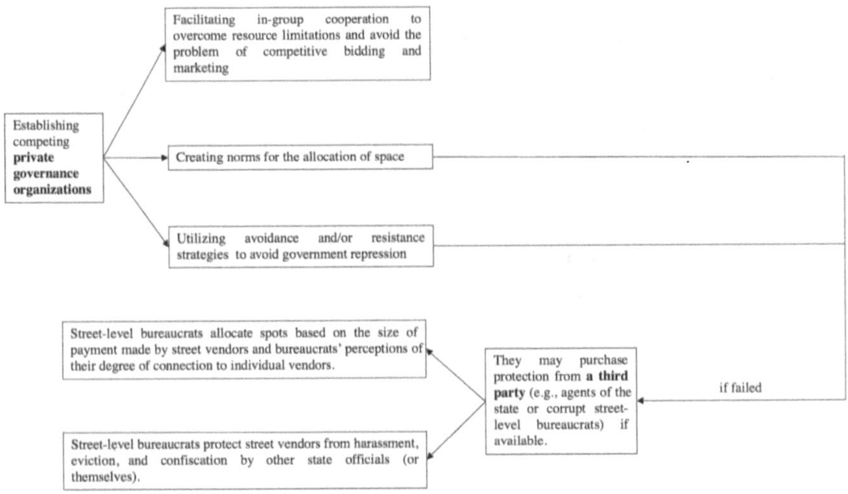

Figure 4.10 A summary of major strategies employed by street vendors.

bureaucrats if that option is available (see Figure 4.10). At our research sites, local authorities deliberately defy higher-level policies of evicting street vending and instead establish "grey spaces," where street vendors who make regular informal payments to local authorities can do business in the officially regulated area. Within these "grey spaces," advantageous physical locations are allocated to vendors who are willing to pay more and who create close social relationships with street-level bureaucrats. These street vendors are also entitled to be free from the harassment, eviction, and confiscation inflicted by street-level bureaucrats.

This case study of street vending in China advances understanding of private governance of informal economies that are illegal but socially acceptable. It contributes to literature on the social order of illegal markets and extralegal governance by illustrating how informal economy participants resolve disputes and handle uncertainty. To survive, street vendors, a significant component of the powerless in urban economies, can develop innovative ways of resolving internal disputes and responding to threats made by groups of the powerful (e.g., agents of the state), which is also examined by Varese (2001) and Chu (2000) in other jurisdictions. Besides the successful cases of deploying private governance institutions to redress uncertainties, our empirical data reveals a number of failed cases: Those who neither managed to develop effective governance organizations nor had the desire or opportunity to purchase protection from a third party eventually withdrew from the business. At our research sites, the successful implementation of a street vendor removal policy compelled a number of street vendors who lacked access to legitimate means of survival to become career criminals, getting involved in a range of criminal activities (e.g., fraud, theft, and robbery) and causing enormous harm to local communities. The unexpected consequence of allowing helpless street vendors to drift into crime suggests that governments in developing countries need not only to reconsider their current hostile policies toward street vending but also to understand and tolerate, and even promote, private governance institutions sustained by street vendors.

5

The Small Property Right Housing Market

5.1 Introduction

How do participants in the extralegal housing market reduce market uncertainty and avoid government interference? This chapter examines China's extralegal housing market, specifically the small property right housing (*xiao chan quan fang*) market, and investigates the major extralegal governance institutions deployed by market participants to mitigate market uncertainty and political risks. Small property right housing refers to houses or apartments built on collectively owned land, including housing plots, by villagers, village committees, or private developers and sold to individuals outside of the villages in China's peri-urban areas. However, the existing law only permits the exchange of user rights to collectively owned land among villagers within the same village and prohibits such exchanges with outsiders. Therefore, the small property right housing that is mainly built for sale to outsiders is considered illegal.

Informality and extralegality have characterized the land use and housing sectors in developing countries and attracted significant scholarly attention (Murtazashvili and Murtazashvili 2016; Roy 2011; Webster et al. 2016; Wu 2016). The land use order in China is a typical example. China's real estate sector, as a formal housing market, has been thriving as a corollary of substantial economic growth and rapid urbanization. Nonetheless, an informal and extralegal housing market (i.e., small property right housing market) exists and runs in parallel to the formal one. The exchange of small property right housing, although illegal, prevails in many Chinese cities, and the exchange of small property right housing is socially legitimate. It is estimated that small property right housing has accommodated more than 71 million households, or a quarter of a billion people, particularly migrant laborers who cannot afford formal housing (Wang and Sun 2014).

Substantial scholarly efforts have facilitated our understanding of the emergence and operation of the small property right housing market. Qiao (2015, 2017) applied focal point theory to examine the coordination between small property right housing builders and buyers and local government, which explains the prosperity of small property right housing in Shenzhen. Zhang (2016) examined the relationships between villagers, village committees and external developers and identified three development patterns in small property right housing: an independent development pattern (i.e., small property right housing operated by individual villages or households); a cooperative development pattern (i.e., small property right housing operated by village committees, which sometimes cooperate with external developers); and a developer development pattern (i.e., small property right housing operated by external developers). Webster et al. (2016) found that small property right housing has both positive and negative effects on social welfare. Specifically, on the one hand it can reduce overall welfare by creating property-rights insecurity, while on the other hand it can raise a household's entitlement mapping and reduce poverty.

The price of small property right housing not only reflects supply and demand in informal housing, as do the prices of commercial housing in legal and liberal markets, but also indicates the degree of certainty and security of informal property rights. The price of the small property right housing, due to its illegal nature, has been much lower than that of formal housing. He et al. (2019) and Zhang and Zhao (2018) found that the price of small property right housing operated by village committees is generally higher than that operated by developers, since the former tend to be stronger in deterring government interference and therefore strengthen (potential) buyers' confidence in its security.

Although past research has uncovered some elements that affect the property rights security of extralegal housing, the set of extralegal governance institutions deployed by small property right housing sellers (including builders) and buyers to mitigate the risks of contract fraud and government interference have not been fully examined. In the small property right housing market, participants encounter two categories of uncertainty. The first is market (internal) uncertainty, referring primarily to the opportunistic behavior of sellers who claim that buyers do not have a right to small property right housing after the buyer makes the payment. The second is political (external) uncertainty, referring to the risk of government interference in the small property right housing market, which could even lead to the demolition of these informal buildings. Based on multiple archival sources and extensive fieldwork, we attempt to provide a more systematic study of the extralegal governance of the small property right housing market from a socio-economic perspective.

We find that a series of extralegal governance institutions (i.e., strategies) have been used by participants to mitigate both the internal and external uncertainties/risks in the market. Specifically, the risk of contract fraud between sellers and buyers is mitigated by (1) codified documents (e.g., informal certificate of title, exchange contract, and lawyer's testimony) and contract-signing rituals, which are used to communicate common/shared knowledge of the extralegal market and screen sellers' trustworthiness; (2) a reputation mechanism sustained by the online WeChat groups that are operated by small property right housing agencies; and (3) a centralized exchange database and system of punishments for opportunists provided by village committees.

Moreover, builders and buyers of small property right housing can reduce the risk of government interference by demonstrating collective action capacity and seeking political patronage. The small property right housing communities managed by village committees are more secure than those managed by private developers. This is because village committees have a strong capacity to organize buyers, which include a large number of villagers and outsiders, for the purpose of resisting government interference collectively. However, private developers have loose ties with buyers, the majority of whom are outsiders rather than locals from the villages where the informal buildings are constructed. As a result, private developers and their buyers do not have a strong collective action capacity. Additionally, village committees are often in an advantageous position for seeking political patronage from local governments due to their strong and extensive connections with local officials from various public sectors. As a result, the property rights of small property right housing managed by village committees are more certain and secure.

The rest of the chapter is organized as follows. Section 5.2 provides an overview of the small property right housing market. It examines the emergence of extralegal housing; compares the social, economic, and physical features of three types of small property right housing; and elaborates on the risks of contract fraud and government interference. Section 5.3 sheds light on how local actors mitigate market uncertainty, especially the risk of contract fraud, and increase property rights enforcement. Section 5.4 elaborates on how local people avoid government interference and why small property right houses managed by village committees are more secure than informal housing managed by private developers. Section 5.5 examines major strategies market participants use to minimize political risk. Section 5.6 makes a concluding remark.

5.2 Small Property Right Housing: An Extralegal Housing Market

5.2.1 Spontaneous Order in the Shadow of a Dual-Track Land System

The small property right housing market is an extralegal housing market that has emerged from the collectively owned land in many of China's peri-urban areas. It is the by-product of ambiguous land property rights under the dual-track land system. China's constitution stipulates that property rights in urban land are owned by the state, while rights in rural land, including housing plots, are held by the villages as collectives. The land administration law provides that any individual or organization that needs land for construction purposes should apply for the use of state-owned land, with the exceptions of collectively owned land used for village housing (only as accommodation for villagers themselves),[1] township and village enterprises, and public welfare facilities (see Figure 5.1). Under such a system, local governments have monopolistic power over formal land use and exchange (Hsing 2010; Lin 2009). The land for commercial housing has to be state-owned and conveyed from local governments to potential users (e.g., real estate developers). According to the China Statistical Yearbook for the years 1999 to 2020, driven by rapid economic growth and urbanization, the national average price of commercial housing surged from RMB 1,854/square meter in 1998 to RMB 9,287/square in 2008; the quantity increased dramatically from 108.27 million square meters in 1998 to 1.501 billion square meters in 1999. By contrast, informal housing built on collectively owned land and sold to nonvillagers is illegal and not recognized by the state. Furthermore, buyers and developers of these informal houses might also encounter government interference.

Despite its illegality and uncertainty, the small property right housing market has emerged and persisted in many cities. The prosperity of the small property right housing market has been driven by both supply and demand. First, although formal law prohibits the exchange of collectively owned land, the enforcement of collective property rights has been ambiguous. To gain the rents left in the public domain, local people compete for access to land that is not assigned to specific individuals or has been allocated but remains unused (Barzel 1997). The thriving real estate

[1] Housing plots are allocated to village households by the village committees based on the decisions of the villagers' assemblies and the approval of local governments. Each household can have only one housing plot, and the housing plot's area must conform to the standards formulated by the provincial or municipal congress or government.

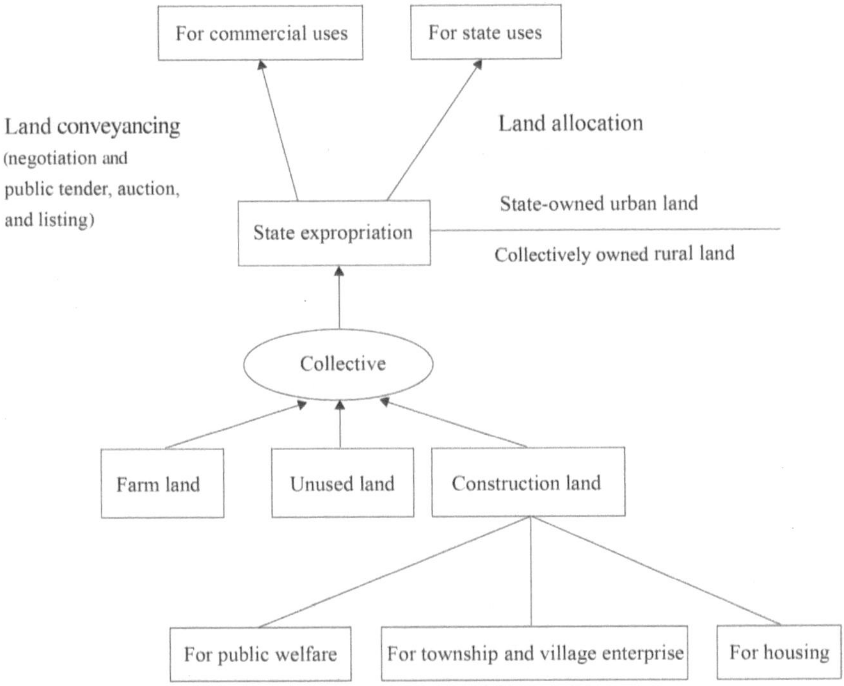

Figure 5.1 China's dual-track land system.[2]

sector has reminded local actors of the beneficial opportunities existing in the extralegal and informal use of collectively owned land. Local actors with entrepreneurship, including villagers, village committees, and private developers/investors, therefore enter the illegal housing market to seek profits.

Second, local people's motivations for earning profits from small property right housing have been reinforced by the high demand for affordable housing from a significant number of migrant laborers. According to the China Statistical Yearbook for the years 1999 to 2020, the past three decades have witnessed more and more migrant laborers flowing from rural or township areas into urban ones, with numbers increasing from 21.4 million in 1990 to 236 million in 2019. The migrant laborers look for job opportunities, need to feed their families (e.g., children and the old left behind in the rural home), and seek to stay in the cities in the future. This has generated a high demand for affordable housing, which cannot be

[2] This figure is created based on insights from Lin (2009: 76, 100).

satisfied by commercial housing. As a result, small property right housing has emerged to bridge the gap.

Empirical evidence suggests that the small property right housing market has extensively and spontaneously emerged and persisted in many cities (e.g., Beijing, Chongqing, Guangzhou, Shenzhen, and Tianjin; see He et al. 2019; Lai et al. 2017; Sun and Ho 2018; Zhang and Zhao 2018). Given the illegal nature of the small property right housing market, it is difficult to fully identify all the sites and precisely calculate the total amount of small property right housing. Nonetheless, according to the estimation made by Zhao (2017), the floor area of small property right housing increased by 7.6 billion square meters between 1995 and 2010, equivalent to 8 percent of the total floor area of housing in cities and towns during the same period. Both media reports and our fieldwork suggest that it continued to rise after 2010 in cities such as Beijing, Sanya, and Shenzhen (Li 2015). Small property right housing is believed to have emerged in Guangdong province, especially in major cities such as Guangzhou and Shenzhen in the early 1990s (Sun and Ho 2018). Taking the city of Shenzhen as an example, the city is a special economic zone and is regarded as the city with the highest percentage of extralegal housing. According to the reports of the Shenzhen Municipality Urban Planning Land and Resources Commission, the floor area of extralegal housing was 172 million square meters in 2014, accounting for around 40 percent of Shenzhen's total floor area of housing, and accommodated more than 7.378 million people, which accounted for around 68 percent of the total population in 2014, according to the Guangdong Statistical Yearbook 2017.

The price of small property right housing has been a powerful indicator of the security of informal property rights and robustness of the extralegal market. On the one hand, the price of small property right housing has been much lower than that of formal and commercial housing. Specifically, the prices of small property right housing are as low as one-half to one-third of the price of commercial housing, although they vary from city to city (Sun and Ho 2018; Zhang 2016). Without high land conveyancing fees, estate taxes, and land value increment taxes, the cost of small property right housing is dramatically lower than the legal alternative. More importantly, the lack of formal title is the main factor contributing to its low price (Alston et al. 1996). For instance, legal title was estimated to account for more than 45 percent of formal housing prices in Beijing (Wang and Sun 2014). The substantial demand for informal housing and the robustness of this informal market sustain, and even drive up, the price of small property right housing. In Shenzhen, the prices of some small property right housing projects, especially those close to the underground stations, have doubled in the last few years (Chen 2020). More notably, the prices of small property right housing built by village committees have been higher than those of small property right housing built by private developers. This reflects how (potential) buyers are more confident in property rights security when managed by the former (He et al. 2019; Zhang and Zhao 2018). We will elaborate on this in Sections 5.2.2.2 and 5.2.2.3.

Briefly, the small property right housing market that spontaneously emerged and evolved from the bottom up can be seen as local actors' responses to the constraints of formal rules and property rights. For small property right housing builders, especially village committees that construct informal housing to enhance villagers' welfare, it is their effort to break local governments' monopolization of exchanges of collectively owned land. For small property right housing buyers, especially labor migrants, small property right housing reduces their accommodation costs in urban areas and might further facilitate their welfare improvement (Bertaud 2018).

5.2.2 Three Types of Small Property Right Housing

Small property right housing can be classified into three categories. This classification is based on who the builders are, as well as the associated physical features and development patterns of small property right housing. China has witnessed a gradual evolution of small property right housing because local actors participating in this informal market continuously learn from and cooperate with each other in order to secure their informal property rights.

5.2.2.1 Farmer Housing

The first category of small property right housing, generally termed "farmer housing," is built on housing plots by individual households in urban villages in developed cities such as Beijing, Guangzhou, and Shenzhen (Webster et al. 2016). Initially, the high demand for affordable apartments led some villagers to construct taller buildings, up to ten floors high, on their housing plots. They would occupy one or two floors for their own accommodation and rent out the remaining empty apartments to young or rural migrant workers (Zhang et al. 2004).

Notably, some villagers rent out their farmer houses, while others may sell them; only in the latter case do farmer houses become small property right housing. A significant spatial feature of these houses is their density;

they are often built so close together that residents in one building can shake hands with their neighbors in the adjoining building. This implies that farmer housing occupies nearly all the available plots in urban villages (Wu et al. 2013). Village households that cannot afford construction costs might enter into a partnership with external developers. In such arrangements, villagers contribute their land, while the developers organize and finance the construction. The resulting buildings are then shared between the two parties according to a previously agreed ratio.

5.2.2.2 Small Property Right Housing Developed by Village Committees

The second category of small property right housing consists of homes built by village committees on collectively owned construction land. These are commonly referred to as "village committee (VC) small property right housing" by the general public. After observing the surge in commercial housing prices in central areas and recognizing the substantial demand for affordable apartments, village committees realized that constructing apartment blocks that resemble commercial ones can be profitable (Zhao 2017). Compared to farmer housing, informal houses built by village committees exhibit several unique physical and institutional features. First, they are often located in peri-urban areas that are somewhat farther away from city centers than farmer houses, and they tend to be better planned and organized. Apartment blocks built by village committees often consist of more than four buildings, each with fifteen to twenty floors. In contrast to farmer housing, these apartment blocks are well planned, with their plot ratios and greening rate similar to those of commercial apartments. Additionally, to attract potential buyers of small property right housing, village committees tend to invest in public infrastructure (e.g., roads, kindergartens, and parks) and property services (e.g., security, cleaning, and leasing). For instance, the village committee in Bai Ge Zhuang village, located in the Changping district of Beijing, constructed a large apartment block consisting of forty buildings and three sizable public parks. Some retired people in Beijing chose to move there for the excellent air quality and public infrastructure. The only factor distinguishing VC small property right housing from commercial apartments is that the buyers of VC small property right housing do not have certificates of title issued by the government.

A second feature of VC small property right housing is that the construction and daily management of these housing units are more organized and institutionalized than is the case with farmer housing. Villagers are often closely involved in this activity. This is because village committees often establish collective economic organizations, often in the form of joint-stock companies, to manage their economic affairs, particularly land-related matters (Chen 2016; Liu et al. 2010; Zhang and Zhao 2018). Villagers are shareholders, and their shares in the stock are distributed by village committees; some villagers may even make additional investments to purchase more shares. Villagers can receive an annual dividend based on their shares of the stock and the scale of the collective economy. When collective economic organizations enter the small property right housing market, they are responsible for nearly everything. This ranges from the planning and construction of the small property right housing to signing sales contracts with buyers and issuing them with informal titles ("green books") in the name of the village collective. They are also in charge of dividing the profits among villagers and managing the public amenities and services (He et al. 2019; Zhao 2017; Zhang and Zhao 2018).

Moreover, villagers are often allocated small property right apartments or enjoy discounts when buying them. This indicates that the development of small property right housing is beneficial for the villagers; as a result, local government interference might trigger collective resistance from the villagers (Zhang 2016). Because collective resistance often effectively deters government interference, buyers are willing to purchase small property right housing managed by village committees, which increases the price of VC small property right housing. Zhang and Zhao (2018) found that the unit price increases significantly, by 23.2 percent, when small property right housing is developed by village committees in Beijing. A similar result was also found by He et al. (2019) in Shenzhen.

5.2.2.3 Small Property Right Housing Constructed by External Developers

The third category of small property right housing consists of housing built by private developers outside villages. For convenience, we term this "external developers' small property right housing." Their projects are often located in peri-urban areas. They are neither high-density, like farmer housing, nor well-planned and large-scale, like VC small property right housing. Developers often buy housing plots from individual villagers or collectively owned land from village committees, which, according to formal rules, is illegal. However, except in a few cases where village committees serve as the third party and witness the deal between private developers and small property right housing buyers, both villagers and village committees are less involved in the operation of external developers' small property right housing.

In other words, neither the builders nor the buyers are bound to local villagers. As a result, developers and buyers have weak collective action capacity, making it difficult to organize collective resistance against government interference. Although external developers' small property right housing accounts for a relatively high percentage of the overall small property right housing market according to the sample survey – over 60 percent in Beijing and 46.75 percent in Shenzhen – its price has been lower than that of VC small property right housing (He et al. 2019; Zhao 2017). The lower price suggests that it is less popular because buyers are more concerned about the insecurity and uncertainty of property rights in small property right housing constructed by external developers (Sun and Ho 2018; Zhang and Zhao 2018).

5.3 Market Uncertainty and Political Risk

The uncertainty surrounding the property rights of small property right housing is twofold. First, there is market uncertainty resulting from coordination and opportunism issues, such as the risk of contract fraud. Second, there is the threat of government interference, which presents a political risk. Market uncertainty presents the first primary challenge faced by participants in the small property right housing market. One issue associated with market uncertainty is the problem of coordination within the extralegal housing market: Sellers (including builders) and buyers of small property right housing cannot rely on state institutions to coordinate their exchanges, as these transactions do not involve the transfer of legal title and registration with the governments' land and housing departments. They also face insufficient information due to the lack of detailed commercial or governmental reports on the demand for and supply of small property right housing. Therefore, extralegal governance institutions are called for to establish the "rules of the game" and generate people's common knowledge and shared understanding about the situation and rules in the market (Basu 2018; Chwe 2013).

Another issue related to market uncertainty is the risk of contract fraud perpetrated by opportunists. This represents a major challenge that sellers and buyers of small property right housing must overcome. Though both buyers and sellers can benefit from engaging in extralegal transactions, the absence of legal title means that these transactions are not recognized or safeguarded by formal rules, and associated disputes cannot be resolved in court. Consequently, participants may be motivated to violate contract terms. A seller might claim that their exchange of the small property right housing is invalid after the buyer has made the payment, particularly when the price of the small property right housing increases, or they may even sell it to more than one buyer (Qiao 2015). Therefore, a robust small property right housing market requires extralegal governance mechanisms capable of eliminating sellers' opportunistic behavior and encouraging cooperation.

The threat of government interference represents the second obstacle faced by participants in the small property right housing market. Small property right housing violates the formal rules of land-use planning and land exchange defined by the dual-track land system and challenges the local governments' monopolistic power over land-use control. Consequently, local governments have the legal authority to interfere in the small property right housing market. Specifically, they can prevent illegal construction activities and even demolish unauthorized buildings. However, the motivation for local governments to interfere in the small property right housing market is complex, with their incentive structure consisting of three main factors.

First, local governments are motivated to interfere in the small property right housing market to reclaim their monopolistic power over land exchange and accrue extra-budgetary revenue. Under the tax-sharing system implemented since 1994, local governments account for more than 65 percent of the nation's total fiscal expenditure, while their revenue accounts for only approximately 45 percent of the nation's total fiscal revenue. This discrepancy prompts local governments to rely heavily on extra-budgetary sources such as land conveyancing fees (Qian and Weingast 1997). As urbanization leads to an increase in land value, land expropriation and conveyance have become favorable strategies for local governments (Liu et al. 2016). Since 2002, land conveyancing fees have made up more than 30 percent of their revenue (Qun et al. 2015).

Second, the decision by local governments to interfere in the small property right housing market is highly relevant to the city's economic growth and industrial structure. Economic development not only generates tax revenues but also demonstrates that officials are competent and capable of improving social welfare in their jurisdictions (Li et al. 2000). Both land-use planning and land conveyance can serve as instruments for planning economic development. This is not to say that government intervention necessarily leads to faster economic growth, but local officials often have their own political and entrepreneurial ideas about achieving growth (Hubbard 1995). It is unsurprising that cities in various geographical locations and at different stages of development often have distinct industrial and investment structures, resulting in divergent strategies for land supply (Cheng and Shaw 2018; Liu et al. 2016; Shen and Tasi 2016).

Informal land use is not necessarily in conflict with the incentives of local governments. It can provide affordable housing for a significant number of labor migrants and lessen the need for public housing assistance (Wang et al. 2009). Local governments' varying demands for affordable housing can lead to them having different responses to the small property right housing market. In other words, small property right housing projects that can be justified as compatible with economic growth and urbanization are more likely to be tolerated by local governments.

Third, although local governments are enthusiastic about directing land use, maintaining social stability is their primary consideration (Cai 2010). Unlike the legitimacy of democratic regimes, which is based on elections, the legitimacy of authoritarian systems often relies on mass mobilization and is measured by social stability (Beetham 2013; Li 2018; Shue 2004). Collective resistance triggered by government interference in informal property rights can undermine the political legitimacy of the authoritarian regime, posing a threat to local officials. They may face criticism from their superior government counterparts or even be removed from office (Cai 2014). It could be costly for local governments to justify their interference with VC small property right housing and to pacify owners' resistance, because VC small property right housing accommodates not only external buyers but also a significant number of villagers. It is also challenging for local governments to justify their interference when the small property right housing projects do not severely violate land-use planning (i.e., they are built on construction land instead of farmland). Another long-term side effect of excluding informal property rights is that it can discourage local villages from providing public services and infrastructure themselves, as they do in the management of small property right housing projects and village township enterprises (Che and Qian 1998).

In summary, local governments face a tolerance/interference dilemma: Intervening in the small property right housing market helps local governments regain control over land use, but the benefits can be outweighed by the costs of collective resistance and the loss of informal yet affordable housing, which is conducive to local economic growth. Therefore, while the small property right housing market is exposed to the risk of government interference, it is possible for sellers and buyers in this market to reduce and avoid this political risk.

5.4 Extralegal Governance Institutions Used to Mitigate Market Uncertainties

The small property right housing market operates outside a legal framework, and state institutions such as statutes and courts do not provide rules, enforce contracts, protect exchanges, or resolve associated disputes. A court might simply refuse to hear such disputes or declare that the small property right housing exchange contracts are legally invalid. Only when non-state institutions exist that can coordinate people's beliefs about the relative certainty and security of the small property right housing market do people become motivated to engage in the market. Moreover, to sustain the extralegal market, participants must overcome the problem of sellers' opportunistic behavior.[3]

Our empirical evidence finds that a series of extralegal governance institutions – codified documents, contract-signing rituals, online WeChat groups, and village committees – have been developed to mitigate market risks and reduce potential disputes. These institutions not only secure the exchange but also help to generate common knowledge and coordinate people's shared beliefs, which makes the extralegal housing market a focal point in people's options concerning housing (Qiao 2015). This section elaborates on the operation of these governance institutions and how they can help enforce property rights and secure exchanges and explains why VC small property right housing tends to be stronger in overcoming the risk of contract fraud than other types of small property right housing.

5.4.1 Codified Documents and Contract-Signing Rituals

Codified documents and contract-signing rituals have been widely adopted in the small property right housing market. Codified documents include informal certificates of title issued by small property right housing builders, exchange contracts between sellers and buyers, and exchange testimonies or notarial certificates offered by third parties (He et al. 2019; Zhang and Zhao 2018). First, nearly all village committees and some developers provide informal certificates of title. The certificates issued by village committees are called "green books," which differ from legal certificates (called

[3] This is because the market risks are more concerned with the buyer side.

"red books") issued by governments to buyers of commercial housing in the legal market. Second, exchange contracts are used in nearly all transactions involving small property right housing. In the case of secondhand exchanges,[4] the secondhand seller (i.e., the firsthand buyer) must not only sign a new exchange contract with the secondhand buyer but also transfer all informal certificates and previous contracts (which are between the small property right housing builder and the firsthand buyer) to the secondhand buyer. Third, exchange testimonies offered by third parties, such as lawyers and/or village committees, or notarial certificates provided by notary offices, demonstrate that they have witnessed the contract-singing process and confirm the establishment of an exchange between small property right housing sellers and buyers. The contracting process, and the third party's witnessing of it, can be seen as a ritual that partially publicizes the extralegal and underground exchange. It often occurs in the third party's offices.

It should be noted that the abovementioned codified documents are not recognized by state institutions; however, interestingly, individuals involved in the small property right housing market are fully aware of this fact. Participants highlight the necessity and significance of these documents and rituals. The series of codified documents and contract-signing rituals collectively build the private governance infrastructure of the small property right housing market. We find that codified documents and signing rituals enhance small property right housing exchanges and help resolve opportunistic behavior. The prevalent use of codified documents and signing rituals in these exchanges clarifies the economic rationality behind seemingly legally meaningless arrangements, which supports Leeson's (2020: 145) argument that "every observed institution is efficient."

5.4.1.1 Creating Common Knowledge

Codified documents and contract-signing rituals are used by participants to create common knowledge, thereby facilitating the resolution of coordination problems. These documents and rituals not only explicitly inform participants of the market rules and their meanings but also publicly confirm that all participants have been informed of the rules and are aware that others are informed as well. In doing so, they effectively establish

[4] It is common that a unit of small property right housing changes hands in the market. The small property right housing builders (villagers, developers, or village committees) are the firsthand sellers. When the firsthand buyer sells the small property right housing to a new buyer, the former is called the secondhand seller and the latter is the secondhand buyer.

rules for the underground market and mediate and align participants' perceptions.

The codified documents used in the small property right housing market are characterized by their marked similarity and formality. First, their forms and content are highly similar and widely used by sellers and buyers of small property right housing, enabling new entrants to quickly understand the exchange rules and significantly reduce their learning and communication costs. Second, the documents exhibit a high degree of formality, resembling those used in the legal housing market. The certificates of title are well designed and affixed with the official stamps of the small property right housing builders. The exchange contracts in the small property right housing market stipulate both parties' rights and obligations, such as the seller's obligation to deliver the property and the buyer's obligation to make payments on time, as well as their liability for delayed payments. The contracts even highlight that the housing will be owned by the buyers if it can be legalized in the future. These codified and easily copied documents are perceived as crucial evidence of de facto ownership for small property right housing. They provide a private governance infrastructure for exchange participants to coordinate their exchange patterns and reduce transaction costs. As an increasing number of individuals adopt these codified documents, they become focal strategies in the exchange process.

The communication of common knowledge about the rules is also reinforced by contracting rituals, where small property right housing sellers and buyers sign exchange contracts in front of third parties as witnesses. Although the contracting ritual might not be as open and public as religious or tribal rituals, or wedding or graduation ceremonies, it is an activity where contracting parties voluntarily expose their deals to a third party and pay for the third party's monitoring of them. By going through the ritual, one contracting party (seller A) can be very confident that the other party (buyer B) knows the deal is done, and buyer B also knows that seller A knows the deal is done (Coyne and Mathers 2011). Two professional third parties, lawyers and notary offices, have been popular choices. Their professions symbolize impartiality and honesty. As one small property right housing agency said, the contracting ritual is much more about symbolic meaning than legal meaning.

5.4.1.2 Screening Trustworthiness

Codified documents and contract-signing rituals are also important institutional arrangements that help to solve the trust problem in the small property right housing market, in which asymmetric information is prevalent. Specifically, a buyer might have strong motivations to purchase small property right housing, but they may be unsure about whether the seller is honest or not. The buyer may worry that the potential seller might act opportunistically, such as claiming the invalidity of the exchange and attempting to take the housing back. Meanwhile, an honest seller has an incentive to mitigate the information asymmetry by informing potential buyers about their trustworthiness. We find that hostage-posting helps exchange partners enhance their trustworthiness and address their concerns.

During contract-signing rituals, small property right housing buyers and builders post two types of hostages, which reduce participants' incentives to breach the contracts. The first type is their home address, which is included in the written exchange contract. Providing one's home address makes it possible to trace a person and their family's whereabouts, leading to potential private retaliation and sanctions (such as using violence) if trust is abused in the small property right housing transaction. As Qiao (2015: 231) found in his fieldwork in the city of Shenzhen, an interviewed small property right housing buyer said, "As long as the seller wanted to stay in Shenzhen, he would not dare void the contract. I know where he lived and who his family is."

The second hostage is one's reputation, which can be regarded as a form of social capital (Allen 2011; Allen and Reed 2006). By resorting to third-party witnesses and contract-singing rituals, small property right housing contracting parties enhance the visibility of their extralegal exchange and promote information sharing. This means that if one party, especially the seller, violates the contract, gossip concerning their dishonest behavior will quickly spread within the local community. The opportunist will be perceived as an untrustworthy person, which bars them from future exchange opportunities in the small property right housing market. The opportunist might also be socially ostracized. In brief, the hostages pose threats to the contracting parties in the form of private revenge and loss of reputation, which, as Shelling (1960: 22) explains, is the "voluntary but irreversible freedom of choice." It increases the possibilities and decreases the costs of extralegal sanction, and therefore discourages opportunistic behavior (Raub 2004; Raub and Keren 1993; Weesie and Raub 1996).

Additionally, hostage-posting is a mechanism contracting parties adopt to signal their reliability and honesty (Raub 2004; Williamson 1985). The goal of signaling is to reveal a person's favorable but unobservable features (e.g., reliable, cooperative, honest, and trustworthy). A signal is credible when people with favorable features can send a signal at relatively lower cost than those with unfavorable features, such that the former find it worthwhile and affordable to reveal such features while the latter do not (Gambetta 2009; Leeson 2008; Skarbek and Wang 2015). In the context of small property right housing exchanges, the cost differential mainly points to the ex post costs after the deal is done. Specifically, for an honest seller who will honor the buyer's trust and respect the exchange, hostage-posting does not incur additional costs. However, for an opportunist who tends to violate contracts, hostage-posting is costly – they or their families might be punished by violent revenge or suffer a loss of reputation. That is to say, honest and reliable small property right housing sellers are more likely and willing to post such hostages to the buyers and thereby overcome the trust problem faced by small property right housing buyers.

5.4.2 Online WeChat Groups

WeChat (*weixin*) is a popular social media platform in China and has been described as "an indispensable tool for daily use" (Zhou et al. 2020: 201). The online WeChat group function allows users to gather with their friends, chat online, and share pictures and documents. It has been widely adopted by various groups and communities and, to some degree, has revolutionized China's channels of information sharing and diffusion. An online WeChat group not only strengthens people's existing personal ties (*guanxi*, in Chinese) by reducing communication and information costs but also helps people expand their networks (*guanxi wang*, in Chinese) by allowing them to easily introduce one friend to another friend.

Online WeChat groups are widely used in the small property right housing market, having become an important governance mechanism. In this market, online WeChat groups are often established and managed by agencies specializing in small property right housing. These agencies not only bridge the gap between small property right housing builders (sellers) and buyers but also facilitate the enforcement of extralegal property rights. A potential small property right housing buyer often relies on an agency to gain essential information about informal apartments, including details about the locality, prices, and the methods for purchasing these apartments.

Moreover, WeChat group members mainly consist of (potential) small property right housing buyers. Initially, these potential buyers are invited to join WeChat groups managed by the agencies. Meanwhile, existing group members (buyers) also invite their friends or relatives who are also interested in purchasing small property right housing to join these groups, which gradually expands the size of the network. WeChat groups are used by participants to discourage opportunistic behavior and enforce property rights, which will be discussed in detail in Sections 5.4.2.1 and 5.4.2.2.

5.4.2.1 Strengthening the Power of the Reputation Mechanism

We pointed out that the contract-signing ritual encourages exchange participants to act honestly and abide by contract terms in order to protect their reputations. Although information concerning the reputations of sellers and buyers can be revealed by professional witnesses, their networks seem to be relatively fragmented, and the information spread in the local community remains limited. WeChat groups, which include almost all buyers, sellers, and agencies, can significantly facilitate and sustain the swift flow and diffusion of information. This is because the effect of reputation tends to be much more pronounced in a dense network than in a fragmented one. A dense network can better inform people about their potential exchange partner's past behavior, thereby contributing to the formation and adjustment of beliefs about the latter's trustworthiness. This, in turn, encourages the latter to seriously consider the long-term effect of their behavior on their reputation (Raub and Weiss 1990).

How do small property right housing buyers share and accumulate information on sellers' behavior in the WeChat group? The answer is gossip. Gossip is a fundamental and spontaneous process in the creation of reputation (Richman 2017). We found that (potential) small property right housing buyers often engage in casual conversations with agencies in daily life. They discuss disputes in the market, especially certain sellers' opportunistic behaviors. Moreover, new entrants often ask questions about how to avoid or mitigate the risk of contract fraud, and experienced buyers and agencies are usually willing to share their tactics, such as the operational details of contract-signing rituals and effecting payment. Cases involving uncooperative and dishonest sellers are often used as illustrations and frequently mentioned when buyers, both experienced and potential, chat with agencies in WeChat groups.

Information sharing in WeChat groups can sufficiently address the free rider problem for two reasons. First, online WeChat group members are not only connected through online networks but also through offline interpersonal relationships (i.e., *guanxi* networks). The norm of reciprocity in the *guanxi* network promotes information flow, sustains the repeated exchange of favors among individuals within the network, and reduces transaction costs (Chang 2011; Hwang 1987; Standifird and Marshall 2000; Wang 2017). The norm of reciprocity is therefore extended to online WeChat groups, which facilitates the sharing of information about participants' (especially sellers') reputations in the small property right housing market (Rooks et al. 2011). Second, using WeChat groups to share information aligns with the agencies' interests. As key participants in the small property right housing market, agencies can gain more detailed information on the behavior and reputations of small property right housing sellers than other actors. Furthermore, to secure the sustainability of their business, agencies are incentivized to encourage cooperation among exchange parties and mitigate opportunistic behavior. Therefore, this accounts for why we often observe agencies sharing exchange dispute cases arising from sellers' dishonesty and recommending effective strategies that can mitigate market risks.

5.4.2.2 Cultivating Institutional Entrepreneurship

The widespread use of WeChat as a communication channel in the small property right housing market has greatly strengthened and expanded the role of agencies. By coordinating the behavior of sellers and buyers and identifying profitable market opportunities, these small property right housing agencies act as institutional entrepreneurs in two ways. First, like codified documents, agencies facilitate the generation of common knowledge about the small property right housing market and the governance institutions commonly used by market participants. WeChat groups managed by agencies serve as public forums for participants to share information about the market, reliable sellers, informal institutions utilized by participants, and the symbolic meanings of rituals. Agencies are also involved in resolving disputes. Some agencies, having completed multiple deals and gained credibility, even provide third-party services such as the witnessing of contract-signing in a similar manner to lawyers and notary offices.

Second, agencies often utilize the Moments feature on WeChat to share and disseminate information about profit opportunities in the small property right housing market. For example, in Shenzhen, besides purchasing small property right housing as their own accommodation, an increasing number of people consider buying such properties as an investment option. This is because these small property right houses are often treated as legitimate properties, and the owners can receive full compensation – significantly higher than the original price – when real estate companies redevelop the villages, demolishing all existing informal housing and replacing them with modern, commercial buildings.

Real estate companies are willing to pay full compensation in order to avoid collective resistance, which could significantly delay redevelopment projects. Purchasing small property right housing as an investment is highly attractive if the village where the housing is built is more likely to be redeveloped in the short term. Such information is more readily available to agencies, which have close ties with local villagers or village committee members, while accessing this information is costly and difficult for outsiders. We found that agencies often post small property right housing options located in villages with upcoming redevelopment projects in WeChat groups and Moments. Through these WeChat groups and Moments, agencies not only share information that is less available to small property right housing buyers but also frame new market opportunities in the extralegal housing sector, which heavily relies on agencies' local knowledge accumulated on the ground.

5.4.3 Village Committees

Although codified documents, contract-signing rituals, and online WeChat groups are helpful in mitigating market uncertainty, the risk of contract fraud cannot be fully avoided. Village committees also play a crucial role in reducing the potential for opportunistic behavior. Village committees have a dual organizational nature. On the one hand, they are defined as self-governing organizations that represent villagers and assume responsibilities for public affairs in their villages. On the other hand, village committees serve as quasi-formal branches of the township government. In theory, township governments only guide rather than lead village committees, but in practice the latter are often treated as organs of township governments (O'Brien and Han 2009).

Village committees facilitate the enforcement of informal property rights in two ways. First, like professional lawyers and notaries, village committees serve as third-party witnesses during contract-signing. The witness service provided by village committees is very much welcomed by both sellers and buyers, especially secondhand buyers. Second, and more obviously, as we discussed in Section 5.2.2.2, village committees are typical small property right housing builders and sellers and in that capacity act as contracting parties in small property right housing exchanges. Consequently, the price of small property right housing built by village committees has been higher than that of small property right housing built by external developers.

5.4.3.1 Pooling Exchange Information

When small property right housing is built by village committees, they issue informal certificates of title, sign contracts with buyers when they are sellers, or witness the contract-signing when the firsthand buyers sell their small property right housing to new (secondhand) buyers. Village committees also establish and manage a database that is a registration system to record all exchanges. Specifically, when a unit of small property right housing is sold by the village committee, a database is used to record the buyer's information, including name, gender, age, occupation, marital status, identity card number, and contact details.[5] When a resale occurs, the old owner and the new owner must register the change of ownership and update owner information in the database (Zhang and Zhao 2018).[6]

Compared to the buying and selling of small property right housing built by external developers, which relies only on a decentralized reputation mechanism, the registration database managed by village committees provides a centralized information pool. Village committees use the database to regulate transactions concerning the small property right housing they have constructed and to solve the problem of information asymmetry. The database effectively helps (potential) buyers to identify the ownership status of the small property right housing and ensures that their exchange is well recognized. Village committees can not only confirm that the sellers they deal with are the actual owners, instead of cheaters, but also avoid the risk of the small property right housing being sold to multiple buyers. Moreover, the registration database reinforces the effect of the reputation mechanism. The functioning of the reputation mechanism requires the availability and diffusion of information. By providing pooled and credible information, the database makes contract fraud behavior widely observable by participants in the small property right housing market and, therefore, promotes the spread of gossip both offline and online.

5.4.3.2 Punishing Opportunistic Behavior

Besides managing the registration system, village committees can also punish opportunists. To increase the value of VC small property right housing, village committees provide property services – such as supplying water and electricity as well as cleaning, security, and leasing services – for small property right housing owners recorded in the registration system.

[5] Interview C5N27 (agent), 2018.
[6] Interview C5N22 (committee member of village), 2019.

If a dishonest seller claims that their exchange with the buyer (who has already become the small property right housing owner recorded in the registration system) is invalid, the seller will be punished and lose access to the property services provided by the village committee. This is because the dishonest seller is not a legitimate owner registered in the registration database. Even if the dishonest seller physically occupies the small property right housing, the value of the property will significantly decrease due to the seller's flawed ownership. Although dishonest sellers can search for alternative services without relying on village committees, such solutions are often costly. It can be argued that the property services provided by the village committee not only function as physical public services that facilitate the establishment of small property right housing communities but also indirectly impose punishments on sellers who behave opportunistically. These punishments can also be viewed as public services that are less available in other types of small property right housing projects.

Why do village committees have the motivation to establish a centralized registration system and property services to minimize contractual disputes? The answer lies in the dual organizational nature of village committees. Firstly, as quasi-formal branches of local governments, village committees are highly sensitive to government interference. If contractual disputes concerning VC small property right housing become public and attract attention, local governments are less likely to turn a blind eye. This is because the local government's ignorance sends clear signals to the public that they are colluding with village committees in the development of the illegal housing market. Preventing disputes from escalating to incidents that attract local government attention not only helps village committees maintain their autonomy over land use within their villages but also helps them avoid punishments from local governments. Grossman (2020) presented a similar finding in the informal market in Lagos, which showed that trade association leaders offer effective services to resolve disputes and promote trade in order to avoid government intervention. Second, as self-governing organizations with committee members elected by villagers, village committees are motivated to secure their VC small property right housing projects, which are often the most essential part of the villages' collective economy. Contractual disputes harm the informal housing market and thus lead villagers to question the trustworthiness and leadership of village committees.

In summary, a set of extralegal and decentralized governance arrangements, such as codified documents, contract-signing rituals, and online WeChat groups, have been adopted in all types of small property right housing markets to promote trade and secure transactions. For small property right housing developed by village committees, these committees establish a centralized registration system and provide property services, which help mitigate the risk of contract fraud and make VC small property right housing more secure and popular than other types of informal housing.

5.5 Strategies Used to Minimize Political Risk

Besides market uncertainties such as opportunism, participants in the small property right housing market must also confront political risks, such as government interference. However, such interference from local governments can be selective. On the one hand, local governments can harshly intervene in the small property right housing market by demolishing the buildings. On the other hand, local governments might choose to tolerate the illegal housing market if interference is too costly. This implies that, despite its illegality, small property right housing developers and buyers may be able to avoid government interference, essentially making tolerance the optimal response for local governments. We find that demonstrating a capacity for collective action and seeking political patronage are two effective strategies. Drawing on empirical evidence from three cities (Beijing, Sanya, and Shenzhen) where the small property right housing market is substantial, this section depicts how the two strategies work to address government interference.

5.5.1 Demonstrating Collective Action Capacity

A strong capacity for collective action, including the ability to provide public services and conduct collective resistance, can enhance the bargaining power of small property right housing builders and buyers when facing government interference. Specifically, the provision of public amenities and services as components or by-products of small property right housing projects can significantly alleviate the fiscal burden of local governments on public infrastructures (Che and Qian 1998). Collective resistance against government interference imposes considerable costs on local government: It may face criticism from upper-level government, as the outbreak of conspicuous resistance threatens social stability, inhibits economic growth (Fu 2018), and imposes massive costs (e.g., policing costs) to restore social order (Cai 2010; Chen 2012). The provision of public services can be seen as a powerful indicator of the small property right housing communities' collective action capacity. Small property right communities with a sufficient supply of public services for residents have a strong capability to organize collective resistance when confronting interference. We find that builders and buyers of VC small property right housing are more capable of addressing collective action problems than those of other types of small property right housing for two reasons.

First, VC small property right housing projects are managed by village committees, which have a strong motivation to represent villagers in managing their village's collective economy. The development of VC small property right housing projects is an essential way for village committees to enhance the welfare of all villagers: A portion of the profits gained through these projects is used to improve public welfare (including the construction of public infrastructures), and the remainder is allocated to villagers who are individual shareholders. Additionally, many villagers purchase small property right housing or exchange their own houses and housing plots (which is legal) with the small property right housing to improve living conditions. The construction of VC small property right housing and associated public infrastructures not only increase the market price of informal housing but also improve villagers' living conditions. To safeguard their collective economy and informal housing, villagers are more likely to ally with external buyers to engage in collective resistance to deter government interference if it occurs.[7]

Second, social norms and close social networks enhance villagers' collective action capacity, discouraging local governments from interfering in the VC small property right housing market. Clan-based networks in villages help mitigate collective action problems (Hu 2007). Social sanctions, such as gossip and ostracism, are very effective in small, tight-knit communities (Ellickson 1991; Zhang and Zhao 2014). As Lu (2014: 58) claimed, "gossip, avoidance, and even ostracism could be used to detrimentally affect the lives of those villagers who misbehaved." This means that if a villager declines to join collective resistance against government interference, the information concerning their inaction will be quickly transmitted in the village, and they will be socially excluded by other villagers. Moreover, shared behavioral norms and moral obligations that formed and evolved in past experiences facilitate villagers' cooperation (Tsai 2006, 2007). Additionally, village elections can enhance the accountability and leadership of village leaders, who must safeguard the interests of the village to win votes (Zhang et al. 2004). In comparison, external developers who build small property right housing are commonly loosely tied to local villagers, which decreases their bargaining power when encountering governmental interference.

[7] Interview C5N7 (buyer), 2019.

The argument that VC small property right housing committees are more capable of deterring government interference is substantiated by our evidence concerning local governments' responses to the small property right housing market in the cities of Beijing and Sanya. In Beijing, the local government has selectively interfered with the small property right housing market on purpose. According to a list reported by the Beijing government (BMBLR 2013), there were about 108 small property right housing projects in peri-urban areas, and the Beijing government intervened in only 23 projects by demolishing 62,000 square meters and confiscating 2.409 million square meters. The Beijing government has tolerated many large-scale VC small property right housing projects equipped with well-developed public infrastructures. A typical example is a large project called Hongfu Yuan, operated by the village committee of Zheng Ge Zhuang village. This project consists of 130 buildings and accommodates almost 1,500 villagers and a significant number of labor migrants. Because the village committee of Zheng Ge Zhuang has an exceptional capability to offer public services for its residents and the committee enjoys the support of residents, the local government opts for tolerance over these informal buildings.

Moreover, the Beijing government's interference, if any, is fairly mild. It often merely requires village committees to either halt the construction or sale of small property right housing or pay a penalty.[8] Demolition, the most aggressive interventionist measure, is less likely to be adopted. In other words, the interference is only on paper and not effectively implemented. In the few instances where Beijing's government attempted serious interference in VC small property right housing, it retreated when confronted with villagers' collective resistance. For instance, in 2012 and 2013 Beijing's government tried to demolish the small property right housing projects in Shang Hao Zhuang village and Song Zhuang village. However, it triggered the collective resistance of local villagers and external buyers, ultimately forcing the government to make compromises (Dong 2012; Liu 2013; Zhang 2013).

In contrast, small property right housing projects developed by external developers often suffer severe government interference. These projects are typically small-scale, consisting of several apartment buildings with fewer public infrastructures. External developers often buy housing plots from individual villagers or collectively owned construction land from village committees, with the land often being exchanged multiple times (Zhang 2013; Zhao 2013). Neither the village committees nor villagers *have de facto ownership*, and

[8] Interview C5N15 (villager), 2018; interview C5N17 (villager), 2018.

they rarely have ties with the builders and buyers. As a result, it is difficult and costly for developers and buyers to organize collective resistance to fight against local authorities' interference. Moreover, small property right housing projects developed by external developers often do not provide as many public services as those developed by village committees, which motivates the government to interfere with projects managed by external developers.

Similarly, external developers' small property right housing projects face serious crackdowns in the city of Sanya, a popular tourist destination on Hainan island. Sanya's pleasant climate and beautiful landscape have attracted many people from outside of Hainan to spend holidays or enjoy their retirement life in Sanya, generating a high demand for housing. Since the early 2000s, waves of external developers have flooded into Sanya. They bought land from villagers or village committees and built a large amount of small property right housing. These small property right housing builders and buyers were neither closely bound to each other nor connected with local villagers. The informal housing market became a strong rival of the formal commercial housing market. It also posed a threat to the Sanya government's monopoly over the formal land-use order and reduced the government's land conveyancing fees in the long term (Lin and Lin 2023). All these factors have incentivized the Sanya government to interfere with the informal housing market.

The primary reason for the Sanya government's crackdown on the informal housing market is the lack of capacity for collective action on the part of buyers and developers, who are only loosely connected.[9] When the Sanya government launched the "Metal Hammer Campaign" (*tiechui xingdong*) in 2010 and tore down the small property right housing, collective resistance rarely occurred. In other words, small property right housing builders and buyers were in a powerless position, and they had to endure the crackdown and bear all the costs. From 2010 to 2015, the Sanya government demolished 8,100 small property right housing buildings, with a floor area of around 4,900,000 square meters (Deng 2016; Infzm 2010; Qian 2010). The small property right housing market managed by external developers ultimately ended up stagnating in the city.

5.5.2 Seeking Political Patronage

Seeking political patronage is the second strategy small property right housing builders use to reduce the risk of government interference. The possibility of political patronage results from the fact that an illegal market

[9] Interview C5N28 (developers), 2019; interview C5N30 (government official), 2018.

is socially legitimate (Beetham 2013; Engwicht 2017), which compels local government officials to tolerate and even protect the market. Although all small property right housing is technically illegal and local governments have the authority to prohibit and interfere with it, in practice small property right housing projects can vary in their level of social legitimacy. Small property right housing that seriously violates government land-use policy and economic growth planning is more vulnerable to political crackdown than those with fewer conflicts with such planning. Some small property right housing projects might have greater social legitimacy when they clearly improve land-use efficiency and enhance the social welfare of local residents, which encourages the local government not to interfere with these illegal projects. However, interfering with small property right housing projects that have a high degree of social legitimacy might lead to public criticism of the local government. Such criticism puts local governments' (violent) interference in the spotlight, reducing their political legitimacy for enforcing laws and regulating the small property right housing market (Tyler 2006a). As a result, builders of small property right housing are motivated to seek political patronage (e.g., recognition and protection from the local government) by enhancing the social legitimacy of their projects or by challenging the legitimacy of local governments' interference.

Incorporating small property right housing projects into village redevelopment programs is often utilized by village committees. To increase land-use efficiency, many villages initiate the redevelopment program to redefine and redistribute the village's collectively owned land, including housing plots. Consequently, numerous villagers move from multistory houses on their housing plots to high-rise apartments within the village committee's small property right housing project. Meanwhile, the village committee's small property right housing projects are able to accommodate a large number of external buyers who are labor migrants, key contributors to local economic development.

The social legitimacy of such VC small property right housing projects stems from the fact that they not only improve the living conditions of villagers but also liberate more land for other uses. Apart from some land used to construct public infrastructure, the remaining land is utilized for commercial and industrial purposes (such as hotels, factories, or office buildings), which aids the development of the village's collective economy and bolsters the local economy and tax revenues. For instance, villages construct and manage hotels, factories, or office buildings, or collaborate with external firms to engage in business using the village's collectively owned land as their investment. If the local government adopts severe interference measures (e.g., demolition) to suppress village redevelopment programs, it can be perceived as tyranny by the public (Zhang and Zhao 2018). The political legitimacy of such government interference could be questioned by the public, enhancing the legitimacy and righteousness of the villagers' collective resistance. As a result, to retain political legitimacy and promote local economic development, the local government tends to tolerate, or safeguard, village committees' redevelopment programs.

In contrast, small property right housing projects consisting of luxury villas built by external developers or village committees are susceptible to government interference. These villas are primarily sold to a select group of high-income individuals for vacation purposes, and their plot ratios are relatively low.[10] In other words, these projects neither provide affordable housing for migrant laborers nor improve the living conditions of local villagers. From the perspective of local governments, both the land-use efficiency and social legitimacy of these projects are low. This makes it difficult for buyers and sellers to justify the projects if the local government interferes with them. Furthermore, their capacity for collective resistance is weak because the projects are not closely tied to villagers. When the Beijing government selectively interfered with the small property right housing market, almost all of the extralegal villa projects were torn down with little to no resistance (BMBLR 2013), whereas projects developed by village committees managed to remain safe. In short, it can be observed that enhancing the social legitimacy of a small property right housing project is one of the ways in which builders seek political patronage and reduce political risk.

5.6 Conclusion

Based on extensive fieldwork and public materials regarding the operation of the small property right housing market in the cities of Beijing, Sanya, and Shenzhen in China, this chapter has provided a systematic analysis of the governance institutions that participants in the extralegal housing market deploy to mitigate market uncertainty and political risk. Lacking state-sponsored institutions to facilitate transactions, participants must overcome coordination problems and opportunism issues (specifically, sellers' opportunistic behavior). Moreover, participants might face government interference. In some situations, local governments might even launch crackdowns, such as demolishing extralegal housing.

[10] Interview C5N25 (developers), 2019.

Empirical evidence suggests that small property right housing can be divided into three categories: farmer housing, VC small property right housing, and external developers' small property right housing. Participants, such as sellers, buyers, and agencies, devise a series of governance mechanisms to mitigate market uncertainty. First, codified documents (e.g., informal certificate of title, exchange contract, and lawyer's testimony) and contract-signing rituals are widely used to equip market participants with common knowledge, which aids in solving the coordination problem. The mechanism of hostage-posting helps buyers screen sellers' trustworthiness, thereby reducing the risk of contract fraud. Second, online WeChat groups established and managed by agencies are utilized to facilitate information sharing and thus sustain the reputation mechanism. Meanwhile, the common use of WeChat groups has established agencies as institutional entrepreneurs, who have a strong motivation to enforce informal property rights and share profitable market opportunities with (potential) buyers. Third, village committees play a crucial role in sustaining the small property right housing market. They establish centralized registration databases to record small property right housing exchanges and recognize the ownership of each small property right housing unit. These databases can effectively regulate market transactions related to small property right housing.

This chapter has also investigated how the builders of small property right housing reduce or avoid government interference. First, a strong capacity for collective action, which includes the ability to provide public infrastructure and conduct collective resistance, can discourage government interference. We find that village committees have a stronger capacity for collective action and are more powerful in deterring and safeguarding small property right housing projects than other types of small property right housing builders. Second, seeking political patronage is another strategy utilized to mitigate political risk. Empirical data suggests that incorporating a small property right housing project into a village redevelopment program can increase its social legitimacy, persuade the local government to protect the market, and thus minimize political uncertainty. As a result, VC small property right housing is more robust and secure than other categories of informal housing.

6

Corrupt Transactions

6.1 Introduction

How do exchange participants facilitate cooperation and resolve uncertainties in corrupt transactions? To address this research question, this chapter examines China's illegal job market within China's public sector (i.e., the buying and selling of government positions), which is neither legitimate nor legal. Participants involved in these corrupt transactions not only need to manage the scarcity of information concerning potential exchange partners and prevent opportunistic behavior, but they also have to mitigate the risks associated with sellers using their power to exploit buyers, and buyers extorting sellers by threatening to report illegal dealings to anti-corruption agencies. Drawing on sixty-two in-depth interviews, this chapter offers an empirical and socio-economic investigation of corrupt transactions and essential extralegal governance institutions that exchange partners have developed to promote cooperation and mitigate transaction risks and uncertainties.

In general, corrupt transactions are regulated by informal mechanisms of network governance, which include *ganqing* (strong feelings of emotional attachment), *mianzi* (face, which refers to reputation and social esteem), and corrupt intermediaries. We argue that corrupt transactions are highly embedded in strong-tie *guanxi* (*guanxi* can be understood as a Chinese version of personal relationships and networks) as a way of handling both behavioral and external uncertainties (see also Barbalet 2018; Granovetter 1985; Li 2011; Luo 2008; Wang 2014; Zhan 2012). Specifically, exchange participants employ a network of relationships to gather information that allows them to identify reputable and capable exchange partners, discover what the relevant prices are, and negotiate and conclude corrupt deals. Among the principal mechanisms used to prevent opportunist behavior in the operation of corrupt exchanges are: (1) "hostages," such as strong emotional attachment and human capital investment in establishing and maintaining the social exchange relationship; and (2) face, which can be understood as social prestige and reputation that are not only "an outcome state of social interaction" (Qi 2011: 281) but also an incentive structure that prevents opportunistic behavior (Barbalet 2014, 2021). Face is a compelling power that implies following social norms and meeting others' expectations rather than pursuing personal benefit at the expense of other members of the network. This is because any failure to fulfil social expectations leads to a negative response from others and the loss of social esteem and reputation (see also Ho 1976; Hwang 1987).

Recent decades have witnessed an increasing power imbalance in the social exchange relationship between favor-seeker and favor-giver, caused primarily by more people buying promotion and a greater amount of corrupt benefits becoming associated with abusing entrusted power. The favor-seeker, as the low-power actor in the exchange relationship, has to develop informal institutions so as to be able to compete with other favor-seekers to obtain exchange opportunities with the favor-giver. Empirical data shows that to seal a corrupt deal with a power-holder, favor-seekers can improve their ability to reward exchange partners by increasing the amount of bribe payment and making payment in advance. Once a corrupt agreement is sealed, the favor-seeker needs to patiently await the delivery of corrupt benefits by the favor-giver.

Meanwhile, favor-seeker and favor-giver face differential levels of punishment, with the former being the low-risk actor and the latter the high-risk actor. If things go wrong, the favor-seeker can threaten to disclose compromising information to anti-corruption authorities in order to compel the favor-giver to deliver the promised benefits or return the bribe payment. But this sanction was seldom used before President Xi's anti-corruption campaign began in 2012. There were two reasons for this reticence: First, a powerholder whose illicit conduct was reported to anti-corruption officers often retaliated; second, favor-seekers usually lost their reputation in the exchange network because network members regarded the disclosure of compromising information to anti-corruption agencies as a betrayal. President Xi's anti-corruption drive significantly changed the situation; today, reports of suspected corrupt conduct often lead to criminal investigation and legal punishment. This makes the threat of revealing damaging information an effective power-balancing option for favor-seekers.

Strong ties with powerholders, as interviewees emphasized, are the key precondition for initiating corrupt exchanges and enforcing agreements;

buyers of government positions have to employ intermediaries if such ties are weak or nonexistent.[1] In corrupt exchanges achieved through intermediaries, the intermediaries play an essential role at three stages: initiation, exchange, and monitoring. We find that face – more specifically, the concern to preserve rather than lose reputation – is a major governance mechanism for corrupt exchanges involving intermediaries. Our empirical data provides details about how intermediaries help buyers and sellers of corrupt benefits overcome these barriers to trade by offering predictability, monitoring the fulfilment of corrupt agreements, and solving the problems of opportunism (see also Bayar 2005; Lambsdorff 2002; Mishra and Samuel 2016). The case study of corrupt transactions in China enhances our understanding of major types of uncertainty encountered by exchange participants and of the various extralegal governance institutions that have been developed to address uncertainty in practice. It therefore contributes to the literature on corruption and institutional complexity.

6.2 Corruption in China: A Brief Literature Review

Corruption has traditionally been understood as the abuse of public office by public officials for personal gain (Gong and Yang 2019). Definitions of corruption have evolved to cover private-sector corruption (Rothstein and Varraich 2017), and participants in corrupt transactions have a range of aims, including personal, departmental and organizational gains. These can be further categorized as monetary or nonmonetary benefits, the latter including reputation and social recognition (Punch 2000, 2009). Major forms of corruption include bribery ("acts of giving financial benefits to the public official in power in exchange for favorable treatment or services"), extortion ("situations in which public officials take money from a private party by means of illegal compulsion"), kickbacks ("commissions paid to a public official as a reward for rendering government contracts to the bribe payer"), and patronage/nepotism/cronyism ("rewarding political supporters, relatives, or exclusive social network members with government employment"; Jancsics 2019: 524–525). Corruption can also be classified as "activities (appointing personnel, buying things, etc.), sectors (construction, health, energy, etc.) and places (countries, regions, locations, etc.)" (Jancsics 2019: 525).

[1] Interviews C6N1 (government official) and C6N20 (government official), 2015.

Corruption is a way of life in developing countries such as China, and since President Xi Jinping launched his nationwide anti-corruption campaign in 2012 corruption and anti-corruption have attracted enormous attention from scholars. The existing literature examines the effects of corruption on China's economic growth at macro (country), meso (local government) and micro (company) levels. For example, Wedeman observes that China's rapidly worsening corruption is due to new opportunities created by the country's economic reforms (see also Pei 2006); he supports the corruption as sand in the wheels argument by suggesting that the reason corruption has not strangled China's economic growth is that the continued anti-corruption efforts "have prevented corruption from spiraling out of control" (Wedeman 2012: 11). In a departure from Wedeman's viewpoint, Wang and Yan (2020) examine the role of corruption in developing economies at local government level by arguing that corruption, in the form of extravagant position-related consumption and gift-giving, increases local government's capacity to attract investment and mobilize development resources; in other words, corruption greases the wheels of economic growth. Researchers who adopt a micro-level perspective also find that corruption greases the wheels of growth in firms not owned by the state (Jiang and Nie 2014; Kong et al. 2017; Wang and You 2012).

A great deal of scholarly attention has also been paid to the campaign-style anti-corruption approach. President Xi's latest anti-corruption campaign, which boasts "longer duration and higher reach" (Manion 2016: 3; see also Broadhurst and Wang 2014; Li 2016), has boosted "public support for the top national leader" (Zhu et al. 2017: 500) and serves "the purpose of cleaning up obstacles to socio-economic reform" (Zhan and Zhu 2016: 1). In-depth comprehensive studies have been conducted to investigate the role, structure, and reform of individual anti-corruption agencies – for example, the Central Commission for Discipline Inspection (see Fu 2015; Guo 2014; Keliher and Wu 2016; Li 2016), the local discipline inspection commissions (see Li and Deng 2016a; Li et al. 2017), central inspection groups (Yeo 2016), local procuratorates (Li and Deng 2016b), and the newly established National Supervisory Commission (Deng 2018; Li and Wang 2019; Liao and Tsai 2020). Researchers have also extended the scope of research by studying corruption in different sectors, including customs and excise (Shieh 2005), police (Chin and Godson 2006; Wang 2013a), courts (Gong 2004; Li 2012; Wang 2013b), education (Ruan 2016, 2021), media (Li 2013; Wang et al. 2018), state-owned enterprises (Cheng 2004; Huang and Snell 2003), mining (Zhan 2017), and the real estate industry (Zhu 2012). However, the hidden, politically sensitive nature of corruption has led to insufficient research into corruption at the interactional (micro) level.

The literature on corruption can be further enriched by bringing two different fields of study together. The socio-economic approach adopted by this book offers a fresh and innovative explanation of the corruption phenomenon in China by integrating new institutional economics with sociological concepts and theories. This method of analysis enables us to understand corruption at the interactional and institutional level: It investigates major uncertainties encountered by participants in corrupt transactions and how participants deploy extralegal governance institutions to redress these uncertainties. Two behavioral assumptions of human agents generated by transaction-cost economics are especially helpful in understanding what causes the high transaction costs associated with corrupt transactions and what the major costs/uncertainties are. These assumptions are bounded rationality, which holds that behavior is of limited rationality (Simon 1961: xxiv), and opportunism, which is "a condition of self-interest with guile" (Williamson 1985: 30).

Sociological theories such as the power-dependence theory (also known as the social exchange theory) complement the transaction cost theory in explaining transaction risks. When used to examine the power structure of relationships, the power-dependence theory shows that power imbalances between exchange parties often lead to social conflicts and transaction uncertainties, the resolution of which demands power-balancing mechanisms (Emerson 1962, 1972a, 1972b). Combining economics and sociology, a socio-economic method of analysis allows researchers to offer a comprehensive examination of uncertainty in corrupt transactions.

6.3 Risks and Uncertainties in the Buying and Selling of Public Appointments

This section examines different categories of risks and uncertainties in corrupt transactions. It utilizes key theories from institutional economics (especially transaction cost theory) and sociology (particularly power-dependence theory) to understand the major risks and uncertainties associated with such transactions.

6.3.1 A Transaction Cost Approach to Understanding Risk in Corrupt Transactions

Transaction cost theory, originated by Coase (1937, 1993) and developed by Williamson (1985), highlights two fundamental issues of human nature: bounded rationality and opportunism. First, the assumption of bounded rationality suggests that economic actors are limited in their cognitive competence and their ability to process and evaluate information and incorporate all possible contingencies in contract drafting and negotiation (Williamson 1985). This gives rise to bounded rationality-induced transaction costs, which can be economized by assigning different transactions to different governance structures depending on the properties of the transactions. Second, Williamson stresses the concept of opportunism, and his theory is "heavily invested in the belief that people lie, steal, and cheat" (Rindfleisch 2019: 94). Opportunism is defined by Williamson (1985: 47) as referring "to the incomplete or distorted disclosure of information, especially to calculated efforts to mislead, distort, disguise, obfuscate, or otherwise confuse." Opportunistic behavior causes exchange hazards or behavioral uncertainties (You et al. 2018). Given that the trustworthiness of the partners in an economic exchange is not transparent ex ante and a transaction is vulnerable to opportunistic behavior, exchange partners need to make "*ex ante* screening efforts" and establish "*ex post* safeguards" (Williamson 1985: 64).

The cognitive and behavioral assumptions of transaction cost economics can be used to analyze corrupt transactions (Husted 1994). Participants in corrupt exchanges face enormous cognitive limitations because it is often difficult for the favor-seeker to gather a wide range of diverse information, such as "who, precisely, will take the bribe" (Oldenburg 1987: 589), the potential favor-giver's reputation for trustworthiness, and how much payment is needed (price being an essential form of information; see Coase 1937). To seal a corrupt deal, the favor-seeker also needs to know about the interaction rituals that are used to preserve the favor-giver's face or public image (Goffman 1955, 1967; Ruan 2019), negotiation tactics, shared meanings of symbols, and the informal rules governing interactions. On the other hand, the favor-giver demands information to assess the reputation of the potential favor-seeker and evaluate their capabilities and personal characteristics. This information is essential for concluding a corrupt agreement, preventing opportunistic behavior, and avoiding criminal investigation. But this information is not in the public domain. As Lambsdorff (2002: 222) points out, the process of seeking and delivering corrupt services is characterized by "a high degree of secrecy, little transparency, and limited participation." Participants in corrupt transactions therefore have to address the high cost of searching for and screening partners in addition to the cost of negotiating a corrupt agreement.

The illicit nature of corrupt transactions and the kind of participants involved in these transactions increase the potential for opportunistic behavior. First, compared to law-abiding citizens, actors in illegal transactions are self-interest seekers and risk-takers and more inclined to systematically distort information for personal benefit (Campana and Varese 2013; Husted 1994; Macrae 1982). Second, economic actors in corrupt exchanges face a high risk of being cheated because the exchange of money and favors is nonsimultaneous and the favor-seeker has to rely on the word of the favor-giver (Della Porta and Vannucci 2012: 153). A nonsimultaneous transaction, as Trebilcock and Prado (2011: 107) note, "creates a significant need for a credible third-party enforcement mechanism." But participants in illegal transactions cannot rely on state-based contracts and courts to settle their disputes and regulate their interactions (Bevan et al. 1989; Husted 1994; Leeson 2007; Leeson and Skarbek 2010; Wang 2017). Moreover, to receive public support and preserve their legitimacy, democratic and nondemocratic governments alike are actively fighting corruption. A government develops different categories of policy (e.g., establishing or reforming anti-corruption agencies, strengthening anti-corruption audits, and launching educational campaigns) to reduce bureaucratic corruption (Bauhr 2017; Di Tella and Schargrodsky 2003; Gans-Morse et al. 2018). To sum up, participants in corrupt transactions need to address both behavioral uncertainty, such as opportunistic acts, and environmental uncertainty, such as criminal detection and punishment.

An analysis of the transaction costs of corruption cannot ignore the concept of asset specificity, which is defined by Williamson (1985) as "durable investments that are undertaken in support of particular transactions" (p. 55). He further notes that "such investments … cannot be redeployed without sacrifice of productive value if contracts should be interrupted or prematurely terminated" (p. 54). The rationale for employing the concept of asset specificity to explain transaction costs in the context of corruption is that asset specificity refers not only to physical assets but also to human capital investments (Williamson 1985). As Husted (1994: 21) points out, corrupt transactions, especially repeated ones, often "involve investments in human capital [e.g., learning highly nuanced knowledge and establishing and maintaining relationships in order to carry out transactions] with little salvage value outside the particular transaction or relationship." Similarly, Della Porta and Vannucci (2012: 159) argue that "the skills, knowledge and information concerning the most effective methods for creating, managing and enforcing corrupt relations are acquired and accumulated with time." These human capital investments, however, have little or no value when they are used for other purposes. Transaction cost economics stresses that the more specific the asset, the greater the demand for establishing ex post safeguards (i.e., the corresponding governance structures) to support economic transactions.

6.3.2 A Power-Dependence Approach to Understanding Risk in Corrupt Transactions

Power-dependence theory, formulated by Emerson (1962) and developed by Molm (1994, 1997) inspires us to focus on power and dependency in exchange relationships when examining risks and uncertainties in corrupt transactions. As mentioned in Chapter 3 on our methodology chapter, the primary reason for selecting the case of corrupt transactions related to the buying and selling of public appointments is that this case study enhances our understanding of the social order of illegal markets from a micro perspective. This perspective stresses the role of imbalanced power relationships between exchange participants and differential punishment faced by favor-seekers and favor-givers according to the risks and uncertainties created by their exchanges.

In most circumstances, participants in a corrupt exchange are embedded in an unequal power relationship: The favor-seeker is the less powerful actor in the relationship because they are more dependent on the favor-giver (i.e., the powerholder), and it is not easy for the favor-seeker to obtain the same corrupt benefits from alternative relationships. When the number of favor-seekers far exceeds the number of favor-givers (i.e., demand is high and supply is scarce), the favor-seeker needs to increase their reward power in order to compete. Furthermore, the favor-seekers have to develop extralegal governance institutions to avoid exploitation by favor-givers, who may have an incentive to ask the favor-seeker to transfer more resources (e.g., money) than the favor-giver gives in return. As high-power actors, favor-givers may break their promises to deliver corrupt benefits and may form new agreements with other favor-seekers in order to maximize their interests.

Moreover, once detected and convicted by anti-corruption agencies, participants in corrupt exchanges face punishment of varying levels of severity. The primary objective for China's anti-corruption campaign and the routine anti-corruption efforts is to identify corrupt officials and punish them according to Party discipline and criminal law. This encourages anti-corruption investigators to show leniency toward, or simply overlook, the criminal responsibility of bribe-givers who are willing to provide evidence that can be used to prosecute the bribe-receivers (i.e., the corrupt officials). This means that corrupt officials who abuse power to deliver favors to buyers are high-risk actors, whilst the buyers are low-risk actors. Even in the buying and selling of public appointments, office-sellers face more severe punishment than office-buyers. This gives rise to a particular risk and uncertainty: The office-buyer may threaten to report their corrupt dealings to anti-corruption agencies in order to coerce the office-seller to not only fulfill their promise but also satisfy the officer-buyer's additional demands.

To sum up, both transaction cost theory and power-dependence theory enable researchers to gain a more comprehensive understanding of the uncertainties inherent in corrupt transactions. First, the transaction cost approach encourages the examination of key characteristics of market actors, such as bounded rationality and opportunism, as a means of identifying bounded rationality-induced and opportunism-based transaction costs. Second, the power-dependence theory, leaving aside key features of economic actors, looks instead at the power structure of an exchange relationship by arguing that low-power actors need to increase their capacity to reward and punish their exchange partners in order to win exchange opportunities and lower the chances of being exploited by high-power actors. In addition, high-risk actors must address the issue of extortion by low-risk actors, who may threaten to report corrupt dealings to anti-corruption agencies in order to achieve their demands.

6.4 The Embeddedness of Corrupt Transactions in Strong-Tie Relationships

This section examines how participants in corrupt transactions manage the risks and uncertainties resulting from such transactions. It firstly discusses the embeddedness of corrupt dealings in strong-tie relationships and emphasizes that *ganqing* (emotional attachments) is one of the essential mechanisms preventing opportunism. It then discusses the informational function of strong-tie relationships in ex ante screening and the significance of the payment of bribe as a power-balancing operation employed by low-power actors (i.e., buyers of corrupt benefits) to win exchange opportunities with high-power actors. This section also examines *mianzi* (face) as an ex post safeguard mechanism and investigates low-power actors' use of the threat of disclosing damaging information to anti-corruption agencies as a punitive/coercive strategy to compel high-power actors to deliver what they promised or return bribe payments. It is worth noting that corrupt exchanges do not occur only between people who are directly connected through strong ties; where favor-seekers do not possess strong ties to favor-givers, corrupt intermediaries will help them obtain corrupt benefits. This will be discussed in Section 6.5.

6.4.1 Strong Ties and *Ganqing*

Tie strength and how it is measured have been thoroughly discussed by sociologists (Barbalet 2015; Bruggeman 2016). According to Granovetter (1973: 1361), the strength of an interpersonal tie is "a combination of the amount of time, the emotional intensity, the intimacy (mutual confiding), and the reciprocal services which characterize the tie." Based on a rigorous empirical examination of Granovetter's intuitive model, Marsden and Campbell (1984: 498) suggest that "closeness (the measure of the emotional intensity of a tie) is the best indicator of tie strength," while the time spent in a relationship – the frequency and duration of contact – is not a useful indicator of tie strength. As Marsden and Campbell (1984: 499) explain, "The use of frequency as a measure of strength will tend systematically to overestimate the strength of ties between persons who are neighbors or co-workers, while the use of duration as a measure of strength will overestimate the strength of ties between relatives."

Tie strength has become an essential factor in job search and internal promotion in different countries (see Brown and Konrad 2001; Lee and Phan 2006). In China's legitimate job market, "jobs are acquired through strong ties [that are characterized by a high level of emotional intensity] more frequently than through weak ties" (Bian 1997: 366). The role of strong ties is not limited to the legitimate labor market; strong ties play an even larger role in the illegal job market, where bribery is used to obtain government positions. As empirical data shows, to solve information asymmetry and prevent opportunistic behavior, corrupt transactions such as buying and selling government appointments are highly embedded in strong-tie relationships.

To be specific, strong ties characterized by *ganqing* (strong emotional feelings of attachment) are a prerequisite for sealing a corrupt deal. A businessman mentioned during an interview that "under-the-table transactions will not happen until help-seekers establish *ganqing* with power-holders."[2] The illegal nature of corrupt exchanges prevents participants from resorting to the formal legal system of resolving disputes. This lack of legal sanction against opportunistic behavior significantly restricts illicit exchanges; in practice, sellers of corrupt benefits have to limit their transactions to persons with whom they have deep and enduring emotional bonds. It is risky for power-holders to conduct corrupt exchanges with persons with whom they do not have strong ties, because the assurance mechanisms

[2] Interview C6A (businessman), 2017.

of *ganqing* and face are absent or ineffective. Corrupt exchanges are usually reiterative, not one-off interactions. Once a buyer (A) and a seller (B) seal a corrupt deal, it will be difficult for B (who is now tainted by the deal) to decline A's future requests, for A will be able to extort B by threatening to make public their previous deal or report it to anti-corruption agencies. As an interviewee told us:

> To give and take a bribe is a process in which people commit a bad deed together. Once people have jointly committed a bad deed, they share a secret that can be used against each other, just like two grasshoppers tied to the same string [for honor and for disgrace]. You satisfied my [illegal] request this time, so I expect you to do the same for me next time ... If you decline my requests, our relationship may turn sour ... this incident may become a fuse, developing into a situation in which either the fish dies, or the net gets torn [by employing shared secrets against each other].[3]

When corrupt transactions are embedded in weak-tie relationships, power-holders who sell corrupt benefits are not always in a strong position, and they may face a significant risk of being extorted. In such circumstances, the buyer is able to put the seller at a disadvantage, for two reasons. First, the mechanisms of *ganqing* and face do not work effectively in corrupt transactions embedded in weak-tie relationships. The buyer is ready to act opportunistically in order to obtain higher corrupt benefits from the exchange, and the loss of *ganqing* and face for the buyer due to the destruction of a weak-tie relationship is negligible when compared with the benefits that could be generated from opportunistic behavior. Second, to gather sufficient information and promote cooperation in their investigations and enforcement, anti-corruption agencies and the criminal justice system are more inclined to prosecute and penalize those who take bribes than those who offer them (Wang 2020a). As a result, bribers receive less severe or even no criminal sanctions. The absence of effective assurance mechanisms and the less punitive attitude toward bribers suggest that corrupt exchanges cannot take place without a guarantee derived from the exchange relationship's affective component (*ganqing*).

Buyers of corrupt benefits often successfully employ their deep emotional bonds with power-holders to form corrupt agreements and encourage power-holders to deliver the favors the buyers need. Strong ties or strong emotional connections are usually established through long-term positive interaction between exchange partners. The strong-tie relationship is characterized by reciprocal obligations; "obligations to reciprocate are often translated into emotional feelings of attachment (*ganqing*),

[3] Interview C6N10 (government official), 2015.

and people lose face (*mianzi*) if they do not reciprocate" (Bian 1997: 369). Once *ganqing* is established, it enhances mutual understanding, removes disagreement between help-seekers and help-givers, and creates a high degree of perceived obligation. Theoretically, the deeper the *ganqing* is, the more likely it is that the help-giver will give face (show respect to the other party by satisfying their demands) and deliver favors to the help-seeker. *Ganqing* is highly valued in social exchanges because "mutual emotional attachments" and "relationship-specific assets" (human capital investments in creating and maintaining emotional bonds) are "hostages" in the social exchange relationship (Yamagishi and Yamagishi 1994: 135). The fear of damaging *ganqing* and relationship-specific assets deters unilateral defection and offers an assurance of compliance because it is difficult for exchange participants to restore emotional bonds once broken.

6.4.2 Ex Ante Screening and Bribe Payments

Both strong ties and weak ties facilitate the sharing of information through interpersonal interactions within a social network. But individuals are "less likely to share novel information across [weak] ties" due to "a lack of trust, an unwillingness to share benefits, or a limited ability to understand one another" (Larson 2017: 1). Information about who wants to buy government positions, who will accept bribe payments, and how much the buyer should pay is shared only in strong-tie relationships because unlimited information flow in weak-tie relationships is associated with a higher risk of detection.

The favor-seeker. Before sealing a corrupt agreement, a favor-seeker needs to assess the reputation of the potential favor-giver. This assessment is usually based on their personal experience of working and interacting with the potential exchange partner. "Reliable pieces of information accumulated over a long history of interactions with the partner" help the favor-seeker decide whether the potential favor-giver will be interested in delivering corrupt benefits and whether they will cheat (see Yamagishi and Yamagishi 1994: 139). Evaluation of the potential partner can also be based on information from network members who are willing to give the favor-seeker their assessment of their previous exchanges with the potential exchange partner and their perception of the trustworthiness of the potential favor-giver.

The favor-seeker seeking to buy a specific government position needs to establish the price. The price of government positions is an open secret within the public sector, and this was so even before President Xi's anti-corruption drive in 2012. But this does not mean that any favor-seeker who is willing to pay the price can obtain a government position or promotion. As a public official noted during an interview, "If you have not established a strong tie with the power-holder, there is no way of delivering the bribe payment and reaching a corrupt agreement."[4] In other words, the bribe payment is necessary, but not sufficient, for a successful corrupt transaction, because the power-holder is reluctant to put themselves at risk by engaging in a corrupt exchange with a person the favor-giver does not know well.

Interview data reveals both the increasing importance and the increasing amount of bribe payments in corrupt transactions. In the 1980s and early 1990s, a favor-seeker who was a close friend of the favor-giver did not need to pay; the common practice was for the seeker to invite the giver to dinner or offer a small gift, such as alcohol or cigarettes, to show appreciation for the giver's help.[5] But in this century buying a government position usually involves a large bribe. For example, a middle-ranking police officer in the city of Chongqing paid Wen Qiang, the city's deputy police chief, RMB 1.77 million (more than twenty years of the buyer's salary at the time) for a same-level transfer to a better job (Wang 2017: 148).

For a combination of reasons, bribes have become increasingly important for winning exchange opportunities. First, alongside the rapid development of the socialist market economy and inspired by the Chinese saying "*sheng guan fa cai*" (to obtain a higher or more important position, and at the same time to gain more material wealth), occupants of government positions are likely to abuse power for personal benefit, and a higher-rank position becomes attractive because it brings more opportunities to obtain corrupt benefits. A government official mentioned the changing perception of money among public officials in past decades:

> In the 1970s and 1980s, under the circumstances of material shortages, you might not be able to buy anything with money. But if you had power or created relationships with those who had power, you were able to obtain a lot of commodities that were essential for the survival of your family. Nowadays, if you have sufficient money to pay bills, you and your family can enjoy a better life. Monetary success becomes even more valuable [than a high-rank position]. In general, government officials have changed their understanding of money.[6]

Gaining promotion and occupying a more powerful position in the public sector is perceived by many public officials as the key strategy for achieving both high social status and monetary success. Buying government

4 Interview C6N8 (government official), 2015.
5 Interview C6N33 (government official), 2016.
6 Interview C6N15 (government official), 2015.

positions therefore becomes a cost-effective investment for a large number of corrupt officials.

Second, and related to the first point, corrupt benefits encourage more and more public officials to buy a position, but government appointments and promotion opportunities are scarce. This leads to an increasing power asymmetry in the exchange relationship between the buyer and the seller of a position. To win exchange opportunities, the favor-seeker has to increase their capacity to reward the exchange partner, which often means paying bribes. In addition, the favor-seeker makes a preemptive bribe payment in order to demonstrate a clear intention to purchase a promotion.

The favor-giver. As with favor-seekers, reliable network information is essential for favor-givers, who need to balance the risk of criminal punishment with the social and financial gains on offer. Information gathered from previous direct interactions with a potential favor-seeker is extremely important in order for the favor-giver to be able to assess the exchange partner's personal traits, intentions, and trustworthiness. From the favor-giver's perspective, the concept of trustworthiness concerns not only whether the favor-seeker is honest and sincere but also to what extent the favor-seeker is loyal to the favor-giver. As a government official noted during an interview, "[In theory,] a key criterion for selecting and promoting a public official is that they must be loyal to the organization and the Party, but in practice impersonal loyalty manifests in personal loyalty, which can be understood as personal and affective attachment to upper-level officials."[7] Personal loyalty to upper-level officials is especially valued in the public sector because the level of loyalty determines whether upper-level officials' orders can be effectively implemented and whether their interests, both legitimate and illegitimate, are effectively safeguarded in their daily work. As a result, corrupt benefits are distributed only within strong-tie relationships:

> For the dispenser of corrupt benefits, rather than distributing according to merits or price competition (if there is an open market for the benefits), there is an order of preference, with those closer to them enjoying higher priorities in receiving the corrupt benefits than those farther away. This feature of *guanxi* network makes the dispenser of corrupt benefits lean toward people with whom they share stronger particularistic ties. (Zhan 2012: 102)

Moreover, upper-level officials must ensure that favor-buyers who eventually gain promotion are not only loyal to them but also capable. Upper-level officials and their subordinates are mutually, albeit unequally, dependent

[7] Interview C6N41 (government official), 2015.

on each other: The latter value promotion opportunities provided by the former, while the former are dependent on the latters' competence in addressing routine and nonroutine challenges and implementing policies. For example, a leader and their *mishu* (secretary) are mutually dependent. A leader's *mishu* is responsible for helping the leader handle routine work, giving the leader time to deal with important issues. As Li and Pye (1992: 925) observe, "a leader becomes highly dependent upon his *mishu* in every aspect of his work and even his private life." As a result, the *mishu* has the opportunity to establish close connections with the leader and has a higher chance of gaining career advancement.

A common misunderstanding about corruption in China's bureaucratic system is that incompetent candidates are selected and promoted to important government positions. Our empirical data, however, shows that, despite the use of bribery, capable candidates are promoted to important positions.[8] This is caused firstly by China's reform of its bureaucratic system: Target responsibilities have been established for government officials at varying levels, and these targets relate officials' performance to their future career development. Upper-level officials are responsible for the mistakes of their subordinates; this encourages upper-level officials to promote subordinates they know very well, following the Chinese saying "*zhigen zhidi*" (knowing all of their backgrounds and knowing them thoroughly).[9] Another reason for promoting capable candidates is to avoid the situation of *renzou chaliang*. A literal translation of this phrase is "When a person leaves, the tea becomes cold." Applied in the present context, it could be interpreted as meaning, "When an official retires, they lose influence within their organization and society."[10] To preserve their influence, upper-level officials seek to promote competent candidates within their strong-tie networks.

6.4.3 Face as Ex Post Safeguard Mechanism

In Chinese society, failing to give and return favors to network members leads to loss of *mianzi* (face). Face refers to one's reputation and social esteem, but it has much deeper significance than that. It means "an individual's social position or prestige, gained by successfully performing one or more specific social roles that are well recognized by others" (Hwang 1987: 960). In China, as Hwang further points out, face can be derived from

[8] Interview C6N48 (government official), 2016.
[9] Interview C6N17 (government official), 2015.
[10] Interview C6N20 (government official), 2015.

one's physical appearance, family background, personal qualities (e.g., knowledge and abilities), and social factors such as wealth, authority, and social connections (see also Buckley et al. 2006; Leung and Chan 2003). But the most important way to save face (avoid humiliation and maintain prestige within one's social relations) is to meet network members' social expectations and act according to the principle of reciprocity. Since "saving *mianzi* rather than losing it becomes a primary objective in Chinese society" (Hwang 1987: 961), individuals, in many circumstances, would be willing to lose money or abuse power in order to safeguard face and protect self-esteem.

In a country like China, where the party-state fails to make and enforce explicit rules against corruption in government agencies, the allocation of public resources is more likely to be influenced by emotional bonds and the reciprocity rule than the rational–legal principle that emphasizes legal entitlement, performance, and qualification (Wang 2017). This helps explain why public officials choose to meet unethical demands made by network members regardless of bureaucratic regulations and laws (Dunfee and Warren 2001; Fan 2002; Lin and Si 2010; Schramm and Taube 2003; Smart and Hsu 2007; Wang 2016).

Hwang (1987) points out that face is a major source of influence on Chinese social behavior. In parallel, Barbalet's ground-breaking discussion of *guanxi* further suggests that face functions as the assurance mechanism in exchange relations. "Assurance" is defined by Yamagishi and Yamagishi (1994: 132) as "an expectation of benign behavior" that is based on "reasons other than goodwill of the partner" and "the knowledge of the incentive structure surrounding the relationship." Barbalet (2014: 61) argues that the structure of *guanxi* is triadic, rather than dyadic, because the importance of third-party observation cannot be neglected in *guanxi* exchanges. The triadic structure of *guanxi* means that exchange participants' behavior is continuously observed, monitored, and commented on by others (Barbalet 2015, 2018). Transgressing social norms leads to loss of reputation and face, seriously limiting transgressors' ability to engage in future social exchanges. Barbalet (2014: 64) also elaborates on the role of gossip in exposing network members' transgressive actions:

> Gossip functions as a kind of moral discourse, directed to the transmission of information concerning departures from the expected norms of behavior, commitment, and decorum. In this sense, then, gossip is not only a means of censure but a basis of assurance for all members of the network that transgressions of the expectations of appropriate behavior shall be exposed, with a consequent loss of reputation and face for the transgressor.

Barbalet's account of face is helpful for researchers seeking to understand why power-holders in China have to follow *guanxi* norms, such as reciprocity and the essence of maintaining face, when exercising their power. The concern for face encourages public officials to share their power and illicit benefits with their family members and close friends:

> For individuals who possess authority (power), apart from enjoying the authority, they have to share the authority with their relatives and friends within their *guanxi* networks. Their relatives and friends will also unite together to share the authority or demand that the authority be shared. This has already become a form of custom or social norm … For Chinese people who become government officials or become rich, they have to offer relatives and friends some benefits; otherwise they will be viewed as failing to understand and act according to *renqing shigu* [the rules that are used to regulate exchanges with others and maintain harmonious *guanxi* relationships]. A person who does not behave according to *renqing shigu* will lose their social prestige in the local community. (Zhai 2013: 213[11])

Zhai shows that public officials have to respect *guanxi* norms when exercising the power with which they have been entrusted, and the sanction for failing to share official powers with their *guanxi* members is loss of social prestige (face). This not only explains the rise of "family corruption" (Denyer and Xu 2016), but also offers insights into the involvement of public officials' family members, relatives, and close friends as intermediaries in corrupt exchanges, which will be discussed in Section 6.5.

Once the power-holder decides to accept a bribe, a corrupt agreement is reached, and the power-holder is usually highly committed to this agreement in order to preserve their reputation in the network. This also means that the power-holder has to decline other candidates' requests. To prevent loss of face among these unsuccessful favor-seekers, the power-holder usually makes a point of turning down their requests nicely. The power-holder will explain why it was difficult to offer help this time (for example, the hiring decision was made collectively, and the criteria for this position were not fully satisfied by the favor-seeker), will offer advice on improving profile and performance, and sometimes promise help in the future. In this way, favor-seekers who fail to obtain corrupt benefits do not lose face; indeed, they usually appreciate the power-holder's honesty and advice. As a result, the power-holder manages to maintain social esteem in the exchange network.

Although decisions concerning personnel matters are decided collectively by a committee consisting of several senior officials, the leader of

[11] Unless stated otherwise, translations from the Chinese are our own.

the department or organization (i.e., unit leader) still wields enormous influence over the process of selecting and promoting officials. Once the unit leader has decided which candidate should be promoted, the leader will usually indicate this to colleagues during the process of gathering their opinions about candidates before the formal meeting.[12] In theory, the process of consultation before formal meetings gathers opinions and comments from colleagues in order to enhance committee members' knowledge about candidates' professional capacity and political integrity, but in practice unit leaders use it to let their preference be known.[13] For example, when the unit leader solicits an opinion from a committee member about a particular candidate, the committee member has to *cha yan guan se* (evaluate the leader's words and facial expression) and provide the response that the leader appears to expect. During the formal meeting to choose appropriate candidates for promotion, committee members usually give face to the unit leader and vote for the leader's preferred candidates.[14]

In most cases, favor-seekers who manage to reach agreement with favor-givers just need to be patient.[15] For the favor-seeker, there is insufficient reason for them to question the favor-giver's intentions because opportunistic behavior leads to loss of reputation and social esteem. The Chinese saying "*haoshi bu chumen, huaishi chuan qianli*" (a good deed goes unnoticed, but a bad deed spreads fast) is very helpful for understanding the relationship between opportunism and loss of reputation in social networks. The favor-seeker who corruptly obtains promotion may not be keen to let it be known that the power-holder facilitated the promotion, but the favor-seeker who is cheated by the power-holder has an exceptionally strong motivation to share negative gossip about the power-holder with network members, many of whom are very interested in gossiping about others' immoral deeds in their social networks. The favor-seeker who accepts bribes but fails to deliver what was promised is labelled by network members as dishonest, greedy, and deceitful. A negative reputation not only leads to the loss of future exchange opportunities within the social network, but also has a detrimental effect on the transgressor's career development because reputation and social esteem are valued by officials at all levels.

12 Interview C6N12 (government official), 2015.
13 Interview C6N30 (government official), 2016.
14 Interview C6N16 (government official), 2015.
15 Interview C6N49 (government official), 2018.

6.4.4 Revealing Compromising Information as Another Ex Post Safeguard Mechanism

A favor-seeker may threaten to report a corrupt deal to the anti-corruption agency in order to coerce a dishonest favor-giver into fulfilling their side of the deal. The threat or use of disclosure of compromising information to anti-corruption agencies is a punitive strategy employed by the low-power actor to force cooperation, because the briber and the bribed face different levels of punishment: The bribed, the main target of China's anti-corruption efforts, are usually punished severely, whereas bribers receive more lenient punishment. This differential punishment policy helps anti-corruption investigators deal with the information asymmetry caused by the hidden nature of corrupt transactions. As a senior anti-corruption official stated, "For many corrupt transactions, it is difficult for us to collect enough evidence if they [exchange participants] do not confess."[16]

Before President Xi's anti-corruption campaign, recourse to the punitive strategy (reporting illegal acts to anti-corruption agencies) usually provoked a hostile emotional response and retaliation from the exchange partner. This was because anti-corruption investigators were not independent of local influence and had insufficient incentive to investigate these reported cases. Their anti-corruption operations were seriously affected by social norms and network expectations. In other words, senior officials who were reported to the anti-corruption agency for violating Party regulations and accepting bribes were often able to obtain confidential information about the report from friends who worked in the same anti-corruption agency.[17] As a result, less powerful actors who reported corruption would pay the price of betrayal: First, they would lose future promotion opportunities or be demoted; second, all members of their network would exclude them from future exchange opportunities, because disclosing damaging information to the anti-corruption agency was viewed as a profound betrayal of trust.[18]

China's latest anti-corruption campaign and its reform of anti-corruption agencies have significantly changed the situation, however. Local anti-corruption officers have become more independent of local influence and more powerful (Fu 2016; Li and Wang 2019) because President Xi has strengthened the Party's vertical control over local discipline inspection

16 Interview C6N50 (government official), 2021.
17 Interview C6N8 (government official), 2015.
18 Interviews C6N15 (government official) and C6N24 (government official), 2015 and 2016.

commissions. Heads of local commissions are now appointed by the immediately superior commission, which directs the subordinate commission's anti-corruption work. Moreover, anti-corruption officers are required to verify all reported cases, which means that a report of suspected illegal exchange to the anti-corruption agency often initiates a corruption investigation.[19] The establishment of a more independent anti-corruption agency has significantly reduced local officials' ability to intervene in investigations conducted by local anti-corruption officers. Consequently, senior officials who abuse power for personal gain are at much greater risk of arrest and incarceration. Favor-seekers are therefore more likely to threaten to report corrupt conduct to anti-corruption agencies if they need to coerce favor-givers into delivering corrupt benefits or to return bribe payments upon failure to deliver.

6.5 Corrupt Intermediaries

Individuals who are perceived as "insiders" by power abusers can become corrupt intermediaries. In order to become "insiders," individuals need to make use of family/kinship ties and/or engage in long-term interactions and exchanges with power-holders. The existence of intermediaries significantly increases the number of corrupt exchanges. This is because corrupt intermediaries help bribers to avoid human capital investments – that is, the time and money spent on cultivating deep emotional attachment with resource allocators. A strong tie between intermediaries and bribers is not always necessary in order to initiate corrupt deals, however, because intermediaries usually face little risk of legal sanction. Senior officers are always the main target of anti-corruption drives, while intermediaries (such as family members, secretaries, and drivers of senior officials) are commonly treated leniently in order to encourage them to cooperate with the Party's discipline inspection officers and supply crucial information against their bosses (Chu and Wang 2017). Added to this, corrupt exchanges are an opaque process: It is not easy for anti-corruption investigators to gather sufficient evidence showing whether intermediaries earn economic profit by facilitating corrupt exchanges.[20]

The involvement of intermediaries greatly expands the pool of qualified exchange partners, exacerbating the difficulty of controlling corruption. This suggests that the study of corrupt intermediaries is particularly

[19] Interview C6N50 (government official), 2021.
[20] Interview C6N33 (government official), 2016.

important. A senior government official asserted that curbing the problem of corrupt intermediaries was an essential step in a successful anticorruption campaign:

> If it is very difficult for the buyers and sellers to locate each another, then this market will probably wither. Because those intermediaries are always there, it is easy [for the buyers and sellers] to locate each other. Thus I believe that, in order to curb corruption, we should not only punish those who give bribes and those who receive bribes, but also identify and penalize these intermediaries. If this link in the middle is disconnected, corruption [in China] will not be so serious.[21]

Face is a major governance and assurance mechanism for corrupt exchanges involving intermediaries. To illustrate this, the operation of corrupt exchanges facilitated by intermediaries deserves close examination. In the following example, a resource allocator (A) and B are connected through a strong tie, which is a prerequisite for a direct corrupt exchange. In addition, B is friends with C. Suppose C wants to buy a government position and wants A to help him. C could ask A directly for this favor, but A is likely to decline C's request, refusing to give face, because A feels no obligation toward C. If, however, C makes the request through B as an intermediary, B can say to A, "'Please take my face into account." In this situation, C's request is much more likely to be accepted because the cost of disregarding B's face is high.

Employing intermediaries to help obtain promotion is usually more complicated than in this example, because more than one intermediary may be needed and obtaining promotion usually requires the payment of bribes. In order to understand the phenomenon of corrupt intermediaries, a thorough examination of the extralegal governance institution that facilitates and assures corrupt exchanges is needed. Based on rich empirical data, Sections 6.5.1–6.5.3 analyze how intermediaries initiate corrupt deals and how they make use of the mechanism of face to regulate corrupt exchanges and prevent opportunistic behavior.

6.5.1 Initiation

The main motivation for favor-seekers who do not possess strong ties with favor-givers to use intermediaries is that intermediaries increase the likelihood of success. Discussing and negotiating an illegal deal with a senior officer with whom the favor-seeker is not familiar is associated with a high risk of being rejected (losing face) and a strong feeling of embarrassment. The

[21] Interview C6N21 (government official), 2016.

senior officer might feel offended by the favor-seeker's visit because the favor-seeker is not welcome or qualified to negotiate due to unequal official status. During an interview conducted in 2015, an officer mentioned that turning to an intermediary for help was common practice in the public sector:

> If he [the favor-seeker] approaches the senior officer directly, he may not know what to say. He is afraid that he may say something that offends the senior officer ... He also does not know what the senior officer likes and what he needs ... It is very different if an intermediary is involved in the process, [since] he is very familiar with what the senior officer needs. Furthermore, the intermediary knows whether his request can be met or not, and how to persuade the senior officer to deliver help to the favor-seeker.[22]

The key criterion for selecting intermediaries is their reputation (face) in the social network and their ability to persuade a power-holder to deliver corrupt benefits. For corrupt exchanges that rely on intermediaries, the intermediaries have face when they have a good track record of engaging in social exchanges based on social norms and of facilitating corrupt exchanges, and when they occupy an important social or government position that obliges the seller of corrupt benefits to give them face. Choosing different intermediaries may bring different outcomes,[23] as an interviewee described:

> There are a lot of people around senior officers who could all become intermediaries; for example, secretaries, drivers and persons who share home ties with senior officers ... but in reality, the intensity of emotional bonding [the depth of *ganqing*] between senior officers and these intermediaries can be very different, which affects the outcome ... For example, both M and N have established social ties with a senior officer; however, N shares deeper *ganqing* with the senior officer. This means that having N as the intermediary [to assist you to conclude the transaction] will have a higher rate of success.[24]

If there are no strong ties (or deep emotional attachments) existing between favor-seekers and favor-givers, favor-givers need intermediaries to facilitate transactions for three reasons. First, it is extremely difficult and risky for officials who do not know each other and who are ranked differently

[22] Interview C6N34 (government official), 2015.

[23] Where there are multiple candidates vying for a single position, there will be multiple corresponding intermediaries competing against one another in their entreaties to the office-seller. The office-seller usually chooses to satisfy the request of the intermediary whose *mianzi* is the most important to the office-seller. At the same time, because of the existence of *ganqing* between the office-seller and other intermediaries, these intermediaries would accept the explanation offered by the office-seller for why it was difficult to get things done. By doing so, mutual understanding is achieved, *mianzi* is maintained and *ganqing* is not harmed.

[24] Interview C6N46 (government official), 2016.

in the public sector to seal a corrupt deal.[25] Coercion originating from the power differences between exchange partners usually prevents them from concluding successful negotiations. Second, the information provided by intermediaries is essential for favor-givers to assess favor-seekers' credibility, ability, and performance. Deep emotional attachment between favor-givers and intermediaries guarantees that such information is reliable. An interviewee noted that:

> Lobbying is an important aspect … If you engage an intermediary to buy you an official position, at the least you have to let the senior officer believe that you are qualified to take on this position, believe that you will not cause him trouble, and that you can even be of service to the senior officer in the future. All this information needs to be passed on through the intermediary.[26]

Third, the involvement of intermediaries in corrupt exchanges significantly reduces the risk of exposure and legal sanction. A driver from a provincial government agency informed the *Southern Weekly*[27] that: "A lot of people offer gifts or bribes to senior officers, not presented directly to the senior officers but through people around the senior officers, such as drivers and secretaries. There is a consensus among drivers, secretaries and senior officers regarding whose gifts can be accepted and whose gifts cannot be accepted (Chu and Wang 2017)." During negotiations between intermediaries and favor-seekers, intermediaries have to evaluate the costs and benefits of exchanges, assess the trustworthiness, reputation, and social standing (face) of help-seekers, and judge the extent to which help-seekers' requests can be satisfied. This selection process reduces the potential for conflict that can arise due to untrustworthy exchange participants and unachievable requests.

Because sellers of government positions make use of intermediaries to hide their involvement, it is difficult for anti-corruption agencies to pinpoint wrongdoers. Unlike the existing literature discussing the role of corrupt intermediaries in solving information asymmetry (Bayar 2005), empirical data gathered in China for this chapter shows that intermediaries can, to a certain extent, be a source of asymmetric information.[28] As an interviewee said:

[25] Interview C6N34 (government official), 2015.

[26] Interview C6N20 (government official), 2015.

[27] The *Southern Weekly* is a leading Chinese newspaper building an international reputation for investigative reporting.

[28] An interviewee mentioned that the information asymmetry is also used by intermediaries to earn a commission fee, because the buyers are not able (or feel embarrassed) to ask the sellers how much money they actually receive. Source: Interview C6N33 (government official), 2016.

The intermediaries function as a protective shield, a "firewall" for the transaction. That is to say, the intermediary's existence reduces as much as possible the risk of the seller being exposed and punished. In many cases, the seller does not want to reveal his identity ... In some cases, the buyer does not know who receives his bribe; he just gives the money to the intermediary, and the intermediary gets the thing done. This reduces the risk of the seller being exposed ... We can say that it is the intermediaries who provide protection to the participants [especially office sellers] ... Since the person selling and the person buying a government position did not deal with each other directly, it is very difficult for investigators to gather evidence.[29]

6.5.2 Exchange

Gaining social standing and reputation (face) is one of primary objectives of social exchanges. The achievement of this objective requires that exchange participants comply with social norms. For corrupt exchanges involving intermediaries, the degree of obligation felt by senior officers (favor-givers) to offer corrupt benefits is dependent on intermediaries' face, which is derived from the intensity of emotional attachment (*ganqing*) between favor-givers and intermediaries as well as from the official status of the intermediaries. Instead of indicating that the principal motivation for public officials to engage in corrupt transactions is only to convert power into money, interviewees emphasized that face, not money, is the primary consideration. An interviewee explained the significance of intermediaries' face in facilitating corrupt exchanges:

For the superior [favor-giver], the reason for helping you get things done is the *mianzi* (face) of the intermediary. You and the favor-giver are neither relatives nor friends. Why should he help you to deal with the matter? He [the superior] does not lack people desiring to establish close connections with him directly and make payments ...What he cares about is *ganqing* between him and the intermediary. This [*ganqing* component] encourages the superior to help you rather than those who can only make bribe payments.[30]

If strong emotional feelings of attachment and face are absent, senior officers usually decline to accept favor-seekers' bribes.[31] As a researcher noted, "Money is not as important as the media has suggested; many senior officers care less about bribe payments offered by junior officers."[32] The reason

[29] Interview C6N21 (government official), 2016.
[30] Interview C6N20 (government official), 2015.
[31] Interview C6N12 (government official), C6N15 (government official) and C6N42 (government official), 2015.
[32] Interview C6N5 (government official), 2015.

money and expensive gifts are less attractive for senior officers is that they have many opportunities to earn money by abusing power – for example, by manipulating department accounts, embezzling collectively owned assets, taking bribes related to construction projects, and associating with local businesspeople who buy scarce resources controlled by the state.[33]

Although the payment of bribes (money and/or expensive gifts) is not a determinative factor, it is still important in corrupt exchanges involving intermediaries. Interestingly, paying bribes has an emotional connotation in China. Bribe payments, as interviewees noted, are a demonstration of loyalty to, and appreciation of, senior officers.[34] For help-seekers, offering money and expensive gifts demonstrates their clear intention to exchange and *xinyi* (literally, kindly heart-intentions) including love, care, gratitude, and appreciation.[35] Making bribe payments has therefore become a major way for junior officers to strengthen emotional bonds (*ganqing*) with senior officers. Interview data also shows that high-ranking officials are more likely than low-ranking officers to pay bribes before obtaining promotion; this is because these officers have a greater opportunity to abuse their power for personal gain.[36] The purchase of a higher-level position is a worthwhile investment: The new position always provides the favor-seeker with more power and more opportunities to earn corrupt benefits, which will more than cover the cost of buying the promotion.[37]

Doing a favor, such as allocating a government position for money, brings prestige for all three participants: The favor-giver enhances face in the exchange network for having helped the intermediary; the intermediary earns face for demonstrating the ability to facilitate a corrupt exchange; and the favor-seeker receives face for obtaining a higher-level position.[38] Detailed information about corrupt transactions will not be disclosed in social networks, but an intermediary can reveal a seller's sound moral compass (e.g., being reliable, warmhearted, trustworthy, and capable) in social networks, enhancing the seller's reputation and social standing.

Intermediaries, especially drivers and secretaries of high-ranking officers, not only are able to persuade their bosses to deliver corrupt benefits to help-seekers but also directly ask other officers (e.g., leaders of subordinate units or departments) to give face to them and satisfy their

[33] Interview C6N11 (government official), 2015.
[34] Interviews C6N10 (government official) and C6N16 (government official), 2015.
[35] Interview C6N10 (government official), 2015.
[36] Interview C6N22 (government official), 2016.
[37] Interviews C6N12 (government official) and C6N22 (government official), 2015 and 2016.
[38] Interview C6N12 (government official), 2015.

illegal demands. Face is a resource or power that can be transferred by others; as Earley (1997: 69) argues, "by associating with people who have much *mianzi*, a person receives *mianzi*." The nature of face explains why secretaries and drivers of senior officers are able to function as corrupt intermediaries. Take secretaries as an example. Despite the fact that their official rank is not high, they are able to influence or even determine the selection and promotion of officers in subordinate units, as an interviewee mentioned:

> When the secretary of a high-ranking official asks for a favor – for example, assisting a candidate in obtaining promotion – from a subordinate unit, the leader of the unit will have to guess: Is this the high-ranking official's idea or is it the secretary's idea? But no matter whose idea it is, face must be given … This is due to two reasons: First, the unit leader feels very embarrassed [emotional pain associated with the loss of face] to check with the leader; and second, there is a possibility that [the subordinate] will seek the secretary's help in the future.[39]

Information supplied by secretaries concerning high-ranking officers' personal preferences, current psychological and physical condition, and recent concerns is essential for subordinates who want to enhance their chances of promotion by pleasing their superiors. An interviewee explained why leaders of subordinate units are willing to give face to high-ranking officials' secretaries:

> The high-ranking official's recent health conditions, as well as his recent concerns, what he likes to eat or drink, all of this is very important information for subordinates … If you wish to meet the high-ranking official, the secretary always knows his whereabouts; if he reveals this information to you, then you can meet the high-ranking official … For example, if the high-ranking official is going to inspect a subordinate unit, the unit leader [who has a close tie with the secretary] can make a phone call to the secretary to enquire, What matters require special attention during the high-ranking official's visit? What is the focus of this inspection? If you can obtain such valuable information and proceed accordingly, the high-ranking official will be very happy and impressed with your work.[40]

6.5.3 Gossip and Monitoring

Face has compelling power in regulating exchange partners' behavior. The study of corruption in the Chinese public sector suggests that subordinates who are less powerful in the exchange relationship have the power to negatively or positively affect the face of more powerful individuals (see also

[39] Interview C6N3 (government official), 2015.
[40] *Ibid.*

Earley 1997: 73).[41] The mechanism employed by less powerful individuals is gossip, which is a major source of information used by network members to make moral judgements on the social behavior of others and affect the reputations of exchange partners (Barbalet 2014). In other words, deliberately generating negative or positive gossip is an effective way for corrupt intermediaries or other network members to monitor, award, or punish a high-power actor's behavior. This encourages, and even compels, senior officers to bestow promotion opportunities on those who are close to them in the exchange network and those who seek promotion by employing intermediaries.

Superiors who accept bribe payments and fulfill promises have much face because they are widely regarded as good leaders and trustworthy persons in the social network. Conversely, disregarding face and failing to behave according to social norms leads to social sanction. For example, those who accept bribes but are unable or unwilling to deliver the requested favor are seen by network members as dishonest and greedy, and those who neither accept gifts nor deliver favors are seen as lacking *renwei* (human feelings).[42] Although Chinese people avoid expressing direct criticism, negative labels such as dishonest, untrustworthy, greedy, or lacking human feelings make favor-givers who transgress social norms lose reputation and face, diminishing their ability to exchange with others in the future.

Face and gossip also regulate intermediaries' behavior. A case mentioned by an interviewee shows how a corrupt intermediary who failed to facilitate a corrupt exchange managed to avoid the negative gossip that would have led to loss of face in the social network. The interviewee's close relative *lao Zhou* (senior Zhou) wanted to find a job for his son in a military-affiliated institution. Zhou's good friend Yao introduced him to a military officer, Liu, who worked in Beijing and was from the same village as Yao. Liu promised to help Zhou's son find a job in the military after the payment of RMB 300,000 (equivalent to three or four years' salary), but the deal did not go as they expected: Liu failed to fulfil his promise and returned all the money to Zhou a year later.[43] This case shows that avoiding loss of face is a major consideration for the intermediary. Liu could have chosen to disregard face and keep the money, but this might have disqualified him from being an intermediary in future social exchanges. The desire to save face

[41] Interview C6N12 (government official), 2015.
[42] Interview C6N10 (government official), 2015.
[43] Interview C6N29 (government official), 2016.

prompts intermediaries and office-sellers to return all payments to buyers if they fail to deliver the promised benefit.[44]

An explicit conclusion from our empirical data is that the mechanism of face governs corrupt exchanges realized through intermediaries and ensures that participants meet the expectations that stem from social networks. A successful corrupt exchange enables all participants (buyer, intermediary, and seller) to earn social standing and face. Furthermore, it can be argued that the rise of corruption in China is due to the fact that decision-makers in government agencies respect social rules, especially the mechanism of face but, in a classic Weberian conflict between traditional and rational–legal authority, disregard the bureaucratic principles that are key to establishing a clean government (Weber 1978). Our empirical data suggests that the likelihood of social sanction is much greater than that of legal sanction.[45] The efficient transmission of gossip and negative labels in social networks makes it a near certainty that the transgressor will lose social prestige and reputation. At the same time, the embeddedness of corrupt exchanges in strong ties prevents outsiders from obtaining information about corrupt exchanges, seriously undermining China's anti-corruption efforts.

6.6 Conclusion

This chapter took a socio-economic approach to investigating the ways in which corrupt transactions are governed without state support. That approach combines transaction cost theory and power-dependence theory to explain the uncertainties encountered by participants in corrupt exchanges. Transaction cost theory examines the transaction costs of corrupt dealings from three aspects: bounded rationality, opportunism, and asset specificity. In corrupt transactions, participants need to overcome serious cognitive limitations that are caused by the lack of sufficient information to evaluate potential exchange partners' trustworthiness and the sincerity of their intention to exchange. Compared with legitimate market transactions safeguarded by state laws and regulatory agencies, participants in a corrupt transaction face a high risk of being cheated, arrested, and incarcerated. Furthermore, a successful corrupt exchange demands long-term investment in creating and maintaining relationships with exchange partners, and the value of this investment cannot be realized in other

[44] Interview C6N3 (government official), 2015.
[45] Interview C6N48 (government official), 2016.

exchange relationships. Power-dependence theory provides a perfect complement to transaction cost theory by using the concepts of dependence, power, and power-balancing operations to analyze uncertainty and conflict in the social exchange relationship. The theory suggests that seekers of corrupt benefits are lower-power actors in exchange relationships, which means they need to develop strategies to get exchange opportunities and avoid exploitation by high-power actors.

Empirical data collected in China suggests that corrupt transactions, such as the buying and selling of government positions, are highly embedded in strong-tie relationships. Exchange participants rely on network information to assess the trustworthiness, intention, and capacity of potential exchange partners. Exchange partners who are connected through strong ties have a great incentive to cooperate with each other and exchange favors because the cost of losing "hostages" (e.g., human capital investments in creating *ganqing* – deep feelings of emotional attachment – and maintaining strong relationships) and face are high and difficult to recover. Favor-seekers, as low-power actors in exchange relationships, develop two major power-balancing strategies. First, increasing the size of bribe payment and making payments in advance are tactics they employ to increase their reward power and signal their clear intention to exchange. Second, threatening to disclose corrupt deals to anti-corruption agencies becomes an increasingly effective strategy that is employed by lower-power actors to coerce high-power actors (favor-givers) to exchange or return bribe payments made by favor-seekers.

Corrupt intermediaries are commonly used by favor-seekers who have not established strong emotional bonds with power-holders. Intermediaries are responsible for identifying favor-seekers and favor-givers, conducting ex ante screening of exchange participants and accepting bribe payments on behalf of favor-givers. Our empirical data shows that the mechanism of face regulates corrupt exchanges involving intermediaries and ensures that exchange participants will follow social norms and meet social expectations. For favor-seekers who do not create strong ties with power-holders, the fear of losing face (e.g., offending power-holders with improper conduct, such as offering bribes or making unexpected visits) leads favor-seekers to employ intermediaries. For power-holders, the decision to deliver corrupt benefits to those offering bribes is mainly prompted by the intermediary's face rather than the bribe payments; for intermediaries, labels and gossip are used to ensure exchange participants follow social rules. Gossip, an effective mechanism for gathering and disseminating information within social networks, enables a low-power actor to influence the face (reputation) of a more powerful individual, encouraging – or even compelling – the power-holder to meet social expectations. Face also regulates the behavior of intermediaries, as evidenced, for example, by the practice of returning all payments in order to avoid loss of face when a promised favor is not delivered.

The study of uncertainty in corrupt transactions and extralegal governance institutions has wider theoretical implications. A socio-economic approach that combines transaction cost theory and power-dependence theory offers a useful analytical tool for explaining risk and uncertainty in various types of illegal and unethical social exchange in public agencies and private organizations. Moreover, theoretical and empirical discussions about the emotional component of strong ties, the essence and operation of face, and the involvement of corrupt intermediaries show how corrupt transactions are governed. An exploration of the uncertainties experienced by exchange participants, and their solutions for addressing those uncertainties, that more faithfully represents the social realities of Chinese society will help Western researchers to formulate theoretical explanations of uncertainty and informal institutions that will enjoy wider applicability. At the same time, the study of corrupt transactions indicates the significance of Chinese cases and non-Western concepts (e.g., *mianzi* and *ganqing*) in knowledge production at the global level.

7

The Illegal Online Lending Market

7.1 Introduction

How do participants facilitate transactions and enforce agreements in the illegal online market? To answer this question, this chapter examines the online peer-to-peer lending market that enables traditional organized criminal groups, such as loan sharks, to lend money to Chinese students at exorbitant interest rates. Illegal lenders employ techniques of deception, the sharing of compromising information (e.g., social contacts and nude photos), and professional legal services to develop internet-based loan scams to trap student borrowers. To enforce loan repayment, lenders have developed a new strategy: relational repression, which is the use of cyber-violence and the threat of revealing damaging information to clients' social contacts. This puts enormous pressure on clients and their families to make payments. The use of relational repression reduces the need to resort to physical violence and bribe police officers.

This chapter aims to enhance our understanding of the social order of illegal markets in cyberspace by theoretically and empirically investigating how conventional organized crime groups harness the internet for instrumental purposes, such as marketing their products/services, enforcing agreements, and avoiding police arrest. Specifically, it focuses on how traditional criminal groups in China use the online peer-to-peer lending market to lend money to college students at exorbitant interest rates.[1] Empirical

This chapter is an updated version of P. Wang, M. Su, and J. Wang, "Organized crime in cyberspace: How traditional organized criminal groups exploit the online peer-to-peer lending market in China," *British Journal of Criminology*, volume 61, issue 2, March 2021, pages 303–324. Permission has been granted by Oxford University Press.

1 Doing business on the internet does not mean that loan sharks no longer do business off-line. In fact, they do both.

data collected from China shows that loan sharks have managed to expand their offline businesses on the internet by taking advantage of the country's booming peer-to-peer lending market (see also Loubere 2016). The data also suggests that although a large number of the illegal lending firms that have come into existence over recent years did so online, they need to cooperate with conventional criminal groups, especially offline loan sharks, in order to obtain finance and enforce loan repayments[2] in an effective manner; in other words, traditional and offline loan sharks still play an essential role in running the illegal online lending business.

The chapter first defines key concepts (e.g., organized crime, loan-sharking, and compromising information) and discusses new challenges that conventional organized crime groups have to face when they move their offline businesses online. Next, the chapter explains the rise of China's online peer-to-peer market in terms of supply and demand and analyzes why loan sharks target college students. It then explores how predatory loan sharks trap student customers by employing deceptive techniques (e.g., false advertising, obfuscating interest rate information, and prolonging the state of indebtedness), compromising information (e.g., social contacts, nude photos, and pornography videos), and professional legal services. Furthermore, it examines how loan sharks rely on relational repression[3] to enforce loan repayments and avoid police attention. Here, relational repression refers to a control technique utilizing cyberviolence (e.g., text bombing) and the threat of revealing damaging information to victims' social and family ties; this generates enormous pressure on victims and their families to make payments.

7.2 Organized Crime, Loan-Sharking, and Their Strategies for Securing Transactions Offline and Online

This section defines key concepts and discusses the major risks and cooperation enhancement strategies (e.g., violence and hostage-taking) adopted by conventional organized crime groups in the illegal market. It then concentrates on loan sharks' traditional risk management strategies and analyzes the new challenges they face on the internet. It suggests that empirical

2 Illegal lending firms that come into existence online need to cooperate with conventional criminal groups, whose tactics include not only forcing victims to share compromising information and carrying out cyberviolence but also delivering offline threats and physical violence.

3 The concept of relational repression was first developed by O'Brien and Deng (2017) in their research on the use of psychological coercion in protest control.

research is needed to understand how conventional crime groups manage risks associated with internet use.

7.2.1 Organized Crime and Loan-Sharking

The term "organized crime" can be understood from three perspectives: organization/structure, activity, and power (Antonopoulos and Papanicolaou 2018; Varese 2010; von Lampe 2008). First, organized crime refers to an organization (e.g., a hierarchical enterprise) or a network of members who are closely or loosely connected (Paoli 2002; Varese 2010). Second, organized crime refers to criminal activities featuring "planning, preparation, complexity, and continuity over time" (Antonopoulos and Papanicolaou 2018: 4). Third, organized crime is a form of extralegal governance that utilizes power to regulate and control the criminal underworld (Gambetta 1993; Lo and Kwok 2017; Varese 2001, 2010). According to the existing literature, a traditional organized criminal group refers to a criminal association (e.g., an illegal enterprise or a network) that derives its main source of income from the unlawful production and/or distribution of goods or services in the physical world.

Illegal moneylending is a major business area for conventional crime groups, but it has rarely been thoroughly examined. Researchers have used a variety of terms, such as loan-sharking (Aldohini 2013), usury (Lewison 1999), or illegal/unlicensed/predatory moneylending (James 2014), to describe broadly similar social phenomena. Kojouharov and Rusev (2016: 106) suggest that illegal moneylending "can be violent as in the traditional loan sharking sense; and it uses deception and aggressive marketing techniques typical for predatory lending." Accordingly, loan sharks are organized groups that employ deception, violence, and intimidation to run illegal moneylending businesses.

7.2.2 Utilizing Violence and Hostage-Taking to Secure Illegal Transactions

Participants in illegal markets are exposed to considerable risk and uncertainty because they are deprived of state protection and have to face police suppression and dishonest exchange partners (Varese et al. 2019; Wang 2020a). The state plays an essential role in maintaining stability for *legal markets* by setting rules and regulations, protecting properties, ensuring market discipline, and regulating fraudulence, whereas it deploys completely different strategies to inhibit the development of *illegal markets*, not only depriving market actors of access to state protection but also imprisoning participants (Beckert and Dewey 2017; Beckert and Wehinger 2013; Varese 2001; von Lampe and Antonopoulos 2018). To lower the risk of prosecution, suppliers in illegal markets develop secret channels to market their products/services and ensure their transactions lack transparency. This limits the information available to purchasers to evaluate product/service quality and compare prices (Campana and Varese 2013). Moreover, compared to actors in legal markets, participants in illegal markets are found to be more unreliable, dishonest, selfish, and untrustworthy, always ready to betray their counterparts in order to make money (Gottfredson and Hirschi 1990; Wright and Decker 1996).

How do exchange participants approach risk and increase cooperation in illegal transactions? Leading organized crime scholars such as Diego Gambetta and Federico Varese examined the employment of informal mechanisms, such as violence and hostage-taking, to reduce risk and enhance cooperation in illegal transactions (Campana and Varese 2013; Flashman and Gambetta 2014; Gambetta 2009, 2018; Gambetta and Przepiorka 2019; Varese et al. 2019). Firstly, organized crime groups are infamous for their use of violence to enforce agreements, punish noncompliance, block new entrants from the market, and control territories and markets (Andreas and Wallman 2009; Campana and Varese 2013; Varese 2010). Criminals' use of violence to ensure compliance is not always desirable, however, because it attracts police attention.

Secondly, in the absence of state enforcement and protection, actors in illegal markets can create informal, credible commitments to increase the likelihood of cooperation (Campana and Varese 2013; Varese et al. 2019). A credible commitment, as Campana and Varese (2013: 267) suggest, refers to certain actions taken by exchange participants to increase other people's expectation that they will comply with the terms of their agreement (see also Schelling 2006). Hostage-taking, as Cook et al. (2005) argue, is a key strategy for making a given commitment credible. *Kinship ties and an individual's social ties beyond kinship* operate as a form of hostage-taking (Campana and Varese 2013). This is because these ties offer easily accessible but valuable information regarding exchange participants' social contacts, reputations, and past interactions with exchange partners (Antonopoulos et al. 2011; Powell 1990; Wang 2020a). Social ties also offer "future-oriented incentives" to motivate compliance: An actor who is embedded in social ties must behave honestly and fulfill agreements in order to obtain exchange opportunities, whereas opportunist behavior will put the actor and those close to them at risk and lead to exclusion from social ties (Barbalet 2014;

Campana and Varese 2013). For security reasons, participants in illegal markets therefore prefer to cooperate and exchange with individuals who are strongly embedded in kinship and extra-kinship ties.

Compromising information is another form of hostage-taking (Schelling 1960). Actors in the underworld share compromising information to gain trust from others and ensure cooperation. Criminals can "resort to blackmail instead [of violence], namely the threat to reveal compromising information … to force people to do what they never agreed or to make them comply with their agreements, especially when these, by being illicit, are unenforceable by law" (Gambetta 2009: 54). For example, sharing information on violent, illegal, and immoral acts (e.g., criminal offenses) functions as a major mechanism outside kinship serving to significantly reduce defection and increase the likelihood of cooperation among criminals (Campana and Varese 2013; Varese et al. 2019). When compromising information is employed as hostage-taking or collateral security, exchange participant A is able to trigger punishment by disclosing the damaging information if exchange partner B defects (Gambetta 2009, 2018). Revealing compromising information gives rise to "a punishing response by law-enforcement agencies" or "a social response in others bound to cause shame, ridicule, and loss of reputation" (Gambetta 2009: 68).

The sharing of compromising information among criminals can be asymmetric or symmetric (Gambetta and Przepiorka 2019). An example of asymmetric sharing of compromising information would be when novices are asked to confess to or commit a crime in front of senior criminals in order to gain admission to a criminal organization; this incriminating evidence can then be used by senior members to control novices and ensure their compliance (Flashman and Gambetta 2014; Gambetta and Przepiorka 2019). Symmetric sharing of compromising information can be observed in corrupt networks: for example, joint commission of a misdeed (e.g., consuming sexual services, embezzling public assets, creating false accounts, or distributing resources and promotion opportunities by violating regulations) leads to the creation of strong bonds between corrupt officials, making them more committed to their promises (Wang 2016). Moreover, the development of technologies, especially camera phones and social media platforms such as Facebook, YouTube, and Twitter, not only enables individuals to make use of photography and video and audio recordings to capture compromising information but also produces "cheap transmission of information" to large groups of people (Gambetta 2009: 71). In other words, the growth of technology facilitates and empowers the use of compromising information as collateral in the criminal underworld.

In addition, to reduce external uncertainties, criminals may bribe state agencies, especially law enforcement agencies, and gain the assistance of professional intermediaries, such as lawyers and financial advisors. Organized crime groups offer large sums of money, expensive gifts, or free sexual services to police officers in order to secure toleration of their illegal activities (Punch 2009; Wang 2013a). The participation of solicitors in criminal planning and money laundering also gives organized crime groups "access to all of the privileges and protections available to lawyers, including receiving legal aid money, transferring money through confidential client accounts, and conducting litigation" (Middleton and Levi 2005: 141; see also Lord et al. 2019; Middleton and Levi 2015).

7.2.3 From Offline to Online: Risks and Risk Management Strategies in the Illegal Lending Market

7.2.3.1 Offline

Loan sharks confront significant risks when providing credit to customers, because customers who resort to loan sharks are "already indebted or financially compromised individuals" (Kojouharov and Rusev 2016: 113), and loan sharks must lend unsecured money to borrowers first and trust that those borrowers will fulfill their obligations. The existing literature shows that loan sharks employ three mechanisms to enforce repayment, reduce opportunistic behavior, and avoid police detection. First, loan sharks screen their clients and assess risk based on information about clients' reputations and their past interactions with those clients gained from social ties. Kojouharov and Rusev (2016: 112) argue that most clients are approached "through acquaintances and established relationships." Similarly, Soudijn and Zhang (2013: 29) highlight the embeddedness of loan-sharking businesses in the local community, arguing that "the lender must have some connection with his customers … Cultural familiarity[4] probably provided ample informal social control."

Second, violence and intimidation remain essential strategies for securing compliance (Marinaro 2017). The chances of default can be mitigated by aggressive collection methods, including "harassment, threats, extortion and, in extreme cases, violence" (Kojouharov and Rusev 2016: 113). In

[4] Soudijn and Zhang (2013) argue that lenders and clients are connected through social ties and suggest that "cultural familiarity" provides strong informal social control over lender–client exchanges.

parallel, Soudijn and Zhang (2013: 29) note that "if there were no credible threats of some kind, borrowers would have little fear to defraud on their obligations." Third, loan sharks may need to bribe corrupt police officers in order to reduce the threat of police anti-crime efforts. After accepting bribes from loan sharks, corrupt police officers reciprocate by turning a blind eye (Lo 1993; Punch 2009). In addition, illegal moneylenders commonly hold collateral properties (e.g., real estate) and charge exorbitant interest rates to lower their investment risk (Soudijn and Zhang 2013).

7.2.3.2 Online

Loan sharks face new challenges when moving their illegal lending online. First, in contrast to the offline lending market, where exchange participants are connected through interpersonal networks, lender and client in the online lending market usually do not have offline connections. As a result, social ties play little part in attracting clients, assessing their trustworthiness, and regulating exchanges, which makes default more likely. Second, offline loan sharks use intimidation and violence to compel defaulting clients to fulfil their obligations, but in the online market exchange participants usually live in different communities and the "unembeddedness" of the business in the local community makes traditional ways of handling instances of default less effective. Distance not only makes it harder for loan sharks to monitor their clients but also increases the difficulty for illegal lenders to make a credible threat through typical offline methods such as physical violence, stalking, and unexpected office/home visits. Third, networked technologies offer illegal moneylenders new, open channels to market their services, which contradicts the core operating principle of offline illegal markets: "keeping criminal practices secret" (Beckert and Dewey 2017: 18). Marketing illegal goods/services on the internet increases the risk of detection and punishment, forcing online loan sharks to develop new avoidance strategies.

Drawing on published materials and empirical data, this chapter examines how traditional crime groups exploit the internet to attract clients, minimize default risk, and enforce repayment. It does not suggest that there is a new mechanism regulating illegal transactions. Instead, it aims to contribute to the understanding of how compromising information is exploited online. Traditional offline moneylenders turn to established social ties to compel clients to fulfil their obligations before resorting to physical violence (Wang 2017), relying on the fact that clients who disregard social expectations lose reputation and social status within that network.

Despite the fact that online moneylenders and clients usually do not have an offline connection, this chapter suggests that moneylenders nevertheless have effective methods of enforcing compliance: They can threaten to reveal compromising information (e.g., nude photos) or use cyberviolence (e.g., text-bombing clients' social contacts) to force victims to make loan payments. Specifically, clients' social contacts are included in the debt collection process and are used to compel clients and their families to pay. The use of relational repression facilitated by cyberviolence and threat of disclosing compromising information has largely removed the need for online loan sharks to use physical violence and bribe police officers.

7.3 The Rise of Cyber Loan-Sharking Targeting University Students in China

China has witnessed a substantial boom in the internet finance industry in the past decade (Loubere 2016; Xu 2017). As Huang (2018: 65) points out, "As of January 2017, there were a total of 2388 P2P [i.e., peer-to-peer] platforms in China; the trading volume in 2015 reached USD 67 billion, which was about four times bigger than that of the US and ten times that of the UK." The sudden expansion of China's internet finance has been "discussed in largely positive terms as facilitating commercial activity … [and] promoting financial inclusion" (Loubere 2017: 9), but its dark manifestations cannot be ignored. As Zhu et al. (2017: 129) state, "as many as one thousand Peer-to-Peer (P2P) lending companies have collapsed in China during 2014–2015 because of suspected Ponzi fraud through Internet-based financing." The involvement of peer-to-peer platforms in Ponzi schemes has been thoroughly examined by Albrecht et al. (2017), Liu et al. (2016) and Zhu et al. (2017), but the exploitation of the peer-to-peer lending market by crime groups, another significant component of the dark side of China's internet finance, remains underexplored. This section proposes an explanation in terms of supply and demand for the emergence and expansion of online loan-sharking targeting university students and examines why students are suitable targets for cyber loan-sharking.

7.3.1 A Supply-and-Demand Explanation

An explanation from the demand perspective looks at the impact of the culture of consumerism on Chinese students' increasing demand for consumer credit. An explanation of the rapid growth in consumer lending highlights "the role of the culture of consumerism" (Rona-Tas and Guseva 2018: 57).

The growth of consumer borrowing is closely associated with overconsumption and status competition, which are pervasive globally, especially among younger adults (Carr et al. 2012). As O'Cass and Siahtiri (2013: 505) argue, "Consumption for many is increasingly underpinned by the search for and creation of identity and status through specific consumption practices, including consumerism and placing a high priority on brands."

The culture of consumerism is helpful for analyzing Chinese students' increasing demand for consumer credit. University students can maintain and increase their social status through improved academic performance, but also by consuming luxury products. Students who lose interest in studying are more likely to overemphasize the links between consumption and status competition. A police officer told us that "student victims of cyber loan-sharking usually come from *sanben* [low-ranked universities] and *zhuanke* (post-secondary specialized colleges that offer two-year or three-year diploma programmes), while the number of student victims from *yiben* (elite public universities) is very few."[5] Many students from low-ranked universities and post-secondary specialized colleges lose interest in their academic studies and are more likely to replace academic performance with competitive consumption to earn status among peers.[6] A clinical psychologist explained: "Although college students have reached adulthood, their mentality is very similar to that of teenagers, who are easily stimulated by consumer advertising. Some college students are more vulnerable than others because of the lack of parental care. They thus hope to get recognition from others through other methods, such as consuming luxury brands."[7] A victim from a post-secondary specialized college mentioned that her parents gave her around RMB 2,000 per month, while her monthly expenses were over RMB 4,000. She explained her overconsumption and her reason for applying for loans from online lenders:

> We university and college students are very vain about our appearance and clothes. We like to compare ourselves with our peers and purchase luxury goods such as cosmetic products produced by Chanel, Saint Laurent, and Givenchy ... Appearance is so important [for girls] ... but I felt uncomfortable about asking my parents [to increase my spending budget], because the money would not be used to buy items like books ... I didn't want to borrow money from my classmates, either. This was why I resorted to the APP [developed by an online peer-to-peer lending company].[8]

[5] Interview C7N35 (police officer), 2018.
[6] Interview C7N23 (lawyer), 2018.
[7] Interview C7N24 (clinical psychologist), 2018.
[8] Interview C7N20 (student victim), 2018.

From a supply perspective, the rapid growth of online loan-sharking targeting university and college students can be explained by students' exclusion from the formal financial system. University and college students are barred from applying for credit cards in China. A bank manager told us that state-owned banks started to offer students credit cards in 2002 but withdrew them in 2009 because of the high rate of default.[9] Students are seen as high-risk clients by state-owned banks, being dependent on their parents and without income of their own. In the words of a legal consultant in the banking sector:

> It is not right for students to have credit cards ... Do you know why? Students don't have the ability to pay their debts. From the perspective of credit card issuers, it is wrong to accord credit to and issue credit cards to people who do not have the ability to repay. That is to say, [if banks issue cards to university students], these banks will face challenges in controlling [default] risk.[10]

The financial exclusion of university and college students by state-owned banks provides an excellent opportunity for China's major e-commerce players, such as Alibaba and JD.com, to take advantage of this demand–supply gap. For example, Alibaba affiliate Ant Financial offers each customer a credit limit of RMB 4,000, and JD.com's Baitiao offers a personalized consumer credit service targeting university and college students, each of whom is offered an RMB 15,000 credit line (Jiang 2016; Weinland 2015). But consumer credit services provided by these e-commerce players are far from sufficient to meet increasing student demand. There are several reasons for this: (1) The consumer credit offered by these e-commerce players can only be used to purchase goods sold on their online platforms. (2) To reduce the risk of default, these e-commerce giants offer students lines of credit that are too small for the purchase of branded luxury goods. (3) Their possession of a large volume of transaction data enables these e-commerce giants to accurately assess client risk, so a student who defaults will be disqualified from applying for consumer credit in future. Students excluded by legitimate lending platforms (e.g., e-commerce giants) and who are unable to control their consumption impulses are attracted by online loan-sharks' promises of quick cash and easily met application requirements.

7.3.2 University Students as Suitable Targets

Routine activity theory, developed by Cohen and Felson (1979), suggests that crime is likely to occur when three things converge in space and time: "a

9 Interview C7N36 (bank manager), 2018. In late 2017, state-owned banks started to issue credit cards to university and college students again to combat online loan-sharking.

10 Interview C7N19 (lawyer), 2018.

motivated offender, a suitable target, and the absence of a capable guardian" (Bottoms and Wiles 1997: 320). This theory offers insights into the rise in the targeting of college students by online loan sharks. The growth of the online peer-to-peer lending market brings previously underground moneylenders (i.e., motivated offenders) into contact with suitable targets on the internet. Criminal opportunities in cyberspace have been fostered by China's loose regulation of internet finance. As Xu (2017: 86) argues, "there were essentially no regulations placed on internet finance" until 2015, when preliminary regulations were finally released. The government's fragmented regulatory architecture encourages the explosive development of internet finance and offers excellent criminal opportunities to fraudsters and loan sharks.

Students are suitable targets for online loan-sharking because they lack both parental supervision (due to geographical distance from parents) and essential financial knowledge about private loans. Interviewees mentioned several significant issues: (1) Due to a lack of financial knowledge and a demand for consumer loans that is not satisfied by the formal financial system, university and college students are easily caught by debt traps disguised as legitimate lending.[11] (2) When students are unable to pay their debts, loan sharks force students' parents to pay.[12] (3) Students who are trapped in online loan-sharking are not seen as victims.[13] On the contrary, students are blamed for being "materialistic" and "foolish" – materialistic because they love to overspend on luxury goods and comfort, and foolish because they are willing to borrow money at exorbitant interest rates from online loan sharks.[14]

Another reason for students being targeted by online loan sharks is the lack of effective guardianship. Parents condemn their foolish, selfish children without noticing what is missing in their parental monitoring and supervision and/or giving their minds to their children's suffering.[15] Universities and colleges do not teach students about financial literacy and try to hide information relating to student entrapment in online loans, attempting instead to persuade parents to settle their children's debts as soon as possible in order to preserve the institution's reputation.[16] As a university's deputy director of

11 Interviews C7N7 (student victim), 2017; C7N30 (student victim), C7N33 (university administrative staff member), 2018.

12 Interviews C7N11 (student victim's relative), 2017; C7N12 (student victim's relative), C7N14 (student victim's parents), C7N15 (student victim's relative), 2018.

13 Interviews C7N3 (student victim's classmate), 2017; C7N35 (police officer), 2018.

14 Interviews C7N11 (student victim's relative), 2017; C7N19 (lawyer), C7N24 (clinical psychologist), 2018.

15 Interview C7N14 (student victim's parents), 2018.

16 Interviews C7N5 (university administrative staff member), 2017; C7N27 (student victim), C7N33 (university administrative staff member), 2018.

student affairs told us, "To avoid negative impact on the reputation of the university, the first thing is to make sure that things are not known by outsiders, and the second thing is to push students' parents to solve the problem quickly."[17] While scolding their students/kids, parents and teachers ignore their duty to protect these students from online loan-sharking.

Nor do local police officers attempt to prevent online loan-sharking. Before 2018, when the Chinese government embarked on its nationwide campaign against gangs and organized crime, police officers adopted a non-interventionist approach when handling illegal moneylending. As a police officer explained, "We cannot interfere in these affairs; government policy does not allow us to solve civil disputes such as private loans."[18] In 2017, our research team member Mei reported a suspected online loan-sharking case to local police in a coastal city. A police officer disclosed to Mei that he and his colleagues had received a number of reports from students from a nearby low-ranked university. The police officer acknowledged the widespread existence of online loan-sharking targeting students but decided not to record the reported case because, as in similar cases, the amount of money involved was "too small" to warrant criminal investigation. The officer "kindly" advised that he might decide to pass the case for investigation if Mei could find more students who were victims of the same loan shark.

7.4 The Internet-Based Loan Scam

In order to exploit online peer-to-peer lending for illegal profits, loan sharks have to meet normative expectations to attain legitimacy by ostensibly respecting laws, following government guidelines, and obeying online platform regulations, all while hiding their illicit strategies and avoiding attention from police and online platform managers. This section examines loan sharks' major strategies of deception, the employment of compromising information (e.g., social contacts and nude photos) to control clients, and the use of lawyers as crime facilitators.

7.4.1 Debt-Trapping Strategies

In the offline lending market, "acquiring customers very often is a product of the social skills of the loan shark" (Kojouharov and Rusev 2016: 108). That is to say, loan sharks have to develop communication skills to build

[17] Interview C7N33 (university administrative staff member), 2018.
[18] Interview C7N9 (lawyer), 2017.

social networks through which to attract clients; but when the business goes online, physical social networks cease to matter. Instead, loan sharks employ the strategy of *false advertising*: the use of false, misleading, and deceptive information in advertising their services. Loan sharks advertise both online (e.g., on WeChat, QQ, and online forums)[19] and offline (e.g., on campus), using terms like "no need for guarantee/collateral," "very low interest rate," and "get loans immediately." The reference to "very low interest rate" is deceptive because loan sharks use complex methods of calculating interest to hide their high interest rates.

The *obfuscation of interest rate information* is a common tactic among online loan sharks. For example, predatory lenders quoted a monthly interest rate of 0.99 percent when they marketed their lending services to students on a peer-to-peer lending platform. This apparently low rate was very attractive to students who were already indebted and who were excluded by formal financial institutions, but the interest rate was deceptive. According to the loan shark's calculations, if a student borrowed RMB 12,000 and the repayment period was twelve months, they would have to repay a total of RMB 13,425.6, including principal and interest (see Table 7.1). But a financial professional calculated the monthly interest rate using the bank's calculation method (the total repayment) and discovered that the monthly interest rate was about 1.77 percent, rather than 0.99 percent, which made the annual interest rate 21.25 percent, around five times the Bank of China interest rate (Chen 2016). Further investigation showed that predatory lenders adopted a completely different method of calculating interest from that used by formal financial institutions. In mainland China, formal financial institutions allow clients to repay their loans through two major methods: equal principal payment,[20] or equal total payment (amortization).[21] For a loan of RMB 12,000 with a monthly interest rate of 0.99 percent and a repayment period of twelve months, a client using the equal principal method pays a total of RMB 12,772.2 (see Table 7.2) and a client using the

[19] WeChat and QQ are multipurpose messaging and social media apps developed by Tencent, one of the world's largest social media companies. To market their services, loan sharks usually add a large number of university students, with whom they have no relationship, on WeChat and/or QQ chat groups.

[20] When the equal principal payment method is used, each payment includes an equal amount of the principal (the original amount of money borrowed divided into equal monthly amounts) and interest calculated on the principal balance.

[21] When the equal amortization method is used, each payment consists of a portion of interest and a portion of the principal. The proportion of interest is largest in the first month and gradually decreases through the payment period, while the proportion of the principal is smallest in the first month and increases through the payment period.

Table 7.1 *Predatory lenders' interest calculation method*

	Loan amount: RMB 12,000; 12 monthly payments	
Month	Payment (equal monthly payment of principal + fixed interest)	Unpaid (principal) balance
0	0	RMB 12,000
1	RMB 1118.81 (RMB 1,000 + RMB 12,000 × 0.99%)	RMB 11,000
2	RMB 1118.81 (RMB 1,000 + 12,000 × 0.99%)	RMB 10,000
3	RMB 1118.81 (RMB 1,000 + RMB 12,000 × 0.99%)	RMB 9,000
4	RMB 1118.81 (RMB 1,000 + RMB 12,000 × 0.99%)	RMB 8,000
	……	
11	RMB 1118.81 (RMB 1,000 + RMB 12,000 × 0.99%)	RMB 1,000
12	RMB 1118.81 (RMB 1,000 + RMB 12,000 × 0.99%)	0

Total (principal + interest) = RMB 13,425.6; student clients may believe that 0.99% is the monthly interest rate, but this is incorrect. A loan with a fixed monthly payment of RMB 1118.81 has a monthly interest rate of 1.77% (not 0.99%) and an annual interest rate as high as 21.25%.[22]

Table 7.2 *Equal principal payment method*

	Loan amount: RMB 12,000; monthly rate: 0.99%; 12 monthly payments	
Month	Payment (equal monthly payment of principal + interest that declines over time[23])	Unpaid (principal) balance
0	0	RMB 12,000
1	RMB 1111.80 (RMB 1,000 + RMB 12,000 × 0.99%)	RMB 11,000
2	RMB 1108.90 (RMB 1,000 + RMB 11,000 × 0.99%)	RMB 10,000
3	RMB 1099.00 (RMB 1,000 + RMB 10,000 × 0.99%)	RMB 9,000
4	RMB 1089.10 (RMB 1,000 + RMB 9,000 × 0.99%)	RMB 8,000
	……	
11	RMB 1019.80 (RMB 1,000 + RMB 2,000 × 0.99%)	RMB 1,000
12	RMB 1009.90 (RMB 1,000 + RMB 1,000 × 0.99%)	0

Total (principal + interest) = RMB 12772.20; annual interest rate = 11.88%.

equal amortization method pays a total of RMB 12,786.14 (see Table 7.3), both of which are lower than the RMB 13,425.6 demanded by predatory lenders (see Table 7.1).

[22] The interest rate is calculated based on the equal total payment (amortization) method.

[23] Interest declines over time because the unpaid principal balance decreases gradually.

Table 7.3 *Equal total payment (amortization) method*

Month	Payment[24] (a portion of principal[25] + a portion of interest[26])	Unpaid (principal) balance
	Loan amount: RMB 12,000; monthly rate: 0.99%; 12 monthly payments	
0	0	RMB 12,000
1	RMB 1065.51 (RMB 946.72 + RMB 118.80)	RMB 11,053.29
2	RMB 1065.51 (RMB 956.09 + RMB 109.43)	RMB 10,097.20
3	RMB 1065.51 (RMB 965.55 + RMB 99.96)	RMB 9,131.65
4	RMB 1065.51 (RMB 975.11 + RMB 90.40)	RMB 8,156.55
	......	
11	RMB 1065.51 (RMB 1,044.73 + RMB 20.79)	RMB 1,055.07
12	RMB 1065.51 (RMB 1,055.07 + RMB 10.45)	0

Total (principal + interest) = RMB 12786.14; annual interest rate = 11.88%.

The reason for this discrepancy, as Table 7.1 shows, is that predatory lenders have their own ways of calculating interest: The monthly repayment is made up of equal amounts of principal[27] plus interest that is fixed regardless of the gradually decreasing principal balance. This is different from interest calculation methods adopted by formal financial institutions. As shown in Table 7.2, legitimate lenders use principal balance when they calculate interest because the borrower's monthly payments reduce the principal balance each month. Two conclusions can be drawn from this: First, predatory lenders use false interest rate information to attract clients, who are not able to identify fraud in the interest calculation due to their lack of financial knowledge; second, the true annual interest rate of 21.25 percent is much higher than the annual rate of 11.88 percent that was based on the advertised monthly rate of 0.99 percent. An interest rate of 21.25 percent is legal in China, where the legal ceiling for annual interest rates is 36 percent; this calculation method allows predatory lenders to avoid penalties from the police and the online lending platform.

The use of false and deceptive information (e.g., "low interest rate") is an important strategy for attracting clients who lack financial literacy, but

[24] Monthly payment = [original principal × monthly interest rate × (1 + monthly interest rate) ^ number of installments] ÷ [(1 + monthly interest rate) ^ number of installments − 1].

[25] Monthly payment of principal = monthly payment − interest.

[26] Interest = principle balance × monthly interest interest.

[27] Equal monthly payment of principal is the total amount of money borrowed divided by the number of payments.

Table 7.4 *An online student loan*

1. Principal	RMB 12,000
2. Service fee (5% of principal)	RMB 600
3. Deposit (20% of principal)	RMB 2,400
Advertised monthly interest rate[28]	0.99%
Default interest rate	1% of principal per day
Amount of loan the borrower finally gets (1 – 2 – 3)	RMB 9,000 (not RMB 12,000)
Total payment (principal + interest)	RMB 13,425.67
Annual interest rate[29]	81.14%

clients' interest payments are not the only source of income for loan sharks. Besides interest on the loan, a client has to pay a service fee (between 2 percent and 6 percent of the original amount of the loan) and a deposit (between 10 percent and 20 percent of the original amount of the loan). That is to say, the client receives only what is left of the loan after deduction of the service fee and deposit but must pay interest calculated on the original amount of the loan. If a client defaults on a loan, they must also pay the default interest at a rate determined by the lender. This rate is typically between 0.5 percent and 8 percent of the principal balance or the original amount of the loan per day.

For example,[30] a female student borrowed RMB 12,000 from an online lender who required 20 percent of the original amount of the loan (principal) as a deposit and 5 percent of the principal as a service fee. As Table 7.4 illustrates, for a loan totaling RMB 12,000, she received only RMB 9,000 but had to repay a total of RMB 13,425.67 (the annual interest rate reached 81.14 percent) and bear an extremely high default interest rate. In most of the cases discovered through our research, the lender did not clearly explain the details of the terms and conditions of the loan contract (e.g., the interest calculation method and default interest rate), and the client did not read the contract carefully before signing.[31] Although the client may not have been happy about the deposit being deducted directly from the principal,

[28] The predatory lender adopts a different method of interest calculation; see Table 7.1.

[29] The annual interest rate is calculated based on the actual loan the borrower gets (RMB 9,000) and the total payment made by the borrower (RMB 13,425.67). The interest rate of 81.14 percent is calculated according to the equal total payment (amortization) method (see Table 7.3).

[30] This example is based on our interview data.

[31] Such were the circumstances revealed in interviews C7N1 (student victim) in 2017 and C7N20 (student victim), C7N27 (student victim), and C7N30 (student victim) in 2018.

they still decided to sign the contract because the lender promised to return the deposit if the client made timely payments.[32] In order to avoid police attention and penalties from the online peer-to-peer platform, lenders did not mention service fees, deposits, and default interest rates in the loan contract. Contracts allowed lenders to give money to the borrower through the peer-to-peer lending platform and off-platform means. The combination of different methods of transferring money to the borrower prevented the online platform from monitoring the process and enabled lenders to manipulate the amount of the loan. These strategies made the loan contracts appear legitimate and legally enforceable.

When the female student borrower failed to make timely payments, she was approached by the lender and his friends, who were also loan sharks, via the online platform and by other means. The lender earned lucrative profits by *prolonging the borrower's indebtedness* and compelling the borrower to sign new contracts. In order to avoid paying an extremely high default interest rate and stop the loan shark's threats and intimidation, she had to agree to sign another contract with a much higher interest rate. When the borrower was deeply trapped in debt, she had to take out new loans with ever higher interest rates to pay off the old loans. The borrower fell deeper and deeper into debt, but what she cared about most was not the interest rate of new loan contracts but avoiding paying the default interest.[33]

7.4.2 Compromising Information as Collateral

Because the lender has to give money to the borrower first, the lender has to trust that the borrower will repay and bear the cost of any default. Traditional ways of reducing risk include careful screening of the client and using real estate and other forms of asset as collateral (Kojouharov and Rusev 2016; Soudijn and Zhang 2013). An offline lender typically uses information from social networks to evaluate the trustworthiness of the potential borrower and assess investment risks. Holding collateral is also important: If the borrower defaults on loan payments, the lender can use the collateral to offset the loan. However, conventional risk-reduction strategies may not be helpful when an offline business goes online. Take online loan-sharking targeting university students as an example: First, there is no

[32] Interview data shows that in most cases the borrower was unable to make timely payments because they were already indebted and/or the lender could not be reached on the due date for repayment; whichever the case, the deposit was not returned to the borrower.

[33] Interview C7N28 (student victim), 2018.

information available from personal networks to help the lender screen the borrower because lender and borrower have usually had no offline interaction; and second, the lender has to offer loans without traditional forms of collateral.

Online loan sharks can reduce risk by requiring clients to share compromising information; social contacts and nude photos can be viewed as innovative forms of collateral.[34] Unlike traditional loan sharks, who screen their clients, online loan sharks who lend to students choose to relax the application requirements in order to include more students. Initially, the most important task for loan sharks is to establish that the client is a currently registered student. Potential clients are required to provide their citizen IDs, student IDs, and their login to the China Higher Education Student Information network.[35] In addition, the client is asked to provide their mobile phone service code, which allows the loan shark to obtain the student's call records and the phone numbers of family members, relatives, teachers, and friends.[36] The client's social contacts have become a new form of collateral, because the lender will text-bomb and harass these contacts if a student defaults on the loan.

Some female students trapped by loan sharks are persuaded or forced to provide naked photos and pornographic videos of themselves (Tatlow 2016). These images and videos allow the lender to control young girls' bodies and enforce repayment (Loubere 2016). Female students may agree to provide nude photos and porn videos to secure loans because (1) loan sharks have persuaded them that these photos and videos will only be used as collateral and will be stored in an encrypted folder only accessible to the lender; (2) offering these images as collateral secures them a larger loan; (3) it is the only way to discharge overdue loans and avoid default interest.[37] Here, the sharing of compromising information is asymmetric because the lender obtains damaging information about the borrower but not vice versa. The use of pornographic images and videos creates an unequal power relation between lender and borrower, and the lender can threaten to make the borrower's images public to ensure repayments. When the borrower fails to make repayments, the lender can simply trigger the punishment by revealing the compromising nude photos or pornographic videos obtained

[34] Interviews C7N1 (student victim), C7N3 (student victim's classmate), 2017; C7N23 (lawyer), 2018.

[35] Interview C7N7 (student victim), 2017.

[36] Interviews C7N3 (student victim's classmate), C7N5 (university administrative staff member), C7N10 (lawyer), 2017; C7N14 (student victim's parents), 2018.

[37] Interviews C7N1 (student victim), 2017; C7N28 (student victim), C7N31 (lawyer), 2018.

when the contract was signed. Along with the general public, the borrower's social contacts are the ones meting out the punishment, causing shame, reproach, and loss of reputation to the borrower and their family members. The lender incurs only minimal costs when making the photos public.

A group of loan sharks who conducted business on Jiedaibao, a Chinese online peer-to-peer lending platform, leaked online an 8 GB zip file containing nude pictures of over 1,000 women, which was widely shared by internet users in China (Luk 2016). The manager of Jiedaibao commented:

> Jiedaibao is a legal and compliant online peer-to-peer lending platform. The platform does not allow loan contracts that are made based on nude photos. "Naked borrowing" contracts are generated through off-platform transactions between a few users and third parties that are illegal lending companies. Illegal lenders bypass the restrictions and supervision of the platform to sign loan contracts with some users who are eager to provide nude photos, through off-platform channels such as QQ, WeChat, and text messages, in order to secure loans. (Zhou 2016)

Jiedaibao's explanation is unconvincing. Its management team should take responsibility for not closing regulatory loopholes and for ineffective monitoring. Female students who become unable to pay and seek to avoid public disclosure of their images are forced to ask their parents to pay instead or work for the loan shark as sex workers. Loan sharks share these workers' photos and videos in online chat groups consisting of a large number of "friends" who are willing to buy sexual services.[38] As a result, loan sharks earn enormous profits not only through charging high interest rates but also by collecting commission fees (e.g., 50 percent of the service fee) for matching sex workers with clients, forcing these female students into prostitution.

7.4.3 Lawyers as Crime Facilitators

Criminologists argue that lawyers are employed by organized criminal groups in Western countries as "fronts" for their criminal activities (Middleton and Levi 2005). Organized criminal groups in China are also aware of the value of involving lawyers as crime facilitators. For example, loan sharks purchase professional services from lawyers to make their contracts comply with the law and online platform regulations (Shanghai Daily 2017). To make loan contracts legally binding and enforceable, legal professionals prepare loan contracts without including information about high interest rates, default rates, deposits, or service fees.

[38] Interviews C7N23 (lawyer), C7N28 (student victim), 2018.

Student victims we interviewed told us that they frequently received or saw the information sent or shared by loan sharks regarding court decisions that were made in favor of the plaintiffs (i.e., the lenders).[39] This encouraged student borrowers to believe that the loan contracts they signed were legally enforceable and they would be imprisoned if they were unable to pay off their debts.[40] Loan sharks usually threaten litigation to force the borrower to pay. A text message sent by a loan shark to a student victim stated as follows:

> You have defaulted on a loan granted by Company XX for a long time. You are suspected of violating Article 224 of the Criminal Law, which constitutes the crime of contract fraud. Legal letters will be mailed to your home address shortly. Please ensure you make repayment in accordance with these letters. Otherwise we will report this case to the police and pursue your criminal responsibility.[41]

By purchasing professional legal services, loan sharks not only avoid criminal proceedings but can harness the formal legal system to enforce repayment of loans. This puts student victims at a disadvantage within the judicial process: It makes it necessary for them to prove that lenders employed deceptive and coercive practices to encourage them to sign the loan agreements.[42] In most cases, student victims' claims are not supported by the court because of students' lack of legal knowledge and professional support.

7.5 Enforcing Loan Repayment through Relational Repression

Online loan sharks seldom resort to "hard" methods. Sharks usually live far from their clients, which makes it harder to credibly threaten violent retaliation. When the original amount of money borrowed is small, it is not cost-effective for lenders to send out debt collectors. Empirical data suggests that loan sharks who exploit China's peer-to-peer online market have developed a new strategy – relational repression facilitated by cyber-violence and the use of compromising information – to enforce repayment of loans.

The concept of cyberviolence refers to psychological, social, and economic damage perpetrated by digital and technological means (Backe et al. 2018: 135). A student interviewee mentioned that what worried her most was that debt collectors (gangsters) would visit her home and use

[39] Interviews C7N7 (student victim), 2017; C7N30 (student victim), 2018.

[40] Interview C7N7 (student victim), 2017.

[41] Interview C7N14 (student victim's parents), 2018.

[42] Interviews C7N19 (lawyer), C7N35 (police officer), 2018.

physical violence against her and her parents, although this had not (yet) happened.[43] As empirical data shows, despite online loan sharks' threats of physical violence and visits to borrowers' homes, they seldom resort to these offline enforcement methods because cyberviolence is more economical than real violence.[44] The use of cyberviolence also avoids police detection and punishment; cyberviolence is not a focus of police work, and officers take action only when serious physical violence occurs (Wang 2017).[45]

When the loan amount (principal, interest, and fees) outstrips the solvency of the borrower's family, loan sharks who have made loan agreements with the borrower will simultaneously enforce repayment by text-bombing all the contacts in the borrower's phone.[46] A university administrative staff member shared his experience of being text-bombed by online loan sharks:

> If our phone numbers are in the contact list [of the student borrower who defaults on the loan], all of us will be harassed by endless phone calls and text messages ... For example, you can receive several hundred, even a thousand, text messages within fifteen or twenty minutes. As far as I know, all my colleagues and a number of students have the experience of being text-bombed.[47]

Loan sharks use software that automatically sends anonymous text messages to specific mobile phone users.[48] This allows loan sharks to diffuse texts massively and simultaneously to multiple targets. It is therefore very economical. Moreover, if student borrowers have provided pornographic images as collateral, their parents or other social contacts will be sent these images. Loan sharks will threaten to post these images online, along with identifying information, if parents refuse to make loan payments (Webb 2016).

Cyberviolence is very effective because the relational repression it produces forces borrowers' parents to make payments on their children's behalf. "Relational repression" refers to the psychological coercion of the borrower's relatives, friends, classmates, and teachers. These people have no connection with the loan shark but assist in compelling the borrower's parents to pay. To be specific, cyberviolence subjects all the borrower's contacts to endless harassment through calls and text messages. Text-bombing encourages these contacts to blame the borrower's foolishness,

43 Interview C7N7 (student victim), 2017.
44 Interviews C7N11 (student victim's relative), 2017; C7N30 (student victim), 2018.
45 Interview C7N35 (police officer), 2018.
46 Interviews C7N5 (university administrative staff member), C7N11 (student victim's relative), 2017; C7N28 (student victim), 2018.
47 Interview C7N5 (university administrative staff member), 2017.
48 Interviews C7N8 (police officer), C7N10 (lawyer), 2017.

materialism, and greed. This generates enormous social and psychological pressure, compelling the borrower's parents to pay back the debt as soon as possible. Student victims trapped by online loan sharks usually decide to give up their studies. One interviewee stated:

> From a student's perspective, borrowing money online is a personal affair, but everyone else [in their networks] knows about it. Their parents, relatives, and friends ask, "Why did you borrow money from them?" or "Why not pay back your debt?" ... They have to explain to everyone [who has been text-bombed by the lenders] ... Such a process places a very heavy psychological burden on the student. In my university, students who can't stand it choose to drop out.[49]

Student borrowers' parents are also victims because they feel obliged to assume the burden of repaying the loan. As a legal professional offering free legal assistance to student victims, one of our research team members was invited to join several "expanded" family meetings, consisting not only of family members but also of friends and relatives who were text-bombed. Based on our research team member's observations, parents in these meetings were very emotional and student victims were very quiet. During one meeting, the mother cried while scolding her son, and the father slapped his son. The student borrower lowered his head and said nothing. Several relatives comforted the parents while criticizing the borrower's foolishness and selfishness. When the parents calmed down, they discussed how much the family needed to pay and how to pay it. Several relatives and friends generously lent money to help the family through this difficult period. Most of them, however, did not realize that the student borrower was also a victim and deserved sympathy and psychological support.

The borrower's relatives, friends, and classmates have a strong incentive to intervene in the borrower's personal lending issues because they wish to stop being text-bombed by loan sharks. They want the borrower's parents to take care of the unpaid loans quickly and efficiently. They therefore play a significant role in persuading the borrower's parents to make timely payments. As a result, online loan sharks find cyberviolence and relational repression so effective that there is no need to employ physical violence.

7.6 Conclusion

In the illegal market, exchange participants cannot turn to the state to enforce illegal "contracts" and must utilize alternative mechanisms, such as violence, social ties, and the sharing of compromising information, to

[49] Interview C7N5 (university administrative staff member), 2017.

avoid risk and increase compliance. When this illegal business goes online, it becomes harder to cost-effectively enforce agreements by visiting clients' homes and offices and threatening or delivering violence. Moreover, social ties can only be employed by exchange partners as collateral to increase compliance where such ties exist. Illegal transactions in cyberspace usually take place between strangers and the lack of social ties increases the risk of default and police arrest. As a result, the sharing of incriminating and/or embarrassing information may be the only effective way to make exchange participants, who share no preexisting social connections, avoid opportunist behavior and increase compliance.

This chapter has examined the methods used by loan sharks to exploit China's online peer-to-peer lending platforms, specifically targeting university and college students. By investigating how participants in illegal online markets enforce agreements, we contribute to the study of how the sharing of compromising information functions online. Furthermore, this research enhances the overall understanding of the intersection between organized crime and cybercrime. Predatory lenders employ deceitful strategies to trap students. Clients are persuaded or forced to give loan sharks compromising images such as nude photos and pornography videos. Clients are also persuaded or coerced into handing over their mobile phone service codes, which are then used to access victims' social contacts. This use of compromising information is asymmetric because it is not reciprocal and the damaging information is then used by loan sharks against clients who break their promises.

Networked technologies and online peer-to-peer lending platforms allow lenders to do business unconstrained by geographical barriers. The problem for the loan sharks is that distance makes offline means of enforcement (e.g., physical violence) too expensive, so they turn to cyberviolence. Cyberviolence drags the client's social contacts into the debt collection process. Pressure from these social contacts cannot be ignored by the client and their family, and relational repression facilitated by cyberviolence and the threat of publicly disclosing compromising information eventually compels the student borrower's parents to make loan repayments. Online loan sharks see bribing police officers as unnecessary: They use professional legal services to make loan contracts legally binding and enforceable and in their enforcement actions rely mainly on cyberviolence and the threat of revealing compromising information rather than offline violence, which attracts police attention.

8

Conclusion

8.1 Introduction

To investigate how extralegal governance institutions are created and function, researchers should examine two basic themes (Leeson 2014). First, in cases where a government is available to facilitate social cooperation, individuals develop extralegal governance institutions that are considered more cost-effective and superior solutions than those supplied by their actual government. Second, in cases where there is no government available, not only to protect property rights and reduce unpredictability but also to actively generate uncertainty by punishing market participants and subverting their activities, individuals still manage to survive and even achieve sizable profits; they manage to do so by deploying extralegal governance institutions to handle market-related uncertainties (e.g., information asymmetry and opportunism) and resolve external risks caused by law enforcement agencies.

The first theme has been thoroughly investigated by several established scholars. For example, a body of literature on community-based governance has revealed that although the state might help to solve people's problems of local collective action, such as the governance of common pool resources, collective enforcement of community property rights, and revival after natural disasters, local communities can craft and develop non-state mechanisms and solutions that are better than state-sponsored mechanisms in achieving efficient cooperation and improving their welfare (see Aldrich 2012; Chamlee-Wright 2010; Ellickson 1991; Ostrom 1990; Storr et al. 2016). Similarly, Bian (1997, 2019), Landa (1981, 1994), and Nee and Opper (2012) find that informal elements such as culture, ethics, and personal ties are often more effective than contract law in sustaining business success in legal markets. Furthermore, extralegal mechanisms are deployed to fight offenses or provide protection for (potential) victims. For example, Jung and Cohen (2020) have revealed that lynching is used to punish offenses against communities in some countries (e.g., Haiti and South Africa) where state governance is poor and state legitimacy is low. Shortland (2018, 2019) unmasks a well-developed private insurance market deployed to ensure that hostages are treated well, keep ransoms moderate and stable, and discourage kidnappers from reneging on agreed-upon ransoms.

The second theme has also attracted the attention of researchers. For example, Gambetta studies how criminals communicate in a lawless universe (Gambetta 2009; see also Densley 2012). Varese and his collaborators study the role of "hostage-taking" in increasing cooperation among co-offenders (Campana and Varese 2013; Varese et al. 2019). Wright et al. investigate informal control (e.g., retaliation, negotiation, avoidance, and tolerance) among drug users and dealers (Dickinson and Wright 2015; Jacques and Wright 2011, 2015; Rosenfeld, Jacobs, and Wright 2003). Leeson conducts an economic analysis of a "pirate code," which was created by late seventeenth- and early eighteenth-century pirates to regulate the ways in which pirates behave on ships (Leeson 2007, 2009); and Skarbek conducts an innovative study of the formation, operation, and evolution of extralegal institutions in the prison underworld (Skarbek 2011, 2012, 2014). Despite these significant achievements, the study of the social order of illegal markets is, in fact, lagging behind because illegal markets, both offline markets and cybercrime black markets, are developing much faster than researchers can keep up with. Therefore, this book fills a much-needed void in the literature by enhancing our understanding of the use of extralegal governance institutions to promote social cooperation under condition of illegality and in the context of transitional authoritarianism.

This concluding chapter is organized as follows: Sections 8.2 and 8.3 summarize what we have done in this book – in other words, the major contributions (i.e., empirical and theoretical) we have made to the literature. This book has utilized rich empirical data collected in China to examine various forms of extralegal governance institutions developed by participants in four different types of illegal markets, enriching the study of illegal markets, informal institutions, and institutional complexity. Combining concepts and theories from new institutional economics and sociology, it has also developed a socio-economic approach to studying illegal markets as well as the risks and extralegal governance institutions within them. After summarizing this book's contributions, this chapter offers recommendations for future research, including the use of a multidisciplinary approach, adoption of a comparative approach of analysis, and investigation of institutional interactions and change. These recommendations are made because (1) they are essential for further development of the research in this field and (2) they are not well addressed by this book because of the nature of our research design, which focuses on investigating uncertainties and institutional complexity rather than institutional diversity and change. The book concludes with policy implications.

8.2 Extralegal Governance Institutions in China's Illegal Markets

Prior studies have investigated extralegal governance institutions in history, in the stateless context, and in democratic and dysfunctional states (Anderson and Hill 2004; Chamlee-Wright 2010; Ellisckon 1991; Gambetta 1993, 2009; Greif 2006; Leeson 2014; Murtazashvili 2016; North 1990; Ostrom 1990; Richman 2017; Skarbek 2014, 2020a; Varese 2001), whereas the study of the formation and operation of extralegal governance institutions in authoritarian China is still underexplored. The present book has aimed to enrich the field by examining institutions and illegal markets in such an authoritarian context. China's rapid economic growth and incomplete political reform have been accompanied by a significant increase in the number of illegal transactions in both the public and private sectors and the development of illegal markets covering a wide range of fields, such as housing, street vending, the credit market, and public sector corruption related to buying public appointments. Many scholarly efforts have been made to understand the establishment and expansion of China's legal markets and state-sponsored, formal institutions (e.g., the police and courts; see Ng and He 2017; Trevaskes 2007; Wong 2012), while insufficient scholarly attention has been given to illegal markets that are not protected by state laws but are rather sustained by a series of extralegal governance mechanisms.

The insufficient number of scholarly works on the social order of illegal markets is largely explained by the enormous challenges of collecting firsthand data in an authoritarian state. In contemporary China, especially in recent decades, the government has noticed the increasing problems of corruption and illegal markets and organized a series of campaigns to address these problems. For example, President Xi has managed to enhance authoritarian rule by employing an anti-corruption campaign against both high-ranking officials ("tigers") and low-ranking officials ("flies") and the "sweep away black" campaign to combat organized crime and illegal markets (Wang 2020b). Meanwhile, the government has become less tolerant of independent and critical research on politically sensitive topics. Local researchers are required to conduct research on politically correct topics and produce knowledge that is beneficial for promoting the national image of the party-state. International scholars are largely blocked by government officials and police officers, who would be ideal interviewees for researchers studying corruption and illegal markets. Public officials are unwilling to become involved in research because exchanging knowledge and ideas with international scholars, especially those from Hong Kong and the United States, may pose risks for their career development. The change in the political atmosphere, which has been hostile for both local and international researchers in recent years, also prevents them from forming research collaborations, making the study of illegal transactions and underground markets extremely difficult. Given that researchers who study sensitive themes in authoritarian China usually experience more psychological stress and risks for their safety than those doing research in democratic states, their efforts in collecting firsthand data should be highly valuable.

Based on field research and 318 in-depth semistructured interviews, this book theoretically and empirically examines the different forms of uncertainty and development of extralegal governance institutions to address these uncertainties in different illegal markets. To illustrate the complexity of extralegal institutions, this book selects four cases: street vending, small property right housing, corrupt transactions relating to the buying and selling of government appointments, and online loan sharks. The first two cases are illegal but legitimate, whereas the latter two are both illegal and illegitimate. Despite the fact that all participants in different markets face both market-based uncertainties (e.g., opportunism) and external uncertainties (e.g., criminal and administrative punishment), they attach different levels of importance to different kinds of uncertainty, hence deploying different forms of institutions. For example, the greatest concern for participants in corrupt transactions, especially favor-givers who are senior public officials, is the risk of criminal detection and punishment; therefore, they develop a series of extralegal governance institutions (e.g., hostages, *mianzi*, and corrupt intermediaries) to address this concern (see Chapter 6). Online loan sharks, however, pay little attention to avoiding criminal punishment because the police usually do nothing to investigate online loan scams, punish loan sharks, and protect victims, especially before the "sweep away black" campaign that started in 2018. The primary challenge for online loan sharks is the opportunistic behavior of lenders who are already deeply trapped in debt when they approach online loan sharks. In response, loan sharks employ the cooperative strategy of using compromising information (e.g., naked photos and personal pornographic videos) to resolve the problem of opportunism (see Chapter 7).

For offline illegal markets, the participants mainly rely on social ties, reputation mechanisms, and emotional attachment to screen potential exchange partners, enforce agreements, and punish opportunistic behavior (see Chapters 4–6). These extralegal governance institutions work effectively to promote cooperation in offline markets, but they play no role when illegitimate business owners (e.g., loan sharks) move their businesses online (see Chapter 7). Moreover, participants not only develop different extralegal governance institutions but also use the same institution differently to address distinct kinds of risk and uncertainty. For example, disclosing damaging information to anti-corruption agencies is perceived as a last resort for the buyers of corrupt benefits because the use of such a mechanism often causes retaliation by those giving corrupt benefits, who are power-holders, and damages buyers' reputations in the social network (see Chapter 6). On the other hand, threatening to reveal damaging information to lenders' contracts and the public is always the first and most effective strategy employed by online loan sharks to coerce lenders and their family members to make repayments (see Chapter 7).

To handle any external uncertainties caused by law enforcement agencies, participants in markets that are neither legal nor legitimate usually develop strategies to hide their illegal exchanges – for example, embedding corrupt transactions in close-tie relations (see Chapter 6) or online loan sharks avoiding attention from police and online platform managers (see Chapter 7). Participants in illegal markets that are socially legitimate also employ collective resistance to address external risks. Collective resistance is organized differently in different cases. For example, street vendors form mutual aid groups that are closely connected and horizontally structured to avoid and resist government intervention (see Chapter 4), while small property right housing builders often increase and signal their capacity for collective action by linking their projects to villages' collective economy or redevelopment programs, which incentivizes local villagers to resist government interference in the small property right housing market (see Chapter 5).

8.3 Socio-economic Analytical Approach

This book has developed a socio-economic approach that integrates new institutional economics with sociology to investigate the characteristics of illegal markets and the nature of exchange relationships among participants. This approach also enables researchers to examine the major types of risk and extralegal governance institutions developed by market participants; it allows researchers to provide a comprehensive picture of illegal markets, along with the uncertainties and strategies used to solve them during various stages of illegal transactions. Specifically, the socio-economic approach focuses on the social order of illegal markets in both the macro and micro dimensions.

The macro dimension is used to examine the nature of illegal markets, combining sociologist Max Weber's concept of legitimacy with the theoretical interpretation of illegal market morality proposed by institutional economists Boettke et al.. This has helped us analyze the social legitimacy of illegal markets. The macro dimension also focuses on the level of state repression against illegal markets and their participants, which is highly relevant to the markets' social legitimacy and the state's willingness and capability to intervene. Further, the macro dimension considers the situation in which illegal businesses go online.

The micro dimension examines the nature of exchange relationships by applying power-dependence theory to analyze power dynamics among participants. In power-imbalanced exchange relationships, the participants can be categorized into high- and low-power actors. Low-power actors must compete for exchange opportunities with high-power actors while developing strategies to avoid exploitation. Additionally, the micro dimension considers differential punishments faced by different exchange partners. High-risk actors, who face severe punishment if detected and convicted, must develop institutions to prevent low-risk actors from reporting their illegal dealings to law enforcement agencies.

Micro level analysis also benefits from institutional economists' transaction cost theory, which highlights how factors such as bounded rationality, opportunism, and asset specificity contribute to risks and uncertainties. Sociological concepts such as social embeddedness, trust, and compromising information, as well as the Chinese sociological concepts of *guanxi* and face, have been employed to offer rich and detailed understandings of local contexts. These concepts provide context-specific explanations of illegal transactions at the micro level.

The present book contributes to the fields of illegal markets and institutions by making use of relevant concepts and theories from new institutional economics and sociology in analyses of risks and institutions in illegal markets. The objective of this book is not to investigate whether economic theories work better than sociological theories or vice versa; rather, the book shows how a combination of knowledge from different academic disciplines better explains the complexity of institutions and illegal transactions. Given that there has been little cooperation between economic sociologists and institutional economists in recent decades, it is hoped this book may inspire researchers who are interested in illegal markets and institutions to carry out cross-disciplinary cooperation.

The socio-economic approach allows us to pursue an analytical narrative and trace the process of the operation and development of a series of illegal markets. In each case, we not only explore what extralegal governance institutions are used by illegal market participants to reduce or mitigate both market-based and external uncertainties but also shed light on how such governance institutions function and interact with each other. Notably, although we do not use game theoretical models (i.e., formal models) in a technical manner to describe the strategic interactions of relevant actors, the ideas of game theory have provided us with insights and useful pointers for elaborating on how the causal process of different governance mechanisms unfolds and for evaluating their effectiveness in helping market participants solve both market-based and external uncertainties (Lorentzen et al. 2017). Although our work does not pretend to uncover all governance mechanisms deployed across all cases – for some governance mechanisms may not be clearly visible – the application of analytical narrative and process tracing approaches underpinned by a socio-economic analytical approach has enabled us to navigate the complexity of institutions and illegal transactions in the real world.

8.4 Recommendations for Future Research

Extralegal governance institutions exist in nearly every corner of human society and in many instances they work better than most people think (Leeson 2014). To better understand market operations and local communities as well as the relationships among the state, the market, and society, studying the ways in which state law protects property rights and enhances social cooperation is far from sufficient, and more scholarly efforts are required to investigate extralegal governance institutions. Therefore, we offer several suggestions for future research. First, and in general, researchers should be more open-minded and flexible when applying theories and concepts from different disciplines. A multidisciplinary approach that integrates knowledge from different disciplines and incorporates diverse perspectives offers the most fruitful way forward. Such an approach encourages researchers from different disciplines to redefine those institutions outside of boundaries set up by new institutional economists. To make multidisciplinary cooperation feasible, theme-based conferences that can bring together researchers from across a range of disciplines as well as cross-disciplinary projects are needed to provide helpful platforms for researchers from different disciplines to share knowledge and initiate collaboration. The objective of adopting a multidisciplinary approach is not only to compare different disciplines and perspectives but also to combine diverse understandings and interpretations from these disciplines and establish a coherent, cross-disciplinary body of knowledge on non-state institutions.

Second, future research can adopt methods of comparative institutional analysis (see Skarbek 2020a). This book adopts a multiple case study design aimed at employing different types of evidence to study illegal markets and the complexity of extralegal institutions, but this research design has limited ability to study institutions from a comparative approach. A single type of institution (e.g., hostages, or the cooperative strategy of using compromising information) may work differently in different markets or in different socio-economic contexts. Hence, it is worthwhile to examine what causes differences in the operation of the institutions. A method of comparative historical research is also helpful for improving our research on institutions. Researchers can adopt this method to directly compare the use of a particular type of institution in different cases throughout history, and this comparison can also be based on other scholars' evidence and historical investigations of single cases. Moreover, illegal transactions of the same type can be diversely governed by different actors. As a result, more research is needed to examine why and how individuals solve the same category of risk and uncertainty in various ways, hence contributing to the emerging area of polycentric governance.

Third, more research efforts should be made to explore the dynamic interaction between formal and extralegal institutions. Extralegal governance institutions exist in many institutional circumstances, regardless of whether formal institutions exist. Extralegal governance institutions emerge when formal institutions are inefficient, insufficient, and weak. Our empirical work on illegal markets in China suggests that when transactions are prohibited by the state, extralegal governance institutions are developed to avoid or reduce state intervention. The workings of these extralegal institutions sometimes vary, and new ones may emerge to more effectively respond to changes in formal institutions (e.g., state laws, policies, and regulations) used to repress illegal transactions. Therefore, further systematic analyses of the interaction between formal and extralegal institutions are needed. Moreover, extralegal governance institutions can facilitate the change and development of formal institutions. One of the themes worthy of scholarly attention is how and under what conditions extralegal institutions can promote changes in formal institutions. When extralegal institutions become focal points coordinating people's beliefs and behaviors in a certain market or within a given territory, a change in formal institutions might occur. In these cases, the resulting changes could include reforms that (partially) legalize certain types of illegal exchanges (such as land institution reform to allow the exchange of collectively owned land) and stringent policies and enforcement measures that crack down on certain types of illegal transactions.

In addition, collecting firsthand data has always been the most effective way to study extralegal governance institutions and illegal markets. Researchers treat sources on the internet (e.g., news articles) with caution because publicly available sources sometimes provide a distorted image of the workings of institutions in illegal markets. It is undeniable that accessing potential interviewees who know a great deal about or are involved in illegal transactions is challenging and even risky, but it is still worth trying to collect empirical data from a few low-risk interviewees because the collected data can be helpful for verifying the reliability and validity of publicly available sources. For example, researchers who study triad societies in Hong Kong and their strategies for regulating the underworld economy can interview police officers from the Organized Crime and Triad Bureau to obtain a clear sense of which media organizations can produce reliable reports on local triads.

8.5 Policy Implications

The present book offers a theoretical and empirical investigation of risks and extralegal governance institutions in China's illegal markets, which has important policy implications for the Chinese government because it helps policymakers understand why and how extralegal governance institutions work better than most people think and how participants manage uncertainties in illegal markets. The book contributes to the development of policies in two ways. First, it contributes directly to the understanding of the impact of laws and policies on both the formation of illegal markets and the development of extralegal governance institutions. Our analysis of empirical evidence enriches Chinese legislators' and policymakers' knowledge about the social order of the underworld economy and the complexity and operation of extralegal governance institutions. Therefore, it enhances legislators' and policymakers' capacity to design and implement cost-effective policies to regulate and/or repress illegal markets. Second, the government can consider legitimizing legitimate illegal markets (e.g., the small property right housing market and street vending) to avoid conflicts between local communities and the local government and thereby promote the social welfare of lower-class people. We suggest that policymakers tolerate and even respect private mechanisms developed by participants in markets that are socially legitimate. This is because, in certain situations, allowing, and even encouraging, private individuals and organizations to govern their own affairs or enforce property rights by themselves is more socially effective and economically beneficial than relying on state institutions.

This book may also help other transitional countries improve the quality of their governance. China's impressive economic growth has been accompanied by the rise of a powerful but predatory state in which formal protection for property rights is in short supply, illegal markets are booming, and rent-seeking is widespread. The China Model of Economic Development cannot be simply copied by other countries that want to promote economic growth. This is because simply following China's top-down rules while ignoring their impact on the expansion of illegal markets and the development of endogenous private mechanisms is likely to be ineffective and perhaps costly. Policies that prove effective in China will not necessarily be so in other regimes, but lessons from China may help other countries to prevent the development of illegal markets. Furthermore, our findings help explain the persistence of illegal markets despite the zero-tolerance approach adopted by the government. The government can consider regulating, rather than simply repressing, illegal markets by decriminalizing certain types of goods and services, especially those that are socially acceptable. After decriminalization, the government needs to break the traditional state–market dichotomy that ignores self-governance developed in the local community, acquire knowledge and skills developed by market participants, and respect and protect non-state institutions as an alternative solution for protecting property rights. A more vibrant and inclusive society will be created if people are encouraged to use local knowledge and skills to develop their own mechanisms of property protection and dispute resolution.

Specifically, four cases have been examined, each with the potential to bring out beneficial effects and valuable changes to public policy, the economy, and society. First, an exploration of street vending in China not only examined major extralegal institutions developed by street vendors to redress uncertainties but also revealed the daily challenges they face to survive and the problem of the "gray area" established by the local government to earn extra-budgetary revenue. We argue that street vendors' survival rights should be well respected by the government, which should establish regulated areas that are large enough to accommodate all street vendors, within which booths are distributed by urban administrative officials in a fair way and street vendors' private properties can be protected. For street vendors who are not willing to perform business in regulated areas, the government can develop an effective reward-and-punishment scheme to incentivize these vendors to obey regulations and conduct business in government-regulated areas. Meanwhile, the government should respect mutual aid groups established by street vendors, allowing these groups to register as formal street vendor associations that can employ context-specific knowledge and skills to redress market-based uncertainties.

Second, this book has investigated the reasons for the prosperity of the small property right housing market, demonstrating to policymakers that informal property rights are secured by informal governance institutions, including reputation-based mechanisms, third-party enforcement provided by lawyers and notary offices, information sharing facilitated by agencies, and a centralized registration and punishment system provided by village committees. Our findings help the government better understand why the small property right housing market is socially legitimate, albeit illegal, why the market is resilient, and why it is extremely costly and ineffective to regulate the market simply by demolishing houses. We argue that policymakers should respect and even protect community-based governance institutions that have become essential tools for improving community welfare and enforcing villages' collective property. These extralegal governance institutions not only supplement China's incomplete protection of villagers' land and property rights but also enable the local society to accommodate more labor migrants and facilitate the cultivation of civil society. Incorporating residents' interests into the public policymaking process will help China achieve more affordable, sustainable, and inclusive urbanization.

Third, the present book has provided details about how corrupt exchanges are regulated by hostages, reputations on social networks, the mechanism of sharing compromising information, and corrupt intermediaries. To make cooperation possible and reduce the risk of arrest and/or imprisonment, corrupt officials manage to credibly commit themselves to a close-tie relation sustained by long-term social capital investments (e.g., gift-giving and wining and dining). Therefore, the government has to design tailored public policies aimed at preventing the formation of close ties, stopping corrupt relations, and cracking down on corrupt networks. Current policies for punishing the misuse of public funds for extravagant consumption (e.g., lavish drinking and dining) and promoting the rotation of government officials are very helpful for preventing the formation of corrupt networks. The anti-corruption policy of differential punishments for bribers and bribees has been effective in securing the cooperation of bribers, especially after 2018 when a single, unitary anti-corruption body, the National Supervisory Commission, was established.

To further solve the problem of corruption, we suggest that policymakers should focus on designing and implementing policies to prevent (potential) conflicts of interest from developing into corrupt acts. Because *guanxi* (personal relations) involves emotional attachment and reciprocal obligations that often conflict with government officials' duties, roles, and responsibilities to the wider public (Provis 2008), the government needs to instill in its officials sufficient knowledge of ethical issues, and government officials should be required to bring up and disclose such conflicts. Although there is a long way to go to ensure that conflicts of interest can be properly managed by government officials in their daily work, establishing and implementing procedures for avoiding and managing potential conflicts of interest should be the starting point for effectively preventing the occurrence of corrupt transactions.

Finally, this book has investigated how traditional loan sharks have moved their offline businesses online, how they devise online scams to attract and trap university students, and how they utilize the strategy of sharing compromising information to compel their student victims to pay. Our findings will help police officers and the general public better understand the nonviolent strategies of online loan sharks – for example, the use of victims' social contacts and nude photos as compromising information to force them and/or their families to pay up. These strategies significantly differ from the methods employed by conventional criminal groups – that is, the use of violence and intimidation to secure cooperation. Police officers have paid insufficient attention to the increasing threat of, and losses caused by, illegal online businesses and the widespread use of compromising information by criminals. Understanding online offenders' nonviolent enforcement strategies is a starting point for shifting major anti-crime policies from focusing on offline violence to placing emphasis on cyberviolence and the harm produced by illegal online markets.

Bibliography

Acemoglu, D., Moscona, J., and Robinson, J. A. (2016). "State capacity and American technology: Evidence from the nineteenth century." *American Economic Review*, 106(5), 61–67.

Albrecht, C., Morales, V., Baldwin, J. K., and Scott, S. D. (2017). "Ezubao." *Journal of Financial Crime*, 24, 256–259.

Aldohni, A. K. (2013). "Loan sharks v. short-term lenders." *Journal of Law and Society*, 40(3), 420–449.

Aldrich, D. P. (2012). *Building resilience: Social capital in post-disaster recovery*. Chicago, IL: University of Chicago Press.

Allen, D. W. (2011). *The institutional revolution: Measurement and the economic emergence of the modern world*. Chicago, IL: University of Chicago Press.

Allen, D. W., and Reed, C. G. (2006). "The duel of honor: Screening for unobservable social capital." *American Law and Economics Review*, 8(1), 81–115.

Alon, I., Farrell, M., and Li, S. (2020). "Regime type and COVID-19 response." *FIIB Business Review*, 9(3), 152–160.

Alston, L. J., Libecap, G. D., and Schneider, R. (1996). "The determinants and impact of property rights: Land titles on the Brazilian frontier." *Journal of Law, Economics, and Organization*, 12(1), 25–61.

Anderson, T. L., and Hill, P. J. (2004). *The not so wild, wild west: Property rights on the frontier*. Stanford, CA: Stanford University Press.

Andreas, P., and Wallman, J. (2009). "Illicit markets and violence." *Crime, Law and Social Change*, 52(3), 225–229.

Antonopoulos, G. A. (2013). "The dragon's shadow: An introduction to the special issue on 'Chinese organized crime'." *Trends in Organized Crime*, 16(1), 1–12.

Antonopoulos, G. A., and Papanicolaou, G. (2018). *Organized crime*. Oxford: Oxford University Press.

Antonopoulos, G. A., Groenhuijsen, M., Harvey, J., Kooijmans, T., Maljevic, A., and von Klaus, L. (2011). *Usual and unusual organising criminals in Europe and beyond*. Belgium: Maklu.

Antonopoulos, G. A., Papanicolaou, G., and Simpson, M. (2009). "Entertainment starts with an E: The ecstasy market in Greece." *Trends in Organized Crime*, 13(1), 31–45.

Aoki, M. (2001). *Toward a comparative institutional analysis*. Cambridge, MA: MIT Press.

Arlacchi, P. (1998). "Some observations on illegal markets." In R. Vincenzo, S. Nigel, and I. R. Taylor (Eds.), *The new European criminology: Crime and social order in Europe* (pp. 203–215). London: Routledge.

Arrow, K. J. (1987). "Reflections on the essays." In G. R. Feiwel (Ed.), *Arrow and the foundations of the theory of economic policy* (pp. 727–734). New York, NY: New York University Press.

Atkinson-Sheppard, S., and Hayward, H. (2019). "Conceptual similarities; distinct difference: Exploring 'the gang' in mainland China." *British Journal of Criminology*, 59(3), 614–633.

Axelrod, R. (1984). *The evolution of cooperation*. London: Basic Books.

Backe, E. L., Lilleston, P., and McCleary-Sills, J. (2018). "Networked individuals, gendered violence." *Violence and Gender*, 5(3), 135–146.

Bai, C. E., Lu, J., and Tao, Z. (2006). "Property rights protection and access to bank loans: Evidence from private enterprises in China." *Economics of Transition*, 14(4), 611–628.

Bakken, B. (Ed.). (2005). *Crime, punishment, and policing in China*. Lanham: Rowman & Littlefield Publishers.

Bakken, B., and Wang, J. (2021). "The changing forms of corruption in China." *Crime, Law and Social Change*, 75(3), 247–265.

Baland, J. M., and Platteau, J. P. (1996). *Halting degradation of natural resources: Is there a role for rural communities?* Rome: Food & Agriculture Organization of the United Nations and Clarendon Press Oxford.

Barbalet, J. (2014). "The structure of guanxi: Resolving problems of network assurance." *Theory and Society*, 43(1), 51–69.

Barbalet, J. (2015). "Guanxi, tie strength, and network attributes." *American Behavioral Scientist*, 59(8), 1038–1050.

Barbalet, J. (2018). "Guanxi as social exchange: Emotions, power and corruption." *Sociology*, 52(5), 934–949.

Barbalet, J. (2021). *The theory of guanxi and Chinese society*. Oxford: Oxford University Press.

Bardhan, D. (2019). "Informality." In A. M. Orum (Ed.), *The Wiley Blackwell encyclopedia of urban and regional studies* (pp. 1–11). Hoboken, NJ: John Wiley & Sons.

Barnes, N. (2017). "Criminal politics: An integrated approach to the study of organized crime, politics, and violence." *Perspectives on Politics*, 15(4), 967–987.

Barzel, Y. (1997). *Economic analysis of property rights*. Cambridge: Cambridge University Press.

Basu, G. (2014). "Concealment, corruption, and evasion: A transaction cost and case analysis of illicit supply chain activity." *Journal of Transportation Security*, 7(3), 209–226.

Basu, K. (2018). *The republic of beliefs: A new approach to law and economics*. Princeton, NJ: Princeton University Press.

Bauhr, M. (2017). "Need or greed? Conditions for collective action against corruption." *Governance*, 30(4), 561–581.

Bayar, G. (2005). "The role of intermediaries in corruption." *Public Choice*, 122(3–4), 277–298.

Becker, G. (1968). "Crime and punishment: An economic approach." *Journal of Political Economy*, 76, 169–217.

Beckert, J. (1996). "What is sociological about economic sociology? Uncertainty and the embeddedness of economic action." *Theory and Society*, 25(6), 803–840.
Beckert, J., and Dewey, M. (2017). "Introduction: The social organization of illegal markets." In J. Beckert and M. Dewey (Eds.), *The architecture of illegal markets: Towards an economic sociology of illegality in the economy* (pp. 1–36). Oxford: Oxford University Press.
Beckert, J., and Wehinger, F. (2013). "In the shadow: Illegal markets and economic sociology." *Socio-Economic Review*, 11(1), 5–30.
Beetham, D. (2013). *The legitimation of power*. London: Palgrave Macmillan.
Beijing Municipality Bureau of Land and Resources (BMBLR). (2013). "Beijing gongbu 108 'ge xiaochanquan fang' yichai 25 ge" [Beijing announces that 25 of 108 small property houses have been demolished]. People.cn, December 5, 2013, available at: http://politics.people.com.cn/n/2013/1205/c1001-23751862.html.
Benkler, Y. (2006). *The wealth of networks: How social production transforms markets and freedom*. New Haven and London: Yale University Press.
Bernstein, L. (1992). "Opting out of the legal system: Extralegal contractual relations in the diamond industry." *Journal of Legal Studies*, 21(1), 115–157.
Bertaud, A. (2018). *Order without design: How markets shape cities*. Cambridge, MA: MIT Press.
Bevan, D., Collier, P., and Gunning, J. W. (1989). "Black markets: Illegality, information, and rents." *World Development*, 17(12), 1955–1963.
Bezemer, D., and Headey, D. (2008). "Agriculture, development, and urban bias." *World Development*, 36(8), 1342–1364.
Bhowmik, S. (2005). "Street vendors in Asia." *Economic and Political Weekly*, May 28th–June 4th: 2256–2264.
Bhowmik, S. (2010). *Street vendors in the global urban economy*. London: Routledge.
Bian, Y. (1997). "Bringing strong ties back in: Indirect ties, network bridges, and job searches in China." *American Sociological Review*, 62(3), 366–385.
Bian, Y. (2019). *Guanxi, how China works*. Cambridge: Polity Press.
Boettke, P. J., Candela, R. A., and Zhukov, K. (2023). "The morality of illicit markets: 'Greasing the wheels' or 'greasing the palm'?" *Journal of Economic Behavior & Organization*, 209, 411–422.
Boittin, M. L. (2013). "New perspectives from the oldest profession: Abuse and the legal consciousness of sex workers in China." *Law & Society Review*, 47(2), 245–278.
Bonnet, F., and Venkatesh, S. (2016). "Poverty and informal economies." In D. Brady and L. M. Burton (Eds.), *Oxford handbook of the social science of poverty* (pp. 637–659). Oxford: Oxford University Press.
Bottoms, A. E., and Wiles, P. (1997). "Environmental criminology." In M. Maguire, R. Morgan, and R. Reiner (Eds.), *The Oxford handbook of criminology* (pp. 305–359). Oxford: Oxford University Press.
Broadhurst, R., and Wang, P. (2014). "After the Bo Xilai trial: Does corruption threaten China's future?" *Survival*, 56(3), 157–178.
Broadhurst, R., Grabosky, P., Alazab, M., Bouhours, B., and Chon, S. (2014). "Organizations and cyber crime." *International Journal of Cyber Criminology*, 8, 1–20.
Brown, D. W., and Konrad, A. M. (2001). "Job-seeking in a turbulent economy: Social networks and the importance of cross-industry ties to an industry change." *Human Relations*, 54, 1015–1044.

Bruggeman, J. (2016). "The strength of varying tie strength: Comment on Aral and Van Alstyne." *American Journal of Sociology*, 121(6), 1919–1930.

Buchanan, J. (1974). "Review of the machinery of freedom: Guide to a radical capitalism." *Journal of Economic Literature*, 12, 914–915.

Buchanan, J. (1975). *The limits of liberty: Between anarchy and Leviathan*. Chicago, IL: University of Chicago Press.

Buckley, P. J., Clegg, J., and Tan, H. (2006). "Cultural awareness in knowledge transfer to China: The role of *guanxi* and *mianzi*." *Journal of World Business*, 41, 275–288.

Cai, M., Fan, J., Ye, C., and Zhang, Q. (2021). "Government debt, land financing and distributive justice in China." *Urban Studies*, 58(11), 2329–2347.

Cai, M., Murtazashvili, I., and Murtazashvili, J. (2020). "The politics of land property rights." *Journal of Institutional Economics*, 16(2), 151–167.

Cai, Y. (2003). "Collective ownership or cadres' ownership? The non-agricultural use of farmland in China." *China Quarterly*, 175, 662–680.

Cai, Y. (2010). *Collective resistance in China: Why popular protests succeed or fail*. Stanford, CA: Stanford University Press.

Cai, Y. (2014). *State and agents in China: Disciplining government officials*. Stanford, CA: Stanford University Press.

Calvert, R. (1995). "Rational actors, equilibrium, and social institutions." In J. Knight and I. Sened (Eds.), *Explaining social institutions* (pp. 57–93). Ann Arbor, MI: University of Michigan Press.

Campana, P., and Varese, F. (2013). "Cooperation in criminal organizations: Kinship and violence as credible commitments." *Rationality and Society*, 25(3), 263–289.

Campana, P., and Varese, F. (2018). "Organized crime in the United Kingdom: Illegal governance of markets and communities." *British Journal of Criminology*, 58(6), 1381–1400.

Carr, D. J., Gotlieb, M. R., Lee, N. J., and Shah, D. V. (2012). "Examining overconsumption, competitive consumption, and conscious consumption from 1994 to 2004." *Annals of the American Academy of Political and Social Science*, 644(1), 220–233.

Casavant, L., and Collin, C. (2001). *Illegal drug use and crime: A complex relationship*. Canada: Paper prepared for the Special Senate Committee on Illegal Drugs. Ottawa, ON: Library of Parliament.

Caulkins, J. P., and Reuter, P. (1998). "What price data tell us about drug markets." *Journal of Drug Issues*, 28(3), 593–612.

Caulkins, J. P., Reuter, P., and Taylor, L. J. (2006). "Can supply restrictions lower price? Violence, drug dealing and positional advantage." *Contributions in Economic Analysis & Policy*, 5(1), 1–18.

Chamlee-Wright, E. (2010). *The cultural and political economy of recovery: Social learning in a post-disaster environment*. Abingdon: Routledge.

Chan, C. S. C. (2009). "Invigorating the content in social embeddedness: An ethnography of life insurance transactions in China." *American Journal of Sociology*, 115(3), 712–754.

Chan, C. S. C., and Yao, Z. (2018). "A market of distrust: Toward a cultural sociology of unofficial exchanges between patients and doctors in China." *Theory and Society*, 47(6), 737–772.

Chang, K. C. (2011). "A path to understanding guanxi in China's transitional economy: Variations on network behavior." *Sociological Theory*, 29(4), 315–339.

Che, J., and Qian, Y. (1998). "Institutional environment, community government, and corporate governance: Understanding China's township-village enterprises." *Journal of Law, Economics, & Organization*, 14(1), 1–23.

Chen, M. A. (2006). "Rethinking the informal economy." In B. Guha-Khansnobis, R. Kanbur, and E. Ostrom (Eds.), *Linking the formal and informal economy* (pp. 93–120). Oxford: Oxford University Press.

Chen, X. (2012). *Social protest and contentious authoritarianism in China*. Cambridge: Cambridge University Press.

Chen, Y. (2016). "Student loans are deceptive and they are not as simple as you think." Newbelink.com, available at: www.newbelink.com/article/16301.html (accessed April 4, 2020; in Chinese).

Chen, Y. (2020). "Shenzhen xiaochanquanfang xiaoshou huobao, quequan hou jiang zouxianghefang, goumaizhe shi zheme xiangde" [Small-property houses in Shenzhen are on hot sales! Where will it end up after the property rights are confirmed? Perspectives from Buyers]. Egsea, June 14, 2020, available at: https://m.thepaper.cn/newsDetail_forward_7845984.

Chen, Z., and Jin, M. (2017). "Financial inclusion in China: Use of credit." *Journal of Family and Economic Issues*, 38(4), 528–540.

Cheng, H., and Shaw, D. (2018). "Polycentric development practice in master planning: The case of China." *International Planning Studies*, 23(2), 163–179.

Cheng, W. (2004). "An empirical study of corruption within China's state-owned enterprises." *China Review*, 4(2), 55–80.

Chin, K., and Godson, R. (2006). "Organized crime and the political-criminal nexus in China." *Trends in Organized Crime*, 9(3), 5–44.

Choo, K. K. R. (2008). "Organised crime groups in cyberspace." *Trends in Organized Crime*, 11, 270–295.

Chu, C., and Wang, L. (2017). "Guanyuan luoma hou, shenbian de ren dou qu na er le" [When officials are sacked, where have the people around them gone?]. *Southern Weekly*, February 17, 2017, available at: www.infzm.com/content/122929 (accessed August 1, 2021).

Chu, Y. K. (2000). *The triads as business*. London: Routledge.

Chwe, M. S. Y. (2013). *Rational ritual: Culture, coordination, and common knowledge*. Princeton, NJ: Princeton University Press.

Clay, K. (1997). "Trade without law: Private-order institutions in Mexican California." *Journal of Law, Economics, and Organization*, 13(1), 202–231.

Coase, R. H. (1937). "The nature of the firm." *Economica*, 4(16), 386–405.

Coase, R. H. (1960). "The problem of social cost." *Journal of Law and Economics*, 3, 1–44.

Coase, R. H. (1984). "The new institutional economics." *Journal of Institutional and Theoretical Economics*, 140(1), 229–231.

Coase, R. H. (1993). "Coase on Posner on Coase: Comment." *Journal of Institutional and Theoretical Economics*, 149(1), 96–98.

Coase, R., and Wang, N. (2016). *How China became capitalist*. London: Palgrave Macmillan.

Cohen, L. E., and Felson, M. (1979). "Social change and crime rate trends." *American Sociological Review*, 44, 588–608.

Cook, K. S., and Emerson, R. M. (1978). "Power, equity and commitment in exchange networks." *American Sociological Review*, 43(5), 721–739.

Cook, K. S., Emerson, R. M., Gillmore, M. R., and Yamagishi, T. (1983). "The distribution of power in exchange networks: Theory and experimental results." *American Journal of Sociology*, 89(2), 275–305.

Cook, K. S., Hardin, R., and Levi, M. (2005). *Cooperation without trust?* London: Russell Sage Foundation.

Copes, H. (2015). "Neutralization theory." In B. M. Huebner (Ed.), *Oxford bibliographies in criminology*. Oxford University Press. DOI: 10.1093/OBO/9780195396607-0140.

Cowen, T. (2020). "What libertarianism has become and will become: State capacity libertarianism," available at: https://marginalrevolution.com/marginalrevolution/2020/01/what-libertarianism-has-become-and-will-become-state-capacity-libertarianism.html.

Coyne, C. J., and Mathers, R. L. (2011). "Rituals: An economic interpretation." *Journal of Economic Behavior & Organization*, 78(1–2), 74–84.

Crawford, S. E., and Ostrom, E. (1995). "A grammar of institutions." *American Political Science Review*, 89(3), 582–600.

Cross, J. C. (1998). "Co-optation, competition, and resistance." *Latin American Perspectives*, 25(2), 41–61.

Crossa, V. (2009). "Resisting the entrepreneurial city." *International Journal of Urban and Regional Research*, 33(1), 43–63.

Darling, K., and Perzanowski, A. (Eds.). (2017). *Creativity without law: Challenging the assumptions of intellectual property*. New York, NY: New York University Press.

De Keyzer, M. (2013). "The impact of different distributions of power on access rights to the common wastelands: The Campine, Brecklands and Geest compared." *Journal of Institutional Economics*, 9(4), 517–542.

De Soto, H. (1989). *Their other path*. New York, NY: Harper & Row.

Décary-Hétu, D., and Dupont, B. (2013). "Reputation in a dark network of online criminals." *Global Crime*, 14(2–3), 175–196.

Della Porta, D., and Vannucci, A. (2012). *The hidden order of corruption: An institutional approach*. Farnham: Ashgate Publishing.

Deng, J. (2018). "The national supervision commission: A new anti-corruption model in China." *International Journal of Law, Crime and Justice*, 52, 58–73.

Deng, S. (2016). "Sanya 2015 nian zhijin gong chaichu weijian chao 1 wan dong, zongmianji 583 wan m2" [More than 10,000 illegal buildings (with 5,830,000 m2) demolished in Sanya since 2015]. Hinews, October 9, 2016, available at: www.hinews.cn/news/system/2016/08/09/030604135.shtml

Densley, J. (2012). "Street gang recruitment: Signaling, screening, and selection." *Social Problems*, 59(3), 301–321.

Densley, J. (2013). *How gangs work*. London: Palgrave Macmillan.

Denyer, S., and Xu, Y. (2016). "China vows to tackle 'family corruption' – but even state media can't hide its skepticism." *The Washington Post*, April 29, 2016, available at: www.washingtonpost.com/news/worldviews/wp/2016/04/29/china-vows-to-tackle-family-corruption-but-even-state-media-cant-hide-its-skepticism/ (accessed August 21, 2021).

Devlin, R. T. (2011). "An area that governs itself." *Planning Theory*, 10(1), 53–65.

Dewey, M. (2019). "The characteristics of illegal markets." In H. N. Pontell (Ed.), *Oxford research encyclopedia of criminology and criminal justice* (pp. 1–24). Oxford: Oxford University Press.

Dewey, M., Míguez, D. P., and Saín, M. F. (2017). "The strength of collusion: A conceptual framework for interpreting hybrid social orders." *Current Sociology*, 65(3), 395–410.

Di Tella, R., and Schargrodsky, E. (2003). "The role of wages and auditing during a crackdown on corruption in the city of Buenos Aires." *Journal of Law and Economics*, 46(1), 269–292.

Dick, A. R. (1995). "When does organized crime pay? A transaction cost analysis." *International Review of Law and Economics*, 15(1), 25–45.

Dickinson, T., and Wright, R. (2015). "Gossip, decision-making and deterrence in drug markets." *British Journal of Criminology*, 55(6), 1263–1281.

Dickinson, T., and Wright, R. (2017). "The funny side of drug dealing: Risk, humor, and narrative identity." *Criminology*, 55(3), 691–720.

Dixit, A. K. (2004). *Lawlessness and economics: Alternative modes of governance*. Princeton, NJ: Princeton University Press.

Dixit, A. K. (2009). "Governance institutions and economic activity." *American Economic Review*, 99(1), 5–24.

Dong, W. (2012). "Chaijie 116 ge xiaochanquan fang chuzhi yangben." [Inveighing samples 116 of intervened small property houses]. Leju, October 15, 2012, available at: http://bj.leju.com/zhuanti/ldgc09/.

Donovan, M. G. (2008). "Informal cities and the contestation of public space." *Urban Studies*: 45(1), 29–51.

Dorn, N., and South, N. (1990). "Drug markets and law enforcement." *British Journal of Criminology*, 30(2), 171–188.

Drugov, M., Hamman, J., and Serra, D. (2014). "Intermediaries in corruption: An experiment." *Experimental Economics*, 17(1), 78–99.

Dunfee, T. W., and Warren, D. E. (2001). "Is guanxi ethical? A normative analysis of doing business in China." *Journal of Business Ethics*, 32(3), 191–204.

Durán-Martínez, A. (2015). "To kill and tell? State power, criminal competition, and drug violence." *Journal of Conflict Resolution*, 59(8), 1377–1402.

Earley, P. C. (1997). *Face, harmony, and social structure: An analysis of organizational behavior across cultures*. Oxford: Oxford University Press.

Ellickson, R. C. (1991). *Order without law: How neighbors settle disputes*. Cambridge, MA: Harvard University Press.

Emerson, R. M. (1962). "Power–dependence relations." *American Sociological Review*, 27, 31–41.

Emerson, R. M. (1972a). "Exchange theory, part I: A psychological basis for social exchange." In J. Berger (Ed.), *Sociological theories in progress*, vol. 2 (pp. 38–57). Boston, MA: Houghton Mifflin.

Emerson, R. M. (1972b). "Exchange theory, part II: Exchange relations and network structures." In J. Berger (Ed.), *Sociological theories in progress*, vol. 2 (pp. 58–87). Boston, MA: Houghton Mifflin.

Engwicht, N. (2017). "'We are the genuine people': Legality and legitimacy in the Sierra Leonean diamond market." In J. Beckert and M. Dewey (Eds.), *The architecture of illegal markets: Towards an economic sociology of illegality in the economy* (pp. 198–217). Oxford: Oxford University Press.

Fan, Y. (2002). "Guanxi's consequences: Personal gains at social cost." *Journal of Business Ethics*, 38(4), 371–380.

Fewsmith, J. (2013). *The logic and limits of political reform in China*. Cambridge: Cambridge University Press.

Flashman, J., and Gambetta, D. (2014). "Thick as thieves." *Rationality and Society*, 26(1), 3–45.

Flock, R., and Breitung, W. (2016). "Migrant street vendors in urban China and the social production of public space." *Population, Space and Place*, 22(2), 158–169.

Frank, H. F. (2015). *Microeconomics and behavior*. New York, NY: McGraw-Hill Education.

Friedman, D. (1979). "Private creation and enforcement of law: A historical case." *Journal of Legal Studies*, 8(2), 399–415.

Friedman, M. (1962). *Capitalism and freedom*. Chicago, IL: University of Chicago Press.

Fu, D. (2018). *Mobilizing without the masses: Control and contention in China*. Cambridge: Cambridge University Press.

Fu, H. (2015). "Wielding the sword: President Xi's new anti-corruption campaign." In S. Rose-Ackerman and P. Felipe Lagunes (Eds.), *Greed, corruption, and the modern state: Essay in political economy* (pp. 134–135). Cheltenham: Edward Elgar.

Fu, H. (2016). "China's striking anti-corruption adventure: A political journey towards the rule of law?" In W. Chen (Ed.), *The Beijing consensus? How China has changed the western ideas of law and economic development* (pp. 249–274). Cambridge: Cambridge University Press.

Fukuyama, F. (2013). "What is governance?" *Governance*, 26(3), 347–368.

Galanter, M. (1981). "Justice in many rooms: Courts, private ordering, and indigenous law." *Journal of Legal Pluralism and Unofficial Law*, 13(19), 1–47.

Gambetta, D. (1993). *The Sicilian mafia: The business of private protection*. Cambridge, MA: Harvard University Press.

Gambetta, D. (2009). *Codes of the underworld: How criminals communicate*. Princeton, NJ: Princeton University Press.

Gambetta, D. (2018). "Why is Italy disproportionally corrupt?" In K. Basu and T. Cordella (Eds.), *Institutions, governance and the control of corruption* (pp. 133–164). New York, NY: Springer.

Gambetta, D., and Przepiorka, W. (2019). "Sharing compromising information as a cooperative strategy." *Sociological Science*, 6, 352–379.

Gans-Morse, J., Borges, M., Makarin, A., Mannah-Blankson, T., Nickow, A., and Zhang, D. (2018). "Reducing bureaucratic corruption: Interdisciplinary perspectives on what works." *World Development*, 105, 171–188.

Geis, G. (1966). "Violence and organized crime." *Annals of the American Academy of Political and Social Science*, 364(1), 86–95.

Gerring, J. (2006). *Case study research: Principles and practices*. Cambridge: Cambridge University Press.

Giardini, F., and Wittek, R. (Eds.). (2019). *The oxford handbook of gossip and reputation*. Oxford: Oxford University Press.

Godfrey, P. C. (2011). "Toward a theory of the informal economy." *Academy of Management Annals*, 5(1), 231–277.

Godson, R. (2017). *Menace to society: Political-criminal collaboration around the world*. London: Routledge.

Goffman, E. (1955). "On face-work: An analysis of ritual elements in social interaction." *Psychiatry*, 18(3), 213–231.

Goffman, E. (1967). *Interaction ritual: Essays in face-to-face behavior*. New Brunswick, NJ: Aldine Transaction.

Gong, T. (2002). "Dangerous collusion: Corruption as a collective venture in contemporary China." *Communist and Post-Communist Studies*, 35(1), 85–103.
Gong, T. (2004). "Dependent judiciary and unaccountable judges: Judicial corruption in contemporary China." *China Review*, 4(2), 33–54.
Gong, T. (2006). "Corruption and local governance: The double identity of Chinese local governments in market reform." *Pacific Review*, 19(1), 85–102.
Gong, T., and Yang, S. L. (2019). "Controlling bureaucratic corruption." In *Oxford Research Encyclopedia of Politics*, available at: https://doi.org/10.1093/acrefore/9780190228637.013.1463.
Gottfredson, M. R., and Hirschi, T. (1990). *A general theory of crime*. Palo Alto, CA: Stanford University Press.
Grabosky, P. (2013). "Organised crime and the internet." *RUSI Journal*, 158(5), 18–25.
Grabosky, P. (2015). "Organized cybercrime and national security." In R. G. Smith, R. C. Cheung, and L. Y. Lau (Eds.), *Cybercrime risks and responses* (pp. 67–80). London: Palgrave Macmillan.
Granovetter, M. (1973). "The strength of weak ties." *American Journal of Sociology*, 78(6), 1360–1380.
Granovetter, M. (1985). "Economic action and social structure: The problem of embeddedness." *American Journal of Sociology*, 91(3), 481–510.
Granovetter, M. (1995). *Getting a job: A study of contacts and careers*. Chicago, IL: University of Chicago Press.
Greif, A. (1989). "Reputation and coalitions in medieval trade: Evidence on the Maghribi traders." *Journal of Economic History*, 49(4), 857–882.
Greif, A. (1994). "Cultural beliefs and the organization of society: A historical and theoretical reflection on collectivist and individualist societies." *Journal of Political Economy*, 102(5), 912–950.
Greif, A. (2000). "The fundamental problem of exchange: A research agenda in historical institutional analysis." *European Review of Economic History*, 4(3), 251–284.
Greif, A. (2006). *Institutions and the path to the modern economy: Lessons from medieval trade*. New York, NY: Cambridge University Press.
Greif, A., and Kingston, C. (2011). "Institutions: Rules or equilibria?" In N. Schofield and G. Caballero (Eds.), *Political economy of institutions, democracy and voting* (pp. 13–43). New York, NY: Springer.
Greif, A., Milgrom, P., and Weingast, B. R. (1994). "Coordination, commitment, and enforcement: The case of the merchant guild." *Journal of Political Economy*, 102(4), 745–776.
Greitens, S. C., and Truex, R. (2020). "Repressive experiences among China scholars: New evidence from survey data." *China Quarterly*, 242, 349–375.
Grossman, S. (2020). "The politics of order in informal markets: Evidence from Lagos." *World Politics*, 72(1), 47–79.
Grossman, S. (2021). *The politics of order in informal markets: How the state shapes private governance*. Cambridge: Cambridge University Press.
Guo, C., and Miller, J. K. (2010). "Guanxi dynamics and entrepreneurial firm creation and development in China." *Management and Organization Review*, 6(2), 267–291.
Guo, X. (2014). "Controlling corruption in the party: China's central discipline inspection commission." *China Quarterly*, 219, 597–624.

Hall, A., and Antonopoulos, G. A. (2016). *Fake meds online: The internet and the transnational market in illicit pharmaceuticals.* New York, NY: Springer.

Haller, T. (2007). *Understanding institutions and their links to resource management from the perspective of new institutionalism.* Bern, Switzerland: NCCR North-South.

Hardy, R. A., and Norgaard, J. R. (2016). "Reputation in the internet black market: An empirical and theoretical analysis of the deep web." *Journal of Institutional Economics*, 12(3), 515–539.

Hart, K. (1973). "Informal income opportunities and urban employment in Ghana." *Journal of Modern African Studies*, 11(1), 61–89.

Hart, K. (2010). "Informal economy." In K. Hart, J.-L. Laville, and A. David Cattani (Eds.), *The human economy* (pp. 142–53). Cambridge: Polity Press.

Hasker, K., and Okten, C. (2008). "Intermediaries and corruption." *Journal of Economic Behavior & Organization*, 67(1), 103–115.

He, B. (2008). "*Chengguan* chase and hawkers resist." *China Legal Science*, 5, 15–169.

He, S., Wang, D., Webster, C., and Chau, K. W. (2019). "Property rights with price tags? Pricing uncertainties in the production, transaction and consumption of China's small property right housing." *Land Use Policy*, 81, 424–433.

He, X., and Ng, K. H. (2017). "'It must be rock strong!' Guanxi's impact on judicial decision making in China." *American Journal of Comparative Law*, 65(4), 841–871.

Helmke, G., and Levitsky, S. (2004). "Informal institutions and comparative politics: A research agenda." *Perspectives on Politics*, 2(4), 725–740.

Hill, P. B. (2003). *The Japanese mafia: Yakuza, law, and the state.* Oxford: Oxford University Press.

Hillman, B. (2010). "Factions and spoils: Examining political behavior within the local state in China." *China Journal*, 64, 1–8.

Hillman, B. (2014). *Patronage and power: Local state networks and party-state resilience in rural China.* Palo Alto, CA: Stanford University Press.

Ho, D. Y. (1976). "On the concept of face." *American Journal of Sociology*, 81(4), 867–884.

Ho, P. (2005). *Institutions in transition: Land ownership, property rights, and social conflict in China.* Oxford: Oxford University Press.

Ho, P. (2017). *Unmaking China's development: The function and credibility of institutions.* Cambridge: Cambridge University Press.

Hobbes, T. (1651) [1955]. *Leviathan.* London: Blackwell.

Holt, T. J. (2013). "Examining the forces shaping cybercrime markets online." *Social Science Computer Review*, 31(2), 165–177.

Holt, T. J., Smirnova, O., Chua, Y. T., and Copes, H. (2015). "Examining the risk reduction strategies of actors in online criminal markets." *Global Crime*, 16(2), 81–103.

Hooghe, L., and Marks, G. (2003). "Unraveling the central state, But how?" *American Political Science Review*, 97(2), 233–243.

Hsing, Y. (2010). *The great urban transformation: Politics of land and property in China.* Oxford: Oxford University Press.

Hu, B. (2007). *Informal institutions and rural development in China.* London: Routledge.

Huang, Y. (2022). "Why did the peer-to-peer lending market fail in China?" *HKUST IEMS Thought Leadership Brief*, no. 61, 1–4.

Huang, G., Xue, D., and Li, Z. (2014). "From revanchism to ambivalence." *Antipode*, 46(1), 170–189.

Huang, G., Zhang, H. O., and Xue, D. (2018). "Beyond unemployment: Informal employment and heterogeneous motivations for participating in street vending in present-day China." *Urban Studies*, 55(12), 2743–2761.

Huang, L. J., and Snell, R. S. (2003). "Turnaround, corruption and mediocrity: Leadership and governance in three state owned enterprises in Mainland China." *Journal of Business Ethics*, 43(1), 111–124.

Huang, R. H. (2018). "Online P2P lending and regulatory responses in China: Opportunities and challenges." *European Business Organization Law Review*, 19(1), 63–92.

Hubbard, M. (1995). "Bureaucrats and markets in China: The rise and fall of Entrepreneurial Local Government." *Governance*, 8(3), 335–353.

Hübschle, A. (2017). "Contested illegality: Processing the trade prohibition of rhino horn." In J. Beckert and M. Dewey (Eds.), *The architecture of illegal markets: Towards an economic sociology of illegality in the economy* (pp. 177–197). Oxford: Oxford University Press.

Human Rights Watch. (2012). *Beat him, take everything away*. New York, NY: Human Rights Watch.

Hummel, C. (2017). "Disobedient markets: Street vendors, enforcement, and state intervention in collective action." *Comparative Political Studies*, 50(11), 1524–1555.

Hummel, C. (2021). *Why informal workers organize: Contentious politics, enforcement, and the state*. Oxford: Oxford University Press.

Husted, B. W. (1994). "Honor among thieves: A transaction-cost interpretation of corruption in third world countries." *Business Ethics Quarterly*, 4(1), 17–27.

Hutchings, A., and Holt, T. J. (2015). "A crime script analysis of the online stolen data market." *British Journal of Criminology*, 55(3), 596–614.

Hwang, K. K. (1987). "Face and favor: The Chinese power game." *American Journal of Sociology*, 92(4), 944–974.

Infzm. (2010). "Sanya gao fangjia ciji zhengfu chaichu weijian xiaochanquanfang fang bu sheng fang." [Sanya's high housing prices stimulate the government to dismantle houses with small property rights]. Infzm, December 20, 2010, available at: http://news.sina.com.cn/c/sd/2010-12-20/140621674508.shtml.

Irwin-Rogers, K., Densley, J., and Pinkney, C. (2018). "Gang violence and social media." In J. L. Ireland, C. A. Ireland, and P. Birch (Eds.), *The Routledge international handbook of human aggression*. London: Routledge.

Jacques, S., and Wright, R. (2011). "Informal control and illicit drug trade." *Criminology*, 49(3), 729–765.

Jacques, S., and Wright, R. (2015). *Code of the suburb: Inside the world of young middle-class drug dealers*. Chicago, IL: University of Chicago Press.

James, D. (2014). "Deeper into a hole?" *Current Anthropology*, 55(S9), S17–S29.

Jancsics, D. (2019). "Corruption as resource transfer: An interdisciplinary synthesis." *Public Administration Review*, 79(4), 523–537.

Jiang, A. (2020). *Regulating street vendors in urban China: Soft law enforcement, dirty institution, and adaptations of vendors*. Doctoral dissertation, University of Macau.

Jiang, A., and Wang, P. (2022). "Governance and informal economies: Informality, uncertainty and street vending in China." *British Journal of Criminology*, 62(6), 1431–1453.

Jiang, G., Lo, T. W., and Garris, C. P. (2012). "Formation and trend of Guanxi practice and Guanxi phenomenon." *International Journal of Criminology and Sociology*, 1, 207–220.

Jiang, T., and Nie, H. (2014). "The stained China miracle: Corruption, regulation, and firm performance." *Economics Letters*, 123(3), 366–369.

Jiang, X. (2016). "Glut of ways to pay." *China Daily*, available at: www.chinadaily.com.cn/business/3rdWuzhenWorldInternetConference/2016-11/18/content_27415834.htm (accessed March 30, 2020).

Johnson, C., Dowd, T. J., and Ridgeway, C. L. (2006). "Legitimacy as a social process." *Annual Review of Sociology*, 32, 53–78.

Jung, D. F., and Cohen, D. K. (2020). *Lynching and local justice: Legitimacy and accountability in weak states*. Cambridge: Cambridge University Press.

Kali, R. (1999). "Endogenous business networks." *Journal of Law, Economics, and Organization*, 15(3), 615–636.

Kaptein, M., and Van Helvoort, M. (2019). "A model of neutralization techniques." *Deviant Behavior*, 40(10), 1260–1285.

Kassab, H. S., and Rosen, J. D. (2019). *Corruption, institutions, and fragile states*. Cham: Palgrave Macmillan.

Kaufman, A. A., and Mackenzie, P. W. (2009). *The culture of the Chinese people's liberation army*. Arlington: CNA China Studies.

Keliher, M., and Wu, H. 2016. "Corruption, anticorruption, and the transformation of political culture in contemporary China." *Journal of Asian Studies*, 75(1), 5–18.

Kelly, R. J. (1999). "The political-criminal nexus in the united states." *Trends in Organized Crime*, 5(2), 85–122.

Khanna, J., and Johnston, M. (2007). "India's middlemen: Connecting by corrupting?" *Crime, Law and Social Change*, 48(3–5), 151.

Kiong, T. C., and Kee, Y. P. (1998). "Guanxi bases, xinyong and Chinese business networks." *British Journal of Sociology*, 49(1), 75–96.

Kleemans, E. R., and Van de Bunt, H. G. (1999). "The social embeddedness of organized crime." *Transnational Organized Crime*, 5(1), 19–36.

Kojouharov, A., and Rusev, A. (2016). "Sharks in sheep's clothing." In G. A. Antonopoulos (Ed.), *Illegal entrepreneurship, organized crime and social control* (pp. 101–121). New York, NY: Springer.

Kong, D., Wang, L., and Wang, M. (2017). "Effects of anti-corruption on firm performance: Evidence from a quasi-natural experiment in China." *Finance Research Letters*, 23, 190–195.

Kundu, D. (2019). "Urban informality." In A. M. Orum (Eds.), *The Wiley Blackwell encyclopedia of urban and regional studies* (pp. 1–5). Hoboken, NJ: John Wiley & Sons.

Ladegaard, I. (2020). "Open secrecy: How police crackdowns and creative problem-solving brought illegal markets out of the shadows." *Social Forces*, 99(2), 532–559.

Lafarguette, R. (2011). "Chongqing: Model for a new economic and social policy?" *China Perspectives*, 2011(2011/4), 62–64.

Lai, Y., Wang, J., and Lok, W. (2017). "Redefining property rights over collective land in the urban redevelopment of Shenzhen, China." *Land Use Policy*, 69, 485–493.

Lambert-Mogiliansky, A., Majumdar, M., and Radner, R. (2009). "Strategic analysis of petty corruption with an intermediary." *Review of Economic Design*, 13(1), 45–57.

Lambsdorff, J. G. (2002). "Making corrupt deals: Contracting in the shadow of the law." *Journal of Economic Behavior & Organization*, 48(3), 221–241.

Lambsdorff, J. G. (2007). *The institutional economics of corruption and reform: Theory, evidence and policy*. Cambridge: Cambridge University Press.

Lambsdorff, J. G. (2013). "Corrupt intermediaries in international business transactions: Between make, buy and reform." *European Journal of Law and Economics*, 35(3), 349–366.

Landa, J. T. (1981). "A theory of the ethnically homogeneous middleman group: An institutional alternative to contract law." *Journal of Legal Studies*, 10(2), 349–362.

Landa, J. T. (1994). *Trust, ethnicity, and identity: Beyond the new institutional economics of ethnic trading networks, contract law, and gift-exchange*. Ann Arbor, MI: University of Michigan Press.

Larson, J. M. (2017). "The weakness of weak ties for novel information diffusion." *Applied Network Science*, 2(1), 1–15.

Lata, L., Walters, P., and Roitman, S. (2019). "A marriage of convenience." *Cities*, 84, 143–150.

Lavorgna, A. (2015). "Organised crime goes online." *Journal of Money Laundering Control*, 18, 153–168.

Lawler, E. J. (1992). "Power processes in bargaining." *Sociological Quarterly*, 33(1), 17–34.

Lee, R., and Thoumi, F. (1997). "The criminal-political nexus in Colombia." *Trends in Organized Crime*, 3(1), 59–65.

Lee, S. H., and Phan, P. H. (2006). "The effects of tie strength and tie diversity on job search, pay increases, and promotions in Singapore and Thailand." *Journal of Social and Personal Relationships*, 23(5), 820–839.

Leeson, P. T. (2006). "Efficient anarchy." *Public Choice*, 130(1–2), 41–53.

Leeson, P. T. (2007). "An-arrgh-chy: The law and economics of pirate organization." *Journal of Political Economy*, 115(6), 1049–1094.

Leeson, P. T. (2008). "Social distance and self-enforcing exchange." *Journal of Legal Studies*, 37(1), 161–188.

Leeson, P. T. (2009). *The invisible hook: The hidden economics of pirates*. Princeton, NJ: Princeton University Press.

Leeson, P. T. (2014). *Anarchy unbound: Why self-governance works better than you think*. Cambridge: Cambridge University Press.

Leeson, P. T. (2020). "Logic is a harsh mistress: Welfare economics for economists." *Journal of Institutional Economics*, 16 (2), 145–150.

Leeson, P. T., and Harris, C. (2018). "Wealth-destroying private property rights." *World Development*, 107, 1–9.

Leeson, P. T., and Skarbek, D. (2010). "Criminal constitutions." *Global Crime*, 11(3), 279–297.

Leeson, P. T., and Williamson, C. R. (2009). "Anarchy and development: An application of the theory of second best." *Law and Development Review*, 2(1), 77–96.

Leukfeldt, E. R., Lavorgna, A., and Kleemans, E. R. (2017). "Organised cybercrime or cybercrime that is organised?" *European Journal on Criminal Policy and Research*, 23(3), 287–300.

Leung, T. K. P., and Chan, Y. K. (2003). "Face, favour and positioning: A Chinese power game." *European Journal of Marketing*, 37(11), 1575–1598.

Levi, M. (2018). "The who, what, and why of performance-based legitimacy." *Journal of Intervention and Statebuilding*, 12(4), 603–610.

Levi, M., and Sacks, A. (2009). "Legitimating beliefs: Sources and indicators." *Regulation & Governance*, 3(4), 311–333.

Levi, M., Sacks, A., and Tyler, T. (2009). "Conceptualizing legitimacy, measuring legitimating beliefs." *American Behavioral Scientist*, 53(3), 354–375.

Lewison, M. (1999). "Conflicts of interest?" *Journal of Business Ethics*, 22(4), 327–339.

Li, F., and Deng, J. (2016a). "The limits of the arbitrariness in anticorruption by China's local Party discipline inspection committees." *Journal of Contemporary China*, 25(97), 75–90.

Li, F., and Deng, J. (2016b). "The power and the misuse of power by China's local procuratorates in anticorruption." *International Journal of Law, Crime and Justice*, 45, 1–25.

Li, J. S. (2003). "Relation-based versus rule-based governance: An explanation of the East Asian miracle and Asian crisis." *Review of International Economics*, 11(4), 651–673.

Li, L. (2011). "Performing bribery in China: Guanxi-practice, corruption with a human face." *Journal of Contemporary China*, 20(68), 1–20.

Li, L. (2012). "The 'production' of corruption in China's courts: Judicial politics and decision making in a one-party state." *Law & Social Inquiry*, 37(4), 848–877.

Li, L. (2016). "The rise of the discipline and inspection commission, 1927–2012: Anticorruption investigation and decision-making in the Chinese communist party." *Modern China*, 42(5), 447–482.

Li, L., and Wang, P. (2019). "From institutional interaction to institutional integration: The national supervisory commission and China's new anti-corruption model." *China Quarterly*, 240, 967–989.

Li, L., Lien, D., Wu, Y., and Zhao, Y. (2017). "Enforcement and political power in anticorruption – Evidence from China." *World Development*, 98, 133–147.

Li, R. (2013). "Media corruption: A Chinese characteristic." *Journal of Business Ethics*, 116(2), 297–310.

Li, S. (2015). "Sanya weijian bian chai bian zhang 5 nian xinzeng 500 wan pingfangmi weijian." [Sanya illegal buildings were expanded as they were dismantled, 5 billion square meters were increased in the past 5 years]. Nanguo Dushibao, April 22, 2015, available at: http://hainan.ifeng.com/app/sanya/detail_2015_04/22/3812061_0.shtml

Li, S., Li, S., and Zhang, W. (2000). "The road to capitalism: Competition and institutional change in China." *Journal of Comparative Economics*, *28*(2), 269–292.

Li, W., and Pye, L. W. (1992). "The ubiquitous role of the *mishu* in Chinese politics." *China Quarterly*, 132, 913–936.

Li, Y. (2014). *The judicial system and reform in post-mao China: Stumbling towards justice*. London: Routledge.

Li, Y. (2018). *Playing by the informal rules: Why the Chinese regime remains stable despite rising protests*. Cambridge: Cambridge University Press.

Liao, X., and Tsai, W. H. (2020). "Strengthening China's powerful commission for discipline inspection under Xi Jinping, with a case study at the county level." *China Journal*, 84(1), 29–50.

Lin, C. S. (2009). *Developing China: Land, politics and social conditions*. London: Routledge.

Lin, J., and Si, S. X. (2010). "Can guanxi be a problem? Contexts, ties, and some unfavorable consequences of social capital in China." *Asia Pacific Journal of Management*, 27(3), 561–581.

Lin, W. (2022). "Garnering sympathy: Moral appeals and land bargaining under autocracy." *Journal of Institutional Economics*. 18(5), 767–784.

Lin, W., and Lin, G. C. (2023). "Strategizing actors and agents in the functioning of informal property rights: The tragicomedy of the extralegal housing market in China." *World Development*, 161, 106111.

Liu, L., and Weingast, B. R. (2017). "Taobao, federalism, and the emergence of law, Chinese style." *Minnesota Law Review*, 102(4), 1563–1590.

Liu, T., Cao, G., Yan, Y., and Wang, R. Y. (2016). "Urban land marketization in China: Central policy, local initiative, and market mechanism." *Land Use Policy*, 57, 265–276.

Liu, Y. (2013). "Beijing songzhuang xiaochanquan fang diaocha: Shiji dong loupan yi tinggong 2 yue." [Research on small property houses of Songzhuang in Beijing: More than ten buildings have been shut for 2 months]. *China Economic Weekly*, August 27, 2013, available at: http://news.sina.com.cn/c/sd/2013-08-27/004528052942.shtml

Liu, Y., He, S., Wu, F., and Webster, C. (2010). "Urban villages under China's rapid urbanization: Unregulated assets and transitional neighbourhoods." *Habitat International*, 34(2), 135–144.

Lo, S. H. (1993). "Bureaucratic corruption and its control in Macao." *Asian Journal of Public Administration*, 15(1), 32–58.

Lo, T. W., and Kwok, S. I. (2017). "Triad organized crime in Macau casinos." *British Journal of Criminology*, 57(3), 589–607.

Lord, N. J., Campbell, L. J., and Van Wingerde, K. (2019). "Other people's dirty money." *British Journal of Criminology*, 59(5): 1217–1236.

Lorentzen, P., Fravel, M. T., and Paine, J. (2017). "Qualitative investigation of theoretical models: The value of process tracing." *Journal of Theoretical Politics*, 29(3), 467–491.

Loubere, N. (2016). "Cyber loan sharks, social credit, and new frontiers of digital control." In J. Golley, L. Jaivin, and L. Tomba (Eds.), *China story yearbook 2016: Control* (pp. 214–223). Canberra: Australian National University Press.

Loubere, N. (2017). "China's internet finance boom and tyrannies of inclusion." *China Perspectives*, 26, 9–18.

Lu, J. (2014). *Varieties of governance in China: Migration and institutional change in Chinese villages*. Oxford: Oxford University Press.

Lu, X. (2000). "Booty socialism, bureau-preneurs, and the state in transition: Organizational corruption in China." *Comparative Politics*, 32(3), 273–294.

Luk, J. (2016). "Hundreds of nude photos sent by desperate women to online loan sharks as guarantees are leaked." *Mail Online*, available at: www.dailymail.co.uk/news/peoplesdaily/article-3989842/Hundreds-nude-photos-sent-desperate-women-online-loan-sharks-guarantees-leaked.html (accessed April 8, 2020).

Luo, Y. (2008). "The changing Chinese culture and business behavior." *International Business Review*, 17(2), 188–193.

Lusthaus, J. (2013). "How organised is organised cybercrime?" *Global Crime*, 14(2), 52–60.

Lusthaus, J. (2018a). "Honour among (cyber) thieves?" *European Journal of Sociology*, 59(2), 191–223.

Lusthaus, J. (2018b). *Industry of anonymity*. Cambridge, MA: Harvard University Press.

Lusthaus, J., and Varese, F. (2021). "Offline and local: The hidden face of cybercrime." *Policing: A Journal of Policy and Practice*, 15(1), 4–14.

Ma, X. (2013). "Less than 10 thousand chengguan regulating 0.3 million to 0.5 million street vendors in Guangzhou." *Southern Metropolis Daily*, available at: http://news.sina.com.cn/c/2013-09-10/083028177550.shtml (accessed April 28, 2020).

Macrae, J. (1982). "Underdevelopment and the economics of corruption: A game theory approach." *World Development*, 10(8), 677–687.

Manion, M. (2016). "Taking China's anticorruption campaign seriously." *Economic and Political Studies*, 4(1), 3–18.

Marinaro, I. C. (2017). "Loan-sharking in a time of crisis." *Trends in Organized Crime*, 20(1–2), 196–215.

Marsden, P. V., and Campbell, K. E. (1984). "Measuring tie strength." *Social Forces*, 63(2), 482–501.

Martin, J., Munksgaard, R., Coomber, R., Demant, J., and Barratt, M. J. (2020). "Selling drugs on darkweb cryptomarkets: Differentiated pathways, risks and rewards." *British Journal of Criminology*, 60(3), 559–578.

Martínez, L., Short, J. R., and Estrada, D. (2018). "The diversity of the street vending." *Cities*, 79, 18–25.

Mayntz, R. (2017). "Illegal markets: Boundaries and interfaces between legality and illegality." In J. Beckert and M. Dewey (Eds.), *The architecture of illegal markets: Towards an economic sociology of illegality in the economy* (pp. 37–47). Oxford: Oxford University Press.

McCusker, R. (2006). "Transnational organized cyber crime." *Crime, Law and Social Change*, 46, 257–273.

McMillan, J., and Woodruff, C. (1999). "Dispute prevention without courts in Vietnam." *Journal of Law, Economics, and Organization*, 15(3), 637–658.

Meramveliotakis, G., and Milonakis, D. (2010). "Surveying the transaction cost foundations of new institutional economics: A critical inquiry." *Journal of Economic Issues*, 44(4), 1045–1072.

Middleton, D., and Levi, M. (2015). "Let sleeping lawyers lie." *British Journal of Criminology*, 55(4), 647–668.

Middleton, D. J., and Levi, M. (2005). "The role of solicitors in facilitating organized crime." *Crime, Law and Social Change*, 42(2–3), 123–161.

Milgrom, P. R., North, D. C., and Weingast, B. R. (1990). "The role of institutions in the revival of trade: The law merchant, private judges, and the champagne fairs." *Economics & Politics*, 2(1), 1–23.

Miron, J. A., and Zwiebel, J. (1995). "The economic case against drug prohibition." *Journal of Economic Perspectives*, 9(4), 175–192.

Mishra, A., and Samuel, A. (2016). "Corruption and hold-up: The role of intermediaries." *European Journal of Law and Economics*, 41(3), 575–599.

Molm, L. D. (1981). "The conversion of power imbalance to power use." *Social Psychology Quarterly*, 44(3), 151–163.

Molm, L. D. (1989). "Punishment power: A balancing process in power-dependence relations." *American Journal of Sociology*, 94(6), 1392–1418.

Molm, L. D. (1994). "Is punishment effective? Coercive strategies in social exchange." *Social Psychology Quarterly*, 57(2), 75–94.

Molm, L. D. (1997). *Coercive power in social exchange*. Cambridge: Cambridge University Press.

Molm, L. D., Takahashi, N., and Peterson, G. (2000). "Risk and trust in social exchange: An experimental test of a classical proposition." *American Journal of Sociology*, 105(5), 1396–1427.

Murphy, R. H., and O'Reilly, C. (2020). "Assessing state capacity libertarianism." *Cato Journal*, 40, 735–767.

Murtazashvili, I., and Murtazashvili, J. (2016). "The origins of private property rights: States or customary organizations?" *Journal of Institutional Economics*, 12(1), 105–128.

Murtazashvili, J. B. (2016). *Informal order and the state in Afghanistan*. New York, NY: Cambridge University Press.

Murtazashvili, J., and Murtazashvili, I. (2020). "Wealth-destroying states." *Public Choice*, 182(3), 353–371.

Murtazashvili, J. B., and Murtazashvili, I. (2021). *Land, the state, and war: Property institutions and political order in Afghanistan*. Cambridge: Cambridge University Press.

Nee, V. (2005). "The new institutionalisms in economics and sociology." In N. J. Smelser and R. Swedberg (Eds.), *The handbook of economic sociology* (pp. 49–74). Princeton, NJ: Princeton University Press.

Nee, V., and Opper, S. (2012). *Capitalism from below: Markets and institutional change in China*. Cambridge, MA and London: Harvard University Press.

Nee, V., and Swedberg, R. (2005). "Economic sociology and new institutional economics." In C. Menard and M. M. Shirley (Eds.), *Handbook of new institutional economics* (pp. 789–818). Boston, MA: Springer.

Ng, K. H., and He, X. (2017). *Embedded courts: Judicial decision-making in China*. New York, NY: Cambridge University Press.

Nip, A. (2020). "Sex-video chatroom under police probe." (updated May 14, 2020), available at: www.thestandard.com.hk/section-news/section/47181603/219017/Sex-video-chatroom-under-police-probe (accessed April 27, 2022).

North, D. C. (1990). *Institutions, institutional change and economic performance*. Cambridge: Cambridge University Press.

North, D. C. (1993). "Institutions and credible commitment." *Journal of Institutional and Theoretical Economics*, 149, 11–23.

Nozick, R. (1974). *Anarchy, state, and utopia*. New York, NY: Basic Books.

O'Brien, K. J., and Deng, Y. (2017). "Preventing protest one person at a time." *China Review*, 17(2), 179–201.

O'Cass, A., and Siahtiri, V. (2013). "In search of status through brands from western and Asian origins." *Journal of Retailing and Consumer Services*, 20(6), 505–515.

Oba, B., and Semerciöz, F. (2005). "Antecedents of trust in industrial districts: An empirical analysis of inter-firm relations in a Turkish industrial district." *Entrepreneurship & Regional Development*, 17(3), 163–182.

O'brien, K. J., and Han, R. (2009). "Path to democracy? Assessing village elections in China." *Journal of Contemporary China*, 18(60), 359–378.

Odabas, M., Holt, T. J., and Breiger, R. L. (2017). "Governance in online stolen data markets." In J. Beckert and M. Dewey (Eds.), *The architecture of illegal markets: Towards an economic sociology of illegality in the economy* (pp. 87–107). Oxford: Oxford University Press.

Oldenburg, P. (1987). "Middlemen in third-world corruption: Implications of an Indian case." *World Politics*, 39(4), 508–535.

Ong, L. H. (2018). "Thugs-for-Hire: Subcontracting of state coercion and state capacity in China." *Perspectives on Politics*, 16(3), 680–695.

Ostrom, E. (1990). *Governing the commons: The evolution of institutions for collective action*. Cambridge: Cambridge University Press.

Özen, Ş., Uysal, Ö. Ö., and Çakar, M. (2016). "Seemingly embedded but obviously exploitative relations: Organizational contingencies of mutual dependence, power imbalance and embedded relations." *European Management Review*, 13(1), 53–68.

Palan, R. (2017). "Futurity, offshore, and the international political economy of crime." In J. Beckert and M. Dewey (Eds.), *The architecture of illegal markets: Towards an economic sociology of illegality in the economy* (pp. 108–120). Oxford: Oxford University Press.

Paletta, D. (2011). "Political legitimacy." In D. K. Chatterjee (Ed.), *Encyclopedia of global justice*. Dordrecht: Springer, available at: https://doi.org/10.1007/978-1-4020-9160-5_201.

Paoli, L. (2002). "The paradoxes of organized crime." *Crime, Law and Social Change*, 37(1), 51–97.

Paoli, L., Greenfield, V. A., and Reuter, P. (2009). *The world heroin market: Can supply be cut?* Oxford: Oxford University Press.

Parodi, G., Pastore, F., Giulietti, C., Ning, G., and Zimmermann, K. F. (2012). "Self-employment of rural-to-urban migrants in China." *International Journal of Manpower*, 33(1), 96–117.

Peerenboom, R., and He, X. (2009). "Dispute resolution in China: Patterns, causes and prognosis." *East Asia Law Review*, 4(1), 1–61.

Pei, M. (2006). *China's trapped transition: The limits of developmental autocracy*. London and Cambridge, MA: Harvard University Press.

Pei, M. (2016). *China's crony capitalism: The dynamics of regime decay*. Cambridge, MA and London: Harvard University Press.

Piano, E. E. (2019). "State capacity and public choice: A critical survey." *Public Choice* 178(1), 289–309.

Polinsky, A. M., and Shavell, S. (2000). "The economic theory of public enforcement of law." *Journal of Economic Literature*, 38(1), 45–76.

Popke, E. J., and Ballard, R. (2004). "Dislocating modernity." *Geoforum*, 35(1), 99–110.

Portes, A., and Haller, W. (2005). "The informal economy." In N. J. Smelser and R. Swedberg (Eds.), *The handbook of economic sociology* (pp. 403–425). Princeton, NJ: Princeton University Press.

Poteete, A. R., Janssen, M. A., and Ostrom, E. (2010). *Working together: Collective action, the commons, and multiple methods*. Princeton, NJ: Princeton University Press.

Powell, B., and Stringham, E. P. (2009). "Public choice and the economic analysis of anarchy: A survey." *Public Choice*, 140(3), 503–538.

Powell, W. W. (1990). "Neither market nor hierarchy." *Research in Organizational Behaviour*, 12, 259–336.

Prieger, J. E., and Kulick, J. (2015). "Violence in illicit markets: Unintended consequences and the search for paradoxical effects of enforcement." *B.E. Journal of Economic Analysis & Policy*, 15(3), 1263–1295.

Provis, C. (2008). "Guanxi and conflicts of interest." *Journal of Business Ethics*, 79(1), 57–68.

Przepiorka, W., Norbutas, L., and Corten, R. (2017). "Order without law: Reputation promotes cooperation in a cryptomarket for illegal drugs." *European Sociological Review*, 33(6), 752–764.

Punch, M. (2000). "Police corruption and its prevention." *European Journal on Criminal Policy and Research*, 8(3), 301–324.

Punch, M. (2009). *Police corruption: Deviance, accountability and reform in policing.* Devon: Willan Publishing.

Pyrooz, D. C., and Moule Jr., R. K. (2019). "Gangs and social media." In *Oxford Research Encyclopedias of Criminology and Criminal Justice*, doi: 10.1093/acrefore/9780190264079.013.439.

Qi, X. (2011). "Face: A Chinese concept in a global sociology." *Journal of Sociology*, 47(3), 279–295.

Qi, X. (2013). "Guanxi, social capital theory and beyond: Toward a globalized social science." *British Journal of Sociology*, 64(2), 308–324.

Qi, X. (2017). "Reconstructing the concept of face in cultural sociology: In Goffman's footsteps, following the Chinese case." *Journal of Chinese Sociology*, 4(1), 1–17.

Qian, Y. (2010). "Sanya 'tiechui xingdong' chaiqian: Zhengfu congzhong yuli." [Sanya's "hammer campaign" demolition: Government profits]. Xinhuanet, October 22, 2010, available at: https://news.qq.com/a/20101022/000642.htm

Qian, Y., and Weingast, B. R. (1997). "Federalism as a commitment to reserving market incentives." *Journal of Economic Perspectives*, 11(4), 83–92.

Qiao, S. (2015). "Small property, big market: A focal point explanation." *American Journal of Comparative Law*, 63(1), 197–238.

Qiao, S. (2017). *Chinese small property: The co-evolution of law and social norms.* Cambridge: Cambridge University Press.

Qun, W., Yongle, L., and Siqi, Y. (2015). "The incentives of China's urban land finance." *Land Use Policy*, *42*, 432–442.

Raub, W. (2004). "Hostage posting as a mechanism of trust: Binding, compensation, and signaling." *Rationality and Society*, 16(3), 319–365.

Raub, W., and Keren, G. (1993). "Hostages as a commitment device: A game-theoretic model and an empirical test of some scenarios." *Journal of Economic Behavior & Organization*, 21(1), 43–67.

Raub, W., and Weesie, J. (1990). "Reputation and efficiency in social interactions: An example of network effects." *American Journal of Sociology*, 96(3), 626–654.

Reuter, P. (1983). *Disorganized crime: The economics of the visible hand.* Cambridge, MA: MIT Press.

Reuter, P. (1985). *The organization of illegal markets: An economic analysis.* Washington, DC: US Department of Justice, National Institute of Justice.

Reuter, P. (2009). "Systemic violence in drug markets." *Crime, Law and Social Change*, 52(3), 275–284.

Rhodes, R. A. W. (1996). "The new governance." *Political Studies*, 44(4), 652–667.

Richman, B. D. (2017). *Stateless commerce: The diamond network and the persistence of relational exchange.* Cambridge, MA: Harvard University Press.

Richter, R. (2015). *Essays on new institutional economics.* Heidelberg: Springer.

Rindfleisch, A. (2019). "Transaction cost theory: Past, present and future." *AMS Review*, 10, 85–97.

Rona-Tas, A., and Guseva, A. (2018). "Consumer credit in comparative perspective." *Annual Review of Sociology*, 44, 55–75.

Rooks, G., Tazelaar, F., and Snijders, C. (2011). "Gossip and reputation in business networks." *European Sociological Review*, 27(1), 90–106.

Rosenfeld, R., Jacobs, B. A., and Wright, R. (2003). "Snitching and the code of the street." *British Journal of Criminology*, 43(2), 291–309.

Rothstein, B., and Varraich, A. (2017). *Making sense of corruption*. Cambridge: Cambridge University Press.

Roy, A. (2011). "Slumdog cities: Rethinking subaltern urbanism." *International Journal of Urban and Regional Research*, 35(2), 223–238.

Ruan, J. (2016). *Guanxi, social capital and school choice in China: The rise of ritual capital*. New York, NY: Springer.

Ruan, J. (2019). "Bribery with Chinese characteristics and the use of guanxi to obtain admission to prestigious secondary schools in urban China." *Critical Asian Studies*, 51(1), 120–130.

Ruan, J. (2021). "Motivations for ritual performance in bribery: Ethnographic case studies of the use of guanxi to gain school places in China." *Current Sociology*, 69(1), 41–58.

Sa, H. (2020). "Do ambiguous property rights matter? Collective value logic in Lin Village." *Land Use Policy*, 99, 105066.

Sagy, T. (2011). "What's so private about private ordering?" *Law & Society Review*, 45(4), 923–954.

Sandberg, S. (2012). "The importance of culture for cannabis markets: Towards an economic sociology of illegal drug markets." *British Journal of Criminology*, 52(6), 1133–1151.

Sanders, A., Young, R., and Burton, M. (2010). *Criminal justice*. New York, NY: Oxford University Press.

Schelling, T. C. (1960). *The strategy of conflict*. Cambridge, MA: Harvard University Press.

Schelling, T. C. (2006). *Strategies of commitment and other essays*. Cambridge, MA: Harvard University Press.

Schmitz, P. W. (2013). "Bargaining position, bargaining power, and the property rights approach." *Economics Letters*, 119(1), 28–31.

Schneider, F. (2005). "Shadow economies around the world." *European Journal of Political Economy*, 21(3), 598–642.

Schotter, A. (1981). *The economic theory of social institutions*. Cambridge: Cambridge University Press.

Schramm, M., and Taube, M. (2003). "The institutional economics of legal institutions, guanxi, and corruption in the PR China." In J. Kidd and F. J. Richter (Eds.), *Fighting corruption in Asia: Causes, effects, and remedies* (pp. 271–296). Danvers, MA: World Scientific.

Sela-Shayovitz, R. (2012). "Gangs and the web." *Journal of Contemporary Criminal Justice*, 28, 389–405.

Shanghai Daily (2017). "Lawyer who joined loan sharks jailed," available at: http://english.china.com/news/china/54/20170829/1059168.html (accessed April 9, 2020).

Shelley, L. I. (1997). "The criminal-political nexus: Russian case study." *Trends in Organized Crime*, 3(1), 12–14.

Shen, A., Antonopoulos, G. A., and Von Lampe, K. (2010). "The dragon breathes smoke: Cigarette counterfeiting in the people's republic of China." *British Journal of Criminology*, 50(2), 239–258.

Shen, X., and Tsai, K. S. (2016). "Institutional adaptability in China: Local developmental models under changing economic conditions." *World Development*, 87, 107–127.

Shenzhen Municipality Urban Planning Land and Resources Commission (SMUPLRC). (2015). *Guanyu chawei he lishi yiliu weijian chuli gongzuo de huibao* [Report on the investigation of illegal buildings and the handling of illegal buildings left over by history].

Shieh, S. (2005). "The rise of collective corruption in China: The Xiamen smuggling case." *Journal of Contemporary China*, 14(42), 67–91.

Shifa, A. B., and Xiao, W. (2022). "Urban bias, migration control and rural land policy: The case of Hukou in China." *Journal of Economic Geography*, available at: https://doi.org/10.1093/jeg/lbac008.

Shirk, D. A. (2010). "Drug violence in Mexico: Data and analysis from 2001–2009." *Trends in Organized Crime*, 13(2–3), 167–174.

Shortland, A. (2018). "Governing criminal markets: The role of private insurers in kidnap for ransom." *Governance*, 31(2), 341–358.

Shortland, A. (2019). *Kidnap: Inside the ransom business*. Oxford: Oxford University Press.

Shortland, A., and Varese, F. (2016). "State-building, informal governance and organised crime: The case of Somali piracy." *Political Studies*, 64(4), 811–831.

Shue, V. (2004). "Legitimacy crisis in China?" In P. Gries and S. Rosen (Eds.), *State and society in 21st century China: Crisis, contention, and legitimation* (pp. 24–49). New York, NY: Routledge.

Simon, H. (1961). *Administrative behavior*. 2nd ed. New York, NY: Macmillan.

Skarbek, D. (2011). "Governance and prison gangs." *American Political Science Review*, 105(4), 702–716.

Skarbek, D. (2012). "Prison gangs, norms, and organizations." *Journal of Economic Behavior & Organization*, 82(1), 96–109.

Skarbek, D. (2014). *The social order of the underworld: How prison gangs govern the American penal system*. Oxford: Oxford University Press.

Skarbek, D. (2020a). *The puzzle of prison order: Why life behind bars varies around the world*. Oxford: Oxford University Press.

Skarbek, D. (2020b). "Qualitative research methods for institutional analysis." *Journal of Institutional Economics*, 16(4), 409–422.

Skarbek, D., and Wang, P. (2015). "Criminal rituals." *Global Crime*, 16(4), 288–305.

Skarbek, E. C. (2014). "The Chicago fire of 1871: A bottom-up approach to disaster relief." *Public Choice*, 160(1–2), 155–180.

Sløk-Madsen, S. K., Skarbek, D., Hansen, A., and Rezaei, A. (2021). "The organization of Danish gangs: A transaction cost approach." *Trends in Organized Crime*, 24(3), 361–377.

Small, M. L. (2009). "'How many cases do I need?' On science and the logic of case selection in field-based research." *Ethnography*, 10(1), 5–38.

Smart, A., and Hsu, C. L. (2007). "Corruption or social capital? Tact and the performance of guanxi in market socialist China." In M. Nuijten and G. Anders (Eds.), *Corruption and the secret of law* (pp. 167–190). London: Routledge.

Smith, R. (2009). "Understanding entrepreneurial behaviour in organized criminals." *Journal of Enterprising Communities: People and Places in the Global Economy*, 3(3), 256–268.

Soudijn, M. R., and Zhang, S. X. (2013). "Taking loan sharking into account." *Trends in Organized Crime*, 16(1), 13–30.

Standifird, S. S., and Marshall, R. S. (2000). "The transaction cost advantage of guanxi-based business practices." *Journal of World Business*, 35(1), 21–42.

Steel, C. M. (2019). "Stolen identity valuation and market evolution on the dark web." *International Journal of Cyber Criminology*, 13(1), 70–83.

Storr, V. H., Haeffele-Balch, S., and Grube, L. E. (2016). *Community revival in the wake of disaster: Lessons in local entrepreneurship*. London: Palgrave Macmillan.

Storrod, M. L., and Densley, J. A. (2017). "Going viral and going country: The expressive and instrumental activities of street gangs on social media." *Journal of Youth Studies*, 20, 677–696.

Stringham, E. (2005). *Anarchy, state and public choice*. Cheltenham: Edward Elgar Publishing.

Stringham, E. (2015). *Private governance: Creating order in economic and social life*. Oxford: Oxford University Press.

Stuart, F. (2020). "Code of the tweet: Urban gang violence in the social media age." *Social Problems*, 67(2), 191–207.

Suchman, M. C. (1995). "Managing legitimacy: Strategic and institutional approaches." *Academy of Management Review*, 20(3), 571–610.

Sugden, R. (2004). *The economics of rights, co-operation and welfare*. London: Palgrave Macmillan.

Sun, L., and Ho, P. (2018). "Formalizing informal homes, a bad idea: The credibility thesis applied to China's 'extra-legal' housing." *Land Use Policy*, 79, 891–901.

Suvilehto, J. T., Glerean, E., Dunbar, R. I., Hari, R., and Nummenmaa, L. (2015). "Topography of social touching depends on emotional bonds between humans." *Proceedings of the National Academy of Sciences*, 112(45), 13811–13816.

Swedberg, R. (2001). "Sociology and game theory: Contemporary and historical perspectives." *Theory and Society*, 30(3), 301–335.

Sykes, G. M., and Matza, D. (1957). "Techniques of neutralization: A theory of delinquency." *American Sociological Review*, 22(6), 664–670.

Tatlow, D. K. (2016). "To secure loans, Chinese women supply perilous collateral." *The New York Times*, available at: www.nytimes.com/2016/06/16/world/asia/to-secure-loans-chinese-women-supply-perilous-collateral-nude-photos.html (accessed April 8, 2020).

Trebilcock, M. J., and Prado, M. M. (2011). *What makes poor countries poor? Institutional determinants of development*. Cheltenham: Edward Elgar Publishing.

Trevaskes, S. (2007). *Courts and criminal justice in contemporary China*. Lanham: Lexington Books.

Trevaskes, S. (2010). *Policing serious crime in China: From strike hard to kill fewer*. London and New York: Routledge.

Tsai, K. S. (2002). *Back-alley banking: Private entrepreneurs in China*. Ithaca and London: Cornell University Press.

Tsai, K. S. (2006). "Adaptive informal institutions and endogenous institutional change in China." *World Politics*, 59, 116.

Tsai, L. L. (2007). "Solidary groups, informal accountability, and local public goods provision in rural China." *American Political Science Review*, 101(2), 355–372.

Tucker, J. L., and Devlin, R. T. (2019). "Uncertainty and the governance of street vending." *International Journal of Urban and Regional Research*, 43(3), 460–475.

Tufekci, Z. (2017). *Twitter and tear gas: The power and fragility of networked protest.* New Haven: Yale University Press.

Tullock, G. (Ed.). (1972). *Explorations in the theory of anarchy.* Blacksburg: Center for Study of Public Choice.

Tullock, G. (Ed.). (1974). *Further explorations in the theory of anarchy.* Blacksburg: University Publications.

Tyler, T. R. (2006a). *Why people obey the law.* Princeton, NJ: Princeton University Press.

Tyler, T. R. (2006b). "Psychological perspectives on legitimacy and legitimation." *Annual Review of Psychology,* 57(1), 375–400.

Tyler, T. R. (2023). "Whither legitimacy? Legal authority in the twenty-first century." *Annual Review of Law and Social Science,* 19(1), 1–17.

Ulyssea, G. (2018). "Firms, informality, and development." *American Economic Review,* 108(8), 2015–2047.

Ulyssea, G. (2020). "Informality." *Annual Review of Economics,* 12, 525–546.

Van de Bunt, H., Siegel, D., and Zaitch D. (2014). "The social embeddedness of organized crime." In L. Paoli (Ed.), *The oxford handbook of organized crime* (pp. 321–339). Oxford: Oxford University Press.

van Uhm, D. P., and Wong, R. W. (2019). "Establishing trust in the illegal wildlife trade in China." *Asian Journal of Criminology,* 14(1), 23–40.

Varese, F. (2001). *The Russian mafia: Private protection in a new market economy.* Oxford: Oxford University Press.

Varese, F. (2010). "General introduction: 'What is organized crime?" In F. Varese (Ed.), *Organized crime* (pp. 1–33). London and New York: Routledge.

Varese, F. (2011). *Mafias on the move: How organized crime conquers new territories.* Oxford: Princeton University Press.

Varese, F., and Wong, R. W. (2018). "Resurgent triads? Democratic mobilization and organized crime in Hong Kong." *Australian and New Zealand Journal of Criminology,* 51(1), 23–39.

Varese, F., Wang, P., and Wong, R. W. (2019). "'Why should I trust you with my money?': Credible commitments in the informal economy in China." *British Journal of Criminology,* 59(3), 594–613.

Velthuis, B. O. (1999). "The changing relationship between economic sociology and institutional economics: From Talcott parsons to mark Granovetter." *American Journal of Economics and Sociology,* 58(4), 629–649.

Vereeck, L., and Mühl, M. (2000). "An economic theory of court delay." *European Journal of Law and Economics,* 10(3), 243–268.

Von Lampe, K. (2008). "Organized crime in Europe." *Policing,* 2(1), 7–17.

Von Lampe, K., and Antonopoulos, G. A. (2018). "An introduction to the special issue on 'organised crime and illegal markets in the UK and Ireland'." *Trends in Organized Crime,* 21, 99–103.

Von Lampe, K., and Ole Johansen, P. (2004). "Organized crime and trust: On the conceptualization and empirical relevance of trust in the context of criminal networks." *Global Crime,* 6(2), 159–184.

Walker, S. (1983). *Sense and nonsense about crime: A policy guide.* Monterey, CA: Brooks/Cole.

Wall, D. S. (2015). "Dis-organised crime: Towards a distributed model of the organization of cybercrime." *European Review of Organised Crime*, 2, 71–90.

Wall, D. S. (2024). *Cybercrime: The transformation of crime in the information age*. Hoboken, NJ: John Wiley & Sons.

Wang, J., and Wang, P. (2024). "Campaign-style law enforcement in China: Causes and consequences." *Journal of Criminology*, available at: https://doi.org/10.1177/26338076241252686.

Wang, L., and Sun, T. (2014). "Capitalization of legal title: Evidence from small-property-rights houses in Beijing." *Habitat International*, 44, 306–313.

Wang, P. (2013a). "The rise of the Red Mafia in China: A case study of organised crime and corruption in Chongqing." *Trends in Organized crime*, 16(1), 49–73.

Wang, P. (2014). "Extra-legal protection in China: How guanxi distorts China's legal system and facilitates the rise of unlawful protectors." *British Journal of Criminology*, 54(5), 809–830.

Wang, P. (2016). "Military corruption in China: The role of guanxi in the buying and selling of military positions." *China Quarterly*, 228, 970–991.

Wang, P. (2017). *The Chinese mafia: Organized crime, corruption, and extra-legal protection*. Oxford: Oxford University Press.

Wang, P. (2020a). "How to engage in illegal transactions: Resolving risk and uncertainty in corrupt dealings." *British Journal of Criminology*, 60, 1282–1301.

Wang, P. (2020b). "Politics of crime control: How campaign-style law enforcement sustains authoritarian rule in China." *British Journal of Criminology*, 60(2), 422–443.

Wang, P., and Antonopoulos, G. A. (2016). "Organized crime and illegal gambling: How do illegal gambling enterprises respond to the challenges posed by their illegality in China?" *Australian & New Zealand Journal of Criminology*, 49(2), 258–280.

Wang, P., and Kwok, S. I. (2023). "Hong Kong triads: The historical and political evolution of urban criminal polity, 1842–2020." *Urban History*, 50(3), 445–467.

Wang, P., and Wang, J. (2018). "How China promotes its military officers: Interactions between formal and informal institutions." *China Quarterly*, 234, 399–419.

Wang, P., and Yan, X. (2020). "Bureaucratic slack in China: The anti-corruption campaign and the decline of patronage networks in developing local economies." *China Quarterly*, 243, 611–634.

Wang, P., Cho, L. F., and Li, R. (2018). "An institutional explanation of media corruption in China." *Journal of Contemporary China*, 27(113), 748–762.

Wang, P., Su, M., and Wang, J. (2021). "Organized crime in cyberspace: How traditional organized criminal groups exploit the online peer-to-peer lending market in China." *British Journal of Criminology*, 61(2), 303–324.

Wang, S., Tan, S., Yang, S., Lin, Q., and Zhang, L. (2019). "Urban-biased land development policy and the urban-rural income gap: Evidence from Hubei Province, China." *Land Use Policy*, 87, 104066.

Wang, Y. (2013b). "Court funding and judicial corruption in China." *China Journal*, (69), 43–63.

Wang, Y. P., Wang, Y., and Wu, J. (2009). "Urbanization and informal development in China: Urban villages in Shenzhen." *International Journal of Urban and Regional Research*, 33(4), 957–973.

Wang, Y., and You, J. (2012). "Corruption and firm growth: Evidence from China." *China Economic Review*, 23(2), 415–433.

Wank, D. L. (2001). *Commodifying communism: Business, trust, and politics in a Chinese city*. Cambridge: Cambridge University Press.

Wank, D. L. (2002). "Business-state clientelism in China: Decline or evolution." In T. Gold, D. Guthrie, and D. Wank (Eds.), *Social connections in China: Institutions, culture, and the changing nature of Guanxi* (pp. 97–116). Cambridge: Cambridge University Press.

Webb, J. W., Bruton, G. D., Tihanyi, L., and Ireland, R. D. (2013). "Research on entrepreneurship in the informal economy." *Journal of Business Venturing*, 28(5): 598–614.

Webb, J. W., Tihanyi, L., Ireland, R. D., and Sirmon, D. G. (2009). "You say illegal, I say legitimate: Entrepreneurship in the informal economy." *Academy of Management Review*, 34(3), 492–510.

Webb, S. (2016). "Dirty money." *The Sun*, available at: www.thesun.co.uk/news/2313351/naked-photos-leaked-online-after-hundreds-of-chinese-women-are-forced-to-send-nude-selfies-to-loan-sharks-as-a-guarantee-theyll-pay-back-the-cash/ (accessed April 9, 2020).

Weber, M. (1956). *Wirtschaft and gesellschaft*. München: C.H. Beck.

Weber, M. (1978). *Economy and society: An outline of interpretive sociology*. Oakland, CA: University of California Press.

Webster, C., Wu, F., Zhang, F., and Sarkar, C. (2016). "Informality, property rights, and poverty in China's 'favelas'." *World Development*, 78, 461–476.

Wedeman, A. H. (2012). *Double paradox: Rapid growth and rising corruption in China*. Ithaca, NY: Cornell University Press.

Wedeman, A. H. (2013). "The challenge of commercial bribery and organized crime in China." *Journal of Contemporary China*, 22(79), 18–34.

Weesie, J., and Raub, W. (1996). "Private ordering: A comparative institutional analysis of hostage games." *Journal of Mathematical Sociology*, 21(3), 201–240.

Weingast, B. R. (1997). "The political foundations of democracy and the rule of the law." *American Political Science Review*, 91(2), 245–263.

Weinland, D. (2015). "The big score." *South China Morning Post*, available at: www.scmp.com/business/banking-finance/article/1878528/big-score-making-or-breaking-chinas-consumer-credit-market (accessed March 30, 2020).

Williams, C. C., and Lansky, M. A. (2013). "Informal employment in developed and developing economies." *International Labour Review*, 152(3–4), 355–380.

Williams, P. (2001). "Organized crime and cybercrime: Synergies, trends, and responses." *Global Issues*, 6(2), 22–26.

Williamson, C. (2011). "Informal institutions rule: Institutional arrangements and economic performance." *Public Choice*, 139(3), 371–387.

Williamson, O. E. (1975). *Markets and hierarchies*. New York, NY: Free Press.

Williamson, O. E. (1979). "Transaction-cost economics: The governance of contractual relations." *Journal of Law and Economics*, 22, 233–261.

Williamson, O. E. (1983). "Credible commitments: Using hostages to support exchange." *American Economic Review*, 73(4), 519–540.

Williamson, O. E. (1985). *The economic institutions of capitalism*. New York, NY: Free Press.

Williamson, O. E. (1986). "Transaction-cost economics: The governance of contractual relations." In J. Barney and W. Ouchi (Eds.), *Organizational economics* (pp. 98–129). San Francisco: Jossey-Bass.

Williamson, O. E. (1993). "Opportunism and its critics." *Managerial and Decision Economics*, 14, 97–107.

Williamson, O. E. (2000). "The new institutional economics: Taking stock, looking ahead." *Journal of Economic Literature*, 38(3), 595–613.

Williamson, O. E. (2002). "The theory of the firm as governance structure: From choice to contract." *Journal of Economic Perspectives*, 16(3), 171–195.

Wong, K. C. (2012). *Police reform in China*. Boca Raton: CRC Press.

Wong, R. W. (2016). "The organization of the illegal tiger parts trade in China." *British Journal of Criminology*, 56(5), 995–1013.

Wong, R. W. (2017). "The role of reputation in the illegal purchase of protected wildlife in China." *Deviant Behavior*, 38(11), 1290–1302.

Wright, R. T., and Decker, S. H. (1996). *Burglars on the job: Streetlife and residential break-ins*. Boston, MA: Northeastern University Press.

Wu, C. (2016). *Regulating government ethics: An underused weapon in China's anti-corruption campaign*. Cambridge: Cambridge University Press.

Wu, F. (2016). "Housing in Chinese urban villages." *Housing Studies*, 31(7), 852–870.

Wu, F., Zhang, F., and Webster, C. (2013). "Informality and the development and demolition of urban villages in the Chinese peri-urban area." *Urban Studies*, 50(10), 1919–1934.

Wu, J., Balliet, D., and Van Lange, P. A. (2016). "Reputation, gossip, and human cooperation." *Social and Personality Psychology Compass*, 10(6), 350–364.

Xia, M. (2008). "Organizational formations of organized crime in China: Perspectives from the state, markets, and networks." *Journal of Contemporary China*, 17(54), 1–23.

Xu, C. (2011). "The fundamental institutions of China's reforms and development." *Journal of Economic Literature*, 49(4), 1076–1151.

Xu, J. (2017). "China's internet finance." *China and World Economy*, 25(4), 78–92.

Xu, J., and Jiang, A. (2019). "Police civilianization and the production of underclass violence." *British Journal of Criminology*, 59(1), 64–84.

Xue, D., and Huang, G. (2015). "Informality and the state's ambivalence in the regulation of street vending in transforming Guangzhou, China." *Geoforum*, 62, 156–165.

Yamagishi, T., and Yamagishi, M. (1994). "Trust and commitment in the United States and Japan." *Motivation and Emotion*, 18(2), 129–166.

Yan, Y. (1996). *The flow of gifts: Reciprocity and social networks in a Chinese village*. Palo Alto, CA: Stanford University Press.

Yang, H., and Zhao, D. (2015). "Performance legitimacy, state autonomy and China's economic miracle." *Journal of Contemporary China*, 24(91), 64–82.

Yang, M. M. H. (1994). *Gifts, favors, and banquets: The art of social relationships in China*. Ithaca, NY: Cornell University Press.

Yeo, Y. (2016). "Complementing the local discipline inspection commissions of the CCP: Empowerment of the central inspection groups." *Journal of Contemporary China*, 25(97), 59–74.

Yeung, G., He, C., and Zhang, P. (2017). "Rural banking in China: Geographically accessible but still financially excluded?" *Regional Studies*, 51(2), 297–312.

Yiftachel, O. (2009). "Theoretical notes on gray cities." *Planning Theory*, 8(1), 88–100.

Yin, R. K. (2009). *Case study research: Design and methods* (4th ed.). Thousand Oaks, CA: SAGE Publications.

Yin, R. K. (2012). *Application of case study research* (3rd ed.). Thousand Oaks, CA: SAGE Publications.

You, J., Chen, Y., Wang, W., and Shi, C. (2018). "Uncertainty, opportunistic behavior, and governance in construction projects: The efficacy of contracts." *International Journal of Project Management*, 36(5), 795–807.

Zelizer, V. A. (2012). "How I became a relational economic sociologist and what does that mean?" *Politics & Society*, 40(2), 145–174.

Zelizer, V. A. (2019). "Why and how social relations matter for economic lives?" Presentation at the Ostrom Speaker Series at George Mason University, October 17, 2019.

Zhai, X. (2013). *Renqing, mianzi yu quanli de zaishengchan [Face, Favor and Reproduction of Power]*. Beijing: Peking University Press.

Zhan, J. V. (2012). "Filling the gap of formal institutions: The effects of Guanxi network on corruption in reform-era China." *Crime, Law and Social Change*, 58(2), 93–109.

Zhan, J. V. (2017). "Do natural resources breed corruption? Evidence from China." *Environmental and Resource Economics*, 66(2), 237–259.

Zhan, J. V., and Zhu, J. (2016). "Explaining China's selective anticorruption efforts in the reform era." Presented at 2016 American Political Science Association Annual Meeting, available at SSRN: https://ssrn.com/abstract=2838087.

Zhang, H. (2013). "Dui songzhuang qiangchai shijian de jianjie." [Insights about forced demolition in Songzhuang]. Art Intern, December 27, 2013, available at: http://collection.sina.com.cn/plfx/20131227/0929138395.shtml

Zhang, M., and Zhao, P. (2018). "The determinants of informal housing price in Beijing: Village power, informal institutions, and property security." *Cities*, 77, 117–129.

Zhang, S. (2016). *Game: The segmentation, implementation and protection of land rights in China*. Hackensack: World Scientific.

Zhang, T., and Zhao, X. (2014). "Do kinship networks strengthen private property? Evidence from rural China." *Journal of Empirical Legal Studies*, 11(3), 505–540.

Zhang, X., Fan, S., Zhang, L., and Huang, J. (2004). "Local governance and public goods provision in rural China." *Journal of Public Economics*, 88(12), 2857–2871.

Zhao, P. (2017). "An 'unceasing war' on land development on the urban fringe of Beijing: A case study of gated informal housing communities." *Cities*, 60, 139–146.

Zhao, S. X., Lao, Q., and Chan, N. Y. M. (2013). "The rise of China and the development of financial centres in Hong Kong, Beijing, Shanghai, and Shenzhen." *Journal of Globalization Studies*, 4(1), 32–62.

Zhou, Y. Y. (2016). "The investigation of the leak of a 10g file concerning naked borrowing." *The Paper*, available at: www.thepaper.cn/newsDetail_forward_1572198 (accessed April 8, 2020; in Chinese).

Zhou, Y., Yu, Y., Chen, X., and Zhou, X. (2020). "Guanxi or justice? An empirical study of WeChat voting." *Journal of Business Ethics*, 164(1), 201–225.

Zhou, Z., and Yau, Y. (2021). "The small property rights housing institution in mainland China: The perspective of substitutability of institutional functions." *Land*, 10(9), 915.

Zhu, A., Fu, P., Zhang, Q., and Chen, Z. (2017). "Ponzi scheme diffusion in complex networks." *Physica A*, 479, 128–136.

Zhu, J. (2002). "Urban development under ambiguous property rights: A case of China's transition economy." *International Journal of Urban and Regional Research*, 26(1), 41–57.

Zhu, J. (2008). "Why are offices for sale in China? A case study of the office-selling chain in Heilongjiang province." *Asian Survey*, 48, 558–579.

Zhu, J. (2012). "The shadow of the skyscrapers: Real estate corruption in China." *Journal of Contemporary China*, 21(74), 243–260.

Zhu, J., and Zhang, D. (2017). "Weapons of the powerful: Authoritarian elite competition and politicized anticorruption in China." *Comparative Political Studies*, 50(9), 1186–1220.

Zhu, J., Huang, H., and Zhang, D. (2017). "Big tigers, big data: Learning social reactions to China's anticorruption campaign through online feedback." *Public Administration Review*, 79(4), 500–513.

Zhu, X., Wei, Y., Lai, Y., Li, Y., Zhong, S., and Dai, C. (2019). "Empirical analysis of the driving factors of China's 'land finance' mechanism using soft budget constraint theory and the PLS-SEM model." *Sustainability*, 11(3), 742.

Zhu, Y. (2011). "'Performance legitimacy' and China's political adaptation strategy." *Journal of Chinese Political Science*, 16(2), 123–140.

Index

www.ingramcontent.com/pod-product-compliance
Lightning Source LLC
LaVergne TN
LVHW091530200926
848483LV00002B/347
* 9 7 8 1 0 0 9 6 2 2 1 4 1 *